# The Ever-Changing American City

# The Ever-Changing American City

## 1945–Present

JOHN F. BAUMAN, ROGER BILES,
AND KRISTIN M. SZYLVIAN

ROWMAN & LITTLEFIELD PUBLISHERS, INC.
*Lanham • Boulder • New York • Toronto • Plymouth, UK*

Published by Rowman & Littlefield Publishers, Inc.
A wholly owned subsidiary of The Rowman & Littlefield Publishing Group, Inc.
4501 Forbes Boulevard, Suite 200, Lanham, Maryland 20706
http://www.rowmanlittlefield.com

Estover Road, Plymouth PL6 7PY, United Kingdom

British Library Cataloguing in Publication Information Available

**Library of Congress Cataloging-in-Publication Data**

Bauman, John F., 1938-
  The ever-changing American city : 1945-present / John F. Bauman, Roger Biles, and Kristin M. Szylvian.
    p. cm.
  Includes bibliographical references and index.
  ISBN 978-1-4422-0181-1 (cloth : alk. paper) — ISBN 978-1-4422-0182-8 (pbk. : alk. paper) — ISBN 978-1-4422-0183-5 (electronic)
  1. Cities and towns—United States. 2. Cities and towns—United States—History. I. Biles, Roger, 1950- II. Szylvian, Kristin M. III. Title.

  HT123.B326 2012
  307.760973—dc23

                                                                        2011035354

∞™ The paper used in this publication meets the minimum requirements of American National Standard for Information Sciences—Permanence of Paper for Printed Library Materials, ANSI/NISO Z39.48-1992.

Printed in the United States of America

# Contents

# Preface

In March 2011, just as this book was being completed, the initial reports of the 2010 census offered additional evidence of the mutability of U.S. cities. The *New York Times* reported on the "grim desertion" of Detroit, noting that the city, the fourth largest in the nation in 1950, had lost a quarter of its population in the previous decade. With the exception of disease-ridden Memphis in the 1870s, no city had ever suffered a larger population decline. Days later, the newspaper reported that many of the people of color who had left Detroit and other northeastern and upper midwestern cities had migrated south. The percentage of the nation's black population residing in the South was higher in 2010 than at any time in the past half century. The Great Migration had largely reversed its course. Today's relocating family of color was likely leaving an ailing industrial city in New York, Pennsylvania, or Ohio for a suburb outside Atlanta or a community near extended family members. What are the economic, political, social, and cultural implications of this demographic shift for U.S. cities? How will elected officials, public policymakers, the leaders of for-profit and nonprofit corporations, and, ultimately, voters respond to these and other related developments? Through the study of urban history, especially the critical years since World War II, we can gain the ability to place such remarkable demographic change into a broader historical context. This book seeks to offer some perspective to urban issues that will help us become more informed voters and caretakers of the nation's cities.[1]

Chapter 1, "The Electronic City," introduces the story of urban America in the decades following World War II, an era when increasing numbers of people left the inner cities for the suburbs, by examining the perceptions that increasingly dominated the mainstream culture. Having relatively little direct contact with inner cities, many Americans formed their impressions of urban life on the images presented by a series of electronic media. During those years, films, television, fiction, a succession of popular music genres, video games, and a variety of handheld devices presented a deeply ambivalent view of American cities as both purveyors of opportunity and dangerous havens for crime and vice. Moreover, a series of powerful images often distorted the important changes ongoing in postwar American cities and suburbs.

Chapter 2, "Shaping the Postwar City: 1945–1960," discusses the state of the nation's cities in 1945 and describes the efforts undertaken to address a host of intractable problems left over from the Great Depression and World War II. Concerned with the spread of blight and rapid suburban growth, defenders of the city devised a series of plans to preserve declining central business districts. In the postwar years, city halls and local business communities worked collaboratively to launch an urban renaissance—and eagerly welcomed assistance from the federal government that contributed money and counsel in unprecedented quantities. Federal programs such as urban renewal and expressway construction remade cityscapes but, contrary to the belief that government intervention could halt metropolitan decentralization, failed to stem the exodus of middle-class residents, industry, and retail to the suburbs.

Chapter 3, "Federal Policy and the American City," describes the effort during the 1960s of Democratic Presidents John F. Kennedy and Lyndon B. Johnson to rescue inner cities from decay and turn flawed government programs around. Attempting to broaden economic opportunities for city residents of all races and concerned that massive urban renewal efforts had displaced low-income families, the two liberal administrations placed greater emphasis on the provision of public housing. Johnson's Great Society allocated huge sums of money to enlarge and expand the construction of urban expressways, resulting in further decentralization of factories, department stores, hotels, and middle- and upper-income families. Despite the best of intentions, an impoverished populace, aging housing stock, and an outmoded infrastructure dominated downtowns and surrounding neighborhoods by the mid-1960s.

Chapter 4, "The Tarnished Face of the American City," reveals how the federal policies of the 1960s failed to offset the powerful forces of decline and decentralization. Riots, protests, and demonstrations, many of which were violent, increased in frequency and scale in cities large and small across the United States beginning in mid-decade and continuing into the early 1970s. As a result of the rioting prevalent during the "red-hot summers," Americans began talking worriedly about an "urban crisis." At the same time, the growth of the ecology movement heightened public awareness of serious pollution problems in the cities. Environmentalists identified automobiles as a leading culprit in the worsening quality of the air, water, and soil in urban America.

Chapter 5, "The American City in the Age of Limits: 1968–1990," recounts a decisive turn in the relationship between the federal government and the cities. For more than two decades, cities found Congress and the White House unwilling to appropriate the funds necessary to maintain rusting bridges, repair leaky water systems, clean up polluted rivers, and help balance municipal budgets. Democratic and Republican political coalitions realigned as voters laid blame for the decline of industrial cities on elected officials and inexorable economic change. The construction of sports arenas, convention centers, and festival marketplaces began to assume greater importance as cities looked to tourism and entertainment both to fill the economic niche vacated by manufacturing and to respond to the growing number of foreign investors in urban real estate markets.

Chapter 6, "The City and the Image Made Real? The 1990s and 2000s," considers how U.S. cities have been forced to adapt to the fact that they were no longer the workshops of the world. With the closing of Chicago's meat-packing plants and Pittsburgh's steel mills, for example, hospitals, universities, prisons, and cultural attractions have loomed larger in urban economies. Pockets of affluence have arisen near universities and trendy neighborhoods where studios, apartments, offices, and restaurants occupied deserted mills, factories, and other commercial buildings. The increasingly bifurcated city became home to affluent financiers and data processors, low-wage service workers, and alarming numbers of the unemployed. As business has become more and more tied to global markets and cyberspace, the American city is being rebuilt again—developing a new function and indeed a new form to meet new demands.

The authors thankfully acknowledge their support from the Edmund
Muskie School of Public Service at the University of Southern Maine, Illinois
State University, Western Michigan University, and St. John's University. A
weeklong trip in July 2009 hosted by John F. Bauman and his wife, Barbara, to
Southport Island, Maine, allowed for a series of invigorating meetings at their
home and at the Muskie School in Portland as well as illuminating research
sessions at the Bowdoin College Library. Michael J. Chiarappa, Andrea M.
Szylvian, Patrick Jouppi, and Matthew A. Schuld provided critical research assistance. Roger Biles wishes to thank Dana Benelli and Tom Powers for sharing their perspectives on American film and television in the postwar decades.

# 1

# The Electronic City

Did you grow up watching public television? If so, you may recall *Mr. Rogers'*
*Neighborhood.* The show began when Mr. Rogers entered his living room,
but within minutes, viewers were onboard a trolley similar to those that
once plied the streets of his native Pittsburgh. After passing through a tunnel (just as if they were arriving in Pittsburgh), they emerged in the city that
constituted the "Neighborhood of Make Believe."[1] It was a welcoming place,
full of infinite possibility, particularly for those who cultivated certain values
and attributes. In his signature song, Mr. Rogers asked, "Please, won't you
be my neighbor?" During the thirty-three years the show was on the air, the
United States became a suburban nation. An increasing number of viewers
lived in subdivisions or neighborhoods that bore little resemblance to Mr.
Rogers' neighborhood. Comedians such as Eddie Murphy, formerly of the
*Saturday Night Live* cast, noticed how the Neighborhood of Make Believe became frozen in time and was not altered to reflect the changes that had taken
place in real American cities. He took Mr. Rogers to task by impersonating
him. As "Mr. Robinson," Murphy invited viewers to become *his* neighbor,
knowing that most would assume this meant taking up residence in a place
where violence and poverty were more visible than neighborliness and mutual
assistance.

Television viewers were familiar with both versions of the city presented
by Mr. Rogers and Mr. Robinson. Long before the emergence of the medium

of television, Americans had been conditioned to accept conflicting images of the city that emerged in art, music, drama, and literature. In Theodore Dreiser's nineteenth-century novel *Sister Carrie*, for instance, the protagonist (Carrie Meeber) leaves the farm for the excitement of Chicago. Like many urban newcomers, she initially stays with family and, lacking skills and connections, settles for a low-paying job in a factory stitching shirt collars. Lonely and naive, Carrie is used by unscrupulous men. Even after she realizes her dream of becoming an actress—not an admirable vocation at that time—happiness eludes her. The novel ends with Carrie sitting in a rocking chair (a symbol of rural "leisure") as though she is a forlorn old woman. In the 1930s film version of *The Wizard of Oz*, the Emerald City turns out to be not quite what Dorothy and her traveling companions hoped it would be. Instead, it is full of people and things that are not what they appear to be. The Wizard himself is a fake who ended up in Oz as a result of his inability to pilot his air balloon skillfully out of Omaha. Some have interpreted the original novel by L. Frank Baum as evidence of the Populist Party's antiurban bent. The popularity of the paintings of Edward Hopper (who spent much of his time at his Cape Cod home in Truro, Massachusetts) can be attributed in part to the artist's ability to capture both the promise and the loneliness of urban life for ordinary people. On the one hand, the city was a place for the realization of economic and social mobility, and, on the other, it was a corrupting force that could lead many astray.

Since the days when you watched television shows such as *Mr. Rogers' Neighborhood* and *Sesame Street*, you have been bombarded with conflicting images of urban life not only in television programs and movies but also in the computer games you have played; in the newspapers, magazines, and books you have read; and in the music you have listened to. As more and more Americans resided in the suburbs, their chief source of information about cities and urban life was electronic. For many suburbanites, the observations of city life that resulted from the occasional visit to a concert, sports event, museum, or city neighborhood where the grandparents once lived proved to be far less influential in shaping notions about the place than the images that emerged from movies, television, songs, video games, and websites. This chapter will show how as more and more affluent Americans of all nationalities and backgrounds moved to the suburbs, the city became known to millions of people not as a place actually experienced in everyday life but through its on-screen, musical, and fictional depictions. Together, these media created and reinforced the dual image of the city as an earthly version of heaven and hell.

In the decades following World War II, the city continued to be depicted as a place where dreams and ambitions could either be realized or shattered. What changed over time was the medium used to deliver the message. In the 1930s and 1940s, when nearly every neighborhood or town had its own theater, motion pictures convinced many Americans that if they avoided temptation and other corrupting forces, the city could be the place for the fulfillment of their hopes and dreams. During the 1950s, although Hollywood productions continued to shape notions of the city, television became the leading purveyor of the city's dual image. In the 1960s, thanks in part to the rise of television and the transistor radio, rock and roll was the most influential shaper of the way cities were viewed. In the decades that followed, disco music, the Music Television (MTV) network, the Internet, and handheld devices, such as smart phones, successively dominated the urban image-making process.

## THE 1950s: THE TELEVISION CITY

During the 1950s, millions of middle-income Americans resumed the migration to the suburbs interrupted by the Great Depression and World War II. For the new suburbanites and those in the countryside, television became the most important medium through which they "knew" the city. Some of the homes built by the famous postwar housing developer William Levitt and Sons included an Admiral television set. Rock and roll music and beat literature poetry also provided a window into urban life and reinforced the dual image of the city.

Although many Americans first encountered or heard about television during the late 1930s and 1940s, it was not until the 1950s when most had a chance to see and hear things regularly that once required travel to a concert hall, theater, museum, sports arena, lecture hall, or natural wonder. As television ownership grew from 9 percent of households in 1950 to 86 percent nine years later, it overtook the neighborhood movie theater as the primary shaper of urban images. The rapid growth of television ownership prompted concern about the impact of the medium on society. In 1954, 74 percent of those polled worried that violence depicted on television might negatively influence children's behavior.[2] It is not known how many of those concerned about television's influence on children were also worried about how gender relations were affected when, for example, New York City bus driver Ralph Kramden, the central character in *The Honeymooners*, threatens to send his wife, Alice, "to the moon" when she disagrees with him.

Many of the most popular of the situation comedies, such as *Ozzie and Harriet*, *Father Knows Best*, and *Leave It to Beaver*, were set in either the suburbs or the city; the location was almost incidental to the family's life. In *I Love Lucy*, starring Lucille Ball and her real-life husband, Cuban band leader Desi Arnaz, a New York City nightclub offers him (but not her) the path to wealth and stardom. The show earned top ratings three seasons in a row beginning in 1952. Representative of many of the decade's comedies and soap operas, *I Love Lucy* presented the big city as a place of promise. The challenges the city presented could be negotiated as long as the characters remained true to themselves and their families.

Despite concerns raised by cultural critics who worried about the influence of the "electronic opiate," by 1959 American families were watching an astonishing six hours of television a day, seven days a week.[3] Viewers began to recognize New York City, Los Angeles, Burbank, and Hollywood as the nation's electronic cultural capitals, in part because variety shows hosted by such celebrities as Milton Berle ("Mr. Television") and Arthur Godfrey usually told audiences where they were broadcasting from—a carryover from their radio days. Game shows such as *What's My Line?* also featured stars who had their start in vaudeville or radio and were often linked to a particular city in an effort to gain credibility among viewers. Regularly scheduled television programs were supplemented with special productions often sponsored by corporations such as the Ford Motor Company and General Electric. The nation's more highbrow television viewers eagerly anticipated the occasional plays, musicals, operas, and symphony orchestra concerts brought to them from leading U.S. cities.

Television shows that presented the darker side of city life were typically police and private detective dramas. One of the most popular of these "cop shows" was NBC's weekly drama *Dragnet*, featuring the laconic leading character Joe Friday famous for his interrogatory style ("Just the facts, ma'am"). The popularity of this Los Angeles–based crime-busting cop was likely influenced by the belief that urban crime was a problem that could easily be solved or managed when a trustworthy law enforcement officer could simply gather "the facts."

Television pioneers quickly embraced the new style of music that had helped to make teenagers 70 percent of all record buyers by 1958. The records they sought fell into the category of rock and roll, the term popularized by Cleveland radio promoter Alan Freed.[4] Some rock-and-roll artists had roots in country and western music; others borrowed elements from gospel, blues, and rhythm and blues. Regardless of its musical origins, the performance and production of rock and roll was purely urban. Among those who gained fame for his success in fusing together knowledge of rural and urban black and white musical genres was Memphis, Tennessee, truck driver Elvis Presley, who first appeared (from the waist up only) on television's popular *The Ed Sullivan Show* in 1956. The Little Gaelic Singers of Derry County appeared in one of the same broadcasts as the "King of Rock and Roll," apparently to add some generational balance to the musical portion of the program.

Despite the debt that rock and roll owed to the music written and pre-formed by people of color such as blues guitarists B. B. King and Bo Didley, most of the performers who achieved stardom during the 1950s were white men. Frankie Avalon enjoyed widespread fame, for example, but found his greatest appeal among the sons, daughters, and grandchildren of urban immigrants to New York, New Jersey, and other urban industrial states. Teens learned about new rock-and-roll artists and dances from watching *Teenorama*, a long-running television show that began in the early 1950s on a Washington, D.C., television station that marketed itself to people of color. Philadelphia's *American Bandstand*, with emcee Dick Clark, targeted primarily white teenagers and became a long-lasting nationwide hit.

As more and more middle-income Americans moved to the suburbs, their view of the city was shaped more by the electronic image of urban life than by the occasional visit. When suburban teenagers saw or heard Elvis Presley sing the lament of a child "born in the ghetto," did they realize that their hero, whose family briefly resided in federally subsidized public housing, had made a narrow and unlikely escape from poverty? Prior to his filmmaking stint, Presley's edgy image and that of film star James Dean, who died in a 1955 automobile accident shortly after the release of the popular film *Rebel Without a Cause*, stood in contrast to stars such as recording artist Pat Boone and television character Dobie Gillis, both of whom seemed to embody the image of the wholesome boy next door in their middle-class subdivisions.

Presley, Dean, and Marlon Brando were one type of 1950s urban rebels. Others embraced bebop, a style of jazz music and form of slang that first originated in the West Coast cities of San Francisco and Los Angeles. The beats were a small group of urban dwellers whose countercultural lifestyle became known to outsiders because of their commitment to challenging convention through writing rather than the speech making and demonstrations of the succeeding generation. Foremost among so-called beat writers was Lowell, Massachusetts, native Jack Kerouac, the son of French Canadian immigrants who briefly attended Columbia University and served in the merchant marine during World War II. His autobiographical novel, *On the Road*, typewritten on a 150-foot-long roll of paper, offered an account of the cross-country journeys Kerouac and his friends took in the late 1940s and early 1950s. They zigzagged back and forth from East Coast to West Coast cities, spending their time in jazz bars, coffeehouses, and flophouses in pursuit of enlightenment or kicks through wine, women, and song (and the stimulant benzene). After witnessing World War II and the Korean War, they had no interest in getting a job, settling down, and raising a family in the suburbs as portrayed in films such as *The Man in the Gray Flannel Suit*. Kerouac's friend, Alan Ginsberg of Patterson, New Jersey, first read and recorded his most famous poem "Howl" in San Francisco in 1957. Early copies of the epic poem of the beats were seized by city police as obscene. For the beats and those who imitated them, city life was what one made it.

The bifurcated image of the city presented in television, rock and roll, and beat literature was reinforced on the stage, in movies, and in fiction. The Broadway musical *West Side Story*, which was made into a 1961 movie, offered a modern retelling of William Shakespeare's *Romeo and Juliet*. Reflecting the changes in patterns of urban immigration, the story focuses on star-crossed lovers from rival teenage gangs of different ethnicities whose weapons of choice were switchblades. Notions of how city schools were affected by the rise of a rebellious youth culture included the 1955 film *Blackboard Jungle*, starring Glenn Ford and Sidney Poitier.

The harsh and seamy side of city life was the focus of many motion pictures known as film noir. Typical of these dark, gritty films was *On the Waterfront*, which showed the difficulties faced by longshoremen and other port workers who eked out a living amidst unscrupulous employers, corrupt unions, and violent criminals. Some film noir scripts were drawn from popular novels of the time period. Many people who never set foot in a large city thought that they knew something about urban life because they read books by best-selling crime novelists such as Brooklyn native Frank Morrison "Mickey" Spillane. The crime novelist created a hard-nosed detective, Mike Hammer, who appeared in six different mysteries with titles such as *Kiss Me, Deadly*. Spillane's detective novels brought him wealth and success (more than 27 million copies of his books were sold), perhaps because he cultivated the image of a regular guy, allowing himself to be photographed in blue jeans and a white T-shirt in his hand-built, knotty pine-paneled Newburgh, New York, bungalow.

Outside of crime and mystery novels, other books from the period remain widely influential in shaping notions of city life. They include the previously mentioned 1957 Kerouac novel *On the Road* and J. D. Salinger's *The Catcher in the Rye*, published in 1951. The latter tells the tale of Holden Caulfield, a habitual prep school flunk-out who is convinced the world is run by "phonies." Caulfield returns to his New York City home in the vain hope of finding his way by visiting the places he once loved and enjoyed, such as the Radio City ice rink and the American Museum of Natural History in Central Park. Instead, he ends up in a sanitarium for mental health treatment.

**THE 1960s: THE ROCK-AND-ROLL CITY**
During the 1960s on the outskirts of nearly every major city, residential subdivisions arose in what had been forests, fields, and orchards. The construction of new schools, office buildings, and shopping centers with ready access to interstate highway interchanges promised to hasten the decline of schools, offices, and shops in the inner city. More and more American families were not only living in suburbia but working and shopping there too. During this time of dramatic societal change, rock and roll became the most influential medium for communicating messages and impressions of cities and urban life. Leading rock-and-roll musicians began to express their opposition to the war in Vietnam and support for civil rights, women's rights, and other social causes. The national capital of rock with a message was San Francisco. One of the main gathering points was a seedy theater in the Filmore section of the city known as Filmore East, where huge crowds listened to such bands as the Mamas and the Papas, Hot Tuna, the Grateful Dead, Janice Joplin, the

Allman Brothers, and Jefferson Airplane. Youth who never witnessed or became a part of the vibrant Bay Area scene during the late 1960s could make a
connection to it through the music. When listening to records of their favorite
bands or hearing songs on the radio, they too could be in San Francisco with
"a flower in their hair" and feel that they were registering their opposition
to the war and "the Establishment." The music suggested that cities such as
San Francisco and Berkeley offered the greatest prospects for the attainment
of social and economic justice. If Americans were ever to "come together," it
would happen in the city. Ironically, it was in 1967, the famous "Summer of
Love" for those who hung out in the Haight-Ashbury section of San Francisco, that brought one of the nation's darkest hours. Detroit's deadly riot
that year not only was a setback for class and race relations but also helped
to justify the economic and social disinvestment that nearly destroyed the
mighty city that literally put America—and many other countries around the
world—on wheels.

Given the violence and turmoil that existed in many U.S. cities during the
1960s, it is hardly surprising that some of television's most popular situation
comedies reinforced the notion of the city as a dangerous or potentially corrupting place. In the opening to *Green Acres*, a popular program that ran from
1965 to 1971, affluent businessman-turned-farmer Oliver Douglas physically
forces his beautiful blonde wife, Lisa (played by Eva Gabor), to leave her New
York "penthouse view" for a shack in the country. Ironically, Lisa fits right in
and wins quick acceptance from the residents of "Pixly." By contrast, Oliver
is baffled by his rustic neighbors, who distrust him for many reasons—including his inability to communicate with a pig named Arnold Ziffle. What
distinguished Oliver and Lisa Douglas most from real-life Americans in the
1960s was their migration to the countryside, not the suburbs, yet the couple
characteristically chose to leave the city.

The popular television situation comedy *The Beverly Hillbillies* mirrored
the awkward adjustment to urban life experienced by so-called hillbillies who
migrated out of Appalachia during the 1930s and 1940s. Like the program's
Jed Clampett and family (including the moonshine-brewing "Granny"), rural
transplants feared the imposing size, fast pace, and depravity of cities. Bound
by a common set of values and assumptions regarding obligation to "kinfolk,"
the blended Clampett family is not corrupted by their new life in Beverly
Hills. They stubbornly wear the same clothes, eat the same food, drive the

same jalopy, and maintain the same values they had before Jed became an oil millionaire. The only thing that is overtly different is that they had abandoned their one-room cabin for a Beverly Hills mansion complete with a "cement pond" (swimming pool). In 1962 and 1963, *The Beverly Hillbillies* was the top-rated television show in the United States.

Television programs playfully poked fun at urban life during a time when the nightly news brought grave images of U.S. cities into living rooms all over the country. In the top-rated network evening newscast during the 1960s, NBC's Chet Huntley typically began each broadcast in New York City with a far-ranging summary of events around the world, and David Brinkley, based in Washington, D.C., appeared via a television monitor to provide the inside scoop on the nation's politics. Regardless of which network news channel viewers selected during the 1960s, they were confronted with one urban tragedy after another and forced to come to grips with scenes of cities erupting in violence, most traumatically after the assassinations of President John F. Kennedy in Dallas in 1963, Black Muslim minister Malcolm X in New York City in 1965, the Reverend Martin Luther King Jr. in Memphis in 1968, and Senator Robert Kennedy in Los Angeles in 1968. The television coverage of the urban rioting played a key role in shifting the view of many whites toward the civil rights movement. Scenes from the rioting in the Watts section of Los Angeles in August 1965 and in Cleveland, Chicago, Newark, Detroit, and more than fifty other cities between 1964 and 1967 fed fear of the city. Images of the Black Power Movement and the Oakland, California–based Black Panther political party reinforced preexisting inclinations to leave the city and relocate in the overwhelmingly white suburbs.

Comedian Dick Gregory compared the Black Panthers' call to arms to the alarm raised by Boston's Paul Revere when the British sought to crush the colonial resistance movement. Gregory was among those who used humor to try to diffuse the social and economic tensions simmering in the cities. The value of this approach was seen in the Burbank, California–produced *Laugh-In*, the leading U.S. television show in 1968 and 1969. In *The Smothers Brothers Comedy Hour*, two folk singers used topical humor to advance progressive causes. Fans of the iconoclastic Smothers brothers picketed the CBS's New York City headquarters when the network terminated its $4.5-million-dollar contract with the famous duo over a censorship battle. As the decade drew to a close, the major networks were forced to acknowledge the widespread appeal of the work of Bill Cosby, Flip Wilson, and other African American comedians, and television executives began to award contracts for prime-time shows to popular black entertainers.

Proof of the growing influence of television in shaping perceptions of urban life in the United States came in the 1960s with the disappearance of over 160 magazines, such as the 148-year-old *Saturday Evening Post*. At the same time, dozens of city newspapers, including the Boston *Traveler*, the San Francisco *News-Call-Bulletin*, and the Portland *Reporter*, ceased publication or merged with other papers. The Portland *Reporter* vanished from newsstands in the midst of a series that examined the regrettable impact of urban renewal and interstate highway building on the city. In 1960, New York City residents could choose from seven newspapers, but by the end of the decade, only three major dailies remained in business. Newspapers became less profitable, closed, or merged with others not only because television news viewing grew in popularity but also because publishers wanted to reduce production and labor costs. In the final analysis, print journalism slipped in popularity because more Americans began relying on television to stay informed.

During the tumultuous 1960s, the notion that America's cities were both places of opportunity and centers of corruption was promoted not only by television and the print media but by popular music as well. Under the impact of the "British invasion," rock and roll developed a harder edge, and the upbeat and harmonious tunes of its early years became passé. For parents whose adolescent children flocked to buy the records produced by or attend concerts given by rock bands from England, the clean-cut members of the Beatles were preferable to the Rolling Stones, who gained a reputation as the bad boys of rock and roll. The upbeat portrayal of life presented in the Beatles' motion pictures *A Hard Day's Night* and *Yellow Submarine*, which offered cartoon depictions of the "Fabulous Four," George Harrison, John Lennon, Paul McCartney, and Ringo Starr, contrasted with the grime of their native Liverpool, a city that was undergoing an industrial and economic decline.

As more and more Americans began to support the dismantling of the so-called color line, African Americans began to take center stage in the rock-and-roll scene and to receive top billing. Their quest for recognition was, in part, satisfied by the rise of the Detroit-based Motown sound. Motown artists celebrated black America's migration out of the rural South, escape from backbreaking agricultural labor, and transition to urban life. City living was not easy, and newcomers faced a series of hurdles to be cleared. The process of learning how to avoid or negotiate the challenges brought a collective strength and shared experience that gave people of color and the sons and daughters of southern and eastern European immigrants the confidence to rise and make their way in American society.

In 1960, "Shop Around," recorded by Smokey Robinson and the Miracles, reached number 2 on the pop chart and number 1 on the rhythm and blues chart, giving Motown its first big crossover hit. Successful Motown singers and bands, including Marvin Gaye, the Temptations, Martha and the Vandellas, Diana Ross and the Supremes, and child star Stevie Wonder, established Detroit as the rock-and-roll capital of the United States. Under the skillful guidance of songwriter, record producer, and former boxer Berry Gordy Jr., singers and musicians who had fused the gospel music many had known as churchgoing youth with rhythm and blues created a new sound with worldwide and enduring appeal. Despite the 1967 race riot and the deep-rooted discrimination people of color faced in Detroit's automobile plants, neighborhoods, stores, offices, and schools, the Motown sound remained upbeat.

At roughly the same time, more and more white performers began to acknowledge their artistic debt to people of color and to condemn racial and class injustice. Janis Joplin of Port Arthur, Texas, sang in a style she acknowledged was borrowed from black blues singers living and performing in the Gulf Coast. Hibbing, Minnesota, a small industrial city whose economic fate was linked to the price of the iron ore extracted nearby, gave rise to the foremost voice of the 1960s Now Generation, Bob Dylan. After a 1962 tour with folksinger Joan Baez, Dylan spent more and more time in New York City; his song "Desolation Row" was reportedly written in the backseat of one of the city's ubiquitous taxi cabs. Dylan's "The Times They Are a Changin'" became the unofficial anthem for disaffected youth in the 1960s.

One of Dylan's protest songwriting contemporaries, Chicago's Phil Ochs, commented on the brutal treatment city police gave protesters outside the 1968 Democratic Convention by singing, "Where were you in Chicago? You know, I didn't see you there." Ochs later committed suicide, and Dylan alienated many of his folk music followers by "going electric" in 1965. Soon, the most popular bands featured a white male lead guitarist capable of producing sounds that greatly deepened the generational void. Even though many of these guitarists such as Eric Clapton—formerly of the Yardbirds, Cream, and Derek and the Dominos—were British, many American parents blamed musicians of color for "killing" the more melodic popular music of earlier generations. Parents and other "squares" liked the popular 1964 hit song "Downtown," which told of a place where "all the lights are bright" even though the lights—the allure and drawing power of many downtowns—had already dimmed in the rush to the suburbs. Popular music suggested that many adolescents did not share their parents' affection for suburban living. The popularity of such films as *The Graduate*, with its popular sound track featuring the Simon and Garfunkel hit "Mrs. Robinson," indicated that many young people felt as though they had missed out on something when the family left the city neighborhood where "those who pray" still resided.

Literature and movies also reinforced the dual cities image in the 1960s. James Baldwin wrote of the racism that divided not only American cities but also the entire nation in *Another Country* (1962) and *The Fire Next Time* (1963). Norman Mailer's *The Armies of the Night* (1968) offered an account of his experiences in Washington, D.C., when he participated in a 1967 antiwar march on the Pentagon. After winning both a Pulitzer Prize and a National Book Award in 1969, Mailer campaigned to be elected mayor of New York, but voters were not convinced that he was the right person for the job.

Biologist Rachel Carson's 1962 book *Silent Spring* focused on how the largely unregulated use of pesticides was helping to "still the song of the birds and the leaping of the fish." The book's influence validated concerns about environmental problems in U.S. cities, where the quality of the air, water, and soil was declining in the face of growing petrochemical and fossil fuel use. Among the events that suggested the growth of an urban environmental consciousness was a 1969 protest organized by Catholic priests in Washington, D.C., who opposed the production and use of napalm, a chemical defoliant widely used by U.S. forces fighting in Southeast Asia.

## THE 1970s: THE DISCO CITY

During the 1970s, U.S. cities reeled under the impact of public and corporate polices that prioritized new suburban development over urban reinvestment. Television, film, and popular music gave most Americans their only view of urban life, and cities were presented as places of nearly irreconcilable differences. Rock and roll still dominated the airwaves, alternately praising and damning the city, but by mid-decade many leading rock-and-roll bands, including the Rolling Stones, released albums that were influenced by the highly processed disco sound. Soon commercial rock radio stations began mixing in disco tunes or rerecording disco or dance versions of certain rock hits. Despite some protests by die-hard rock and rollers, disco gained ground on rock perhaps in large measure because adults found its lack of message more palatable. High school gym class teachers soon added the "Hustle" to the dance lineup right after the "chicken dance."

In spite of the rising popularity of disco, with its emphasis on beat rather than lyrics, popular media continued to address social change in urban settings. Crosby, Stills, Nash, and Young, a popular band of American and Canadian musicians that fused rock and folk traditions, recorded "Four Dead in Ohio" shortly after the May 1970 shooting deaths of four students at Kent State University in northern Ohio by National Guardsmen. The demonstrations and marches that resulted in the temporary closing of roughly 450 college and university campuses in the wake of the shooting coupled with growing publicity about urban crime to convince many that the nation and its cities were out of control. Hollywood (and actor Clint Eastwood) created a movie character to ease this anxiety and give America a hero who was fighting back against the criminals on the streets and the crooked cops and judges who let them prey on ordinary people. In three Eastwood films during the decade, San Francisco movie cop "Dirty Harry" Callahan encourages the thugs he runs down to "make his day" and give him an excuse to fire his intimidating .44 magnum and help restore order to the beleaguered city.

The most highly rated television program from 1971 to 1975 was *All in the Family*, a situation comedy steeped in political satire. In 1971, television producer Norman Lear created a character, Archie Bunker, who expressed the angst and bewilderment felt by many white Anglo-Saxon Protestant males whose long-standing economic and social dominance seemed under siege from people of color, women, and white ethnics, including Jews and Catholics. Played by actor Carroll O'Connor, Bunker is a fifty-something dockworker who resides in a mainly white neighborhood in the New York City borough of Queens. When he is not at work or sitting in his favorite chair next to his long-suffering wife, Edith, Archie can be found drinking beer and commiserating with his friends (other white blue-collar working men) down at Kelsey's Bar. Archie's placid existence is shaken not only by the disturbing international and national events taking place around him but also by the changes within his own household. His "little girl" and only child, adult daughter Gloria, falls in love with and marries Michael Stevic, a Catholic of Polish descent and a political liberal who attended college while his wife worked. Archie's disdain for his son-in-law and for Poles, Catholics, and political liberals in general is underscored by the nickname he gives him: "meathead." Not only has Gloria failed to marry the kind of man Archie expected, but she has also embraced feminism and civil rights and encouraged her mother (who Archie often refers to as a "dingbat") to do the same and to challenge her husband's autocratic ways.

Archie's world goes into a further tailspin when George and Louise Jefferson and their handsome, college-educated son, Lionel, become their neighbors. The Jeffersons, who own a small chain of dry-cleaning stores, prosper, and their son becomes close friends with Gloria and Mike. The black family's economic and social rise is exemplified in their mobility, their hard work, and financial risk rewarded by the pleasure of "movin' on up to the East Side—to a deluxe apartment in the sky." The family then became the focus of their own spin-off situation comedy, *The Jeffersons.* Lear created another television family of color to illustrate further the difficulties faced by those in poverty who wished to better themselves financially and socially. In *Good Times*, Florida and James Evans and their three children are forced by low wages and the lack of steady employment to live in "the projects," what in real life was then the world's largest public housing development: Chicago's Robert Taylor Homes. The crime and deprivation they were surrounded with adversely affect them, but they do not succumb to it because of the strong bonds of family and community. Despite James's frequent absences in search of work, the family stays together and refuses to abandon its dreams of mobility. They survive, in part, because their son, J.J. (Jimmy Walker), keeps them laughing with his carefully honed "ghetto humor."

The way in which the dreams of economic and social betterment held by urban dwellers were frustrated by discrimination and the lack of steady, gainful employment was best illustrated in three 1970s motion pictures focusing on Italian Catholics. *The Godfather*, released in 1972, starring Marlon Brando, Robert De Niro, and Al Pacino, was based on a novel by Mario Puzo. Vito Corleone leaves his native Sicily for New York City, but on discovering that the conventional avenues of social and economic gain are closed to Italian Catholics, he returns to the family structure and culture of organized crime he had known in the old country. Two additional *Godfather* films explored the mob boss's efforts to resist involvement in the illegal drug trade and to go legitimate by investing heavily in legal gambling palaces in Las Vegas.

In 1976, the first of several *Rocky* films appeared. Sylvester Stallone, a real-life native of South Philadelphia's Italian neighborhood, created and played a local fictional character, Rocky Balboa. A meat plant worker who tries his best to steer clear of the organized crime endemic in his neighborhood, Rocky uses boxing as his ticket to fame and fortune. The physical and mental toughness he carefully cultivates is rewarded in the ring, but for the multidimensional Rocky, it is best symbolized when at the peak of his physical prowess, he races up the lengthy steps of the city's Philadelphia Museum of Art, a magnificent edifice modeled on the Acropolis, and raises his arms in triumph. Rocky fights his way out of the urban jungle and can provide economic stability for his beloved Adrian.

In *Saturday Night Fever*, Tony Manero, a Brooklyn, New York, hardware store clerk played by Italian American actor John Travolta, uses a different route to cope with the limitations placed on him by his family and the larger society. Whereas earlier generations of Italians turned to sports such as boxing and baseball, Tony pins his hopes on his ability to excel on the disco dance floor. The movie's enormously successful sound track, written and recorded by the Australian Gibb brothers, who sang together as the Bee Gees, includes a song played as Tony walks down a New York City street delivering paint. The lyrics describe Tony's plight, "I'm goin' nowhere. Somebody help me." He wins a disco dance contest after dropping a local girl who shares his interest in dance and teams up with a better dancer from outside the neighborhood. Her ambitions to go to college and become middle class appeal to him, but at the movie's conclusion it is not at all clear whether Tony can transfer the energy and discipline that went into becoming a disco king to achieve these new goals. Just "Stayin' Alive," as the 1977 film's hit song indicates, seems to be hard enough. In real life, the disco scene was covered in magazines such as *People*, and rumors circulated about the stars and celebrities who danced the night away (in platform shoes) at New York's Studio 54 fueled by cocaine and alcohol.

New York City's Woody Allen, who had earlier made a name for himself doing stand-up comedy on television shows such as *The Steve Allen Show*, made a number of films that helped establish or, rather, reestablish the urban-based, romantic comedy. The most widely recognized of these films is *Annie Hall*, which won four Academy Awards in 1977. On the magical streets of New York, it was still possible for a nerdy guy whose brain was better cultivated than his physique to win the heart of a smart and beautiful woman played by Diane Keaton.

Rock and roll reached the height of its popularity in the 1970s, and many rock bands either formed in cities or sang of their virtues. Journey's "City by the Bay," Foghat's "Fool for the City," and the Lovin' Spoonful's "Summer in the City" were among the popular rock tunes that celebrated the city and the possibilities of urban life. Leading rock bands of the day—the Rolling Stones, Led Zeppelin, Bruce Springsteen and the E Street Band, the Grateful Dead, and others—had such huge followings that they were capable of filling the nation's largest stadiums and arenas for live performances. With music blasting and lyrics practically unintelligible, fans went to concerts at places such as New York's Madison Square Garden and the now-razed Boston Garden more to take in the scene than for the quality of the music delivered in that setting. Many adolescents saved their money to buy pricey home and car stereos and amass a collection of favorite records and eight-track or cassette tapes.

At the apex of rock's influence, popular music saw further splintering with the rise of disco in the mid-1970s. Some disco dancers reached the level of fitness, agility, and strength necessary to engage in break dancing and were capable of literally throwing themselves on the ground without missing a beat. Break dance routines were soon incorporated into marching band routines. Historically black college and university bands attracted talented dancers and enjoyed an interracial following for their expert choreography and performance. Taken together, rock, disco, and rap music helped unify listeners across geographical boundaries. Those who sought celebrity or economic gain were warned of the risks and temptations that city life would place before them. "Jukebox Hero," a song by Foreigner, told of a youth who goes to the city with stars in his eyes, only to succumb to drug and alcohol addiction and to be taken advantage of by unscrupulous managers, booking agents, and record producers. In the end, however, the city was still the place aspiring performers needed to be to achieve success. As Detroit rock vocalist Bob Seger sang, regardless of whether you went east or west, strivers had no choice but to "keep running against the wind."

## 1980s: THE MTV CITY

During the 1980s, millions of U.S. households discarded the rooftop television antennae and had cable television hook-ups installed in their homes and businesses. Soon, "cable guys" seemed to be everywhere as the percentage of households with cable television increased from 19.4 percent in 1979 to 55.6 percent in 1989. From the day of its premier on August 1, 1981, one of the most popular cable channels was the music television network known as MTV. Despite being panned by some critics as "empty TV," it became an immediate hit. MTV offered a compelling new medium for the communication of urban images by fusing television with rock-and-roll music. The rock videos were introduced by hosts and hostesses selected by the network because they were attractive and enthusiastic, not for their insight into or knowledge of rock and roll or American cultural history. The music videos broadcasted on MTV and, later, Video Hits One (VH-1) were filmed in a choppy, quick sequence style. For millions of suburban and rural dwellers, the videos offered a compelling representation of city life. Even if they never set foot in the places where Detroit's Madonna; Michael Jackson of Gary, Indiana (whose career began with Motown as the child star of the Jackson Five); former Los Angeles Lakers cheerleader Paula Abdul; and other stars filmed their videos, MTV viewers could still partake of the urban experience by adopting the popular dances, clothes, hairstyles, and expressions of speech.

During the 1980s, video cameras improved in quality and shrank in size and cost. Although they were not inexpensive for most wage earners, many people purchased them to make their own motion pictures of their family, friends, and travels. Footage shot by videographers was recorded and played on videocassette recorders (VCRs) that were hooked up to televisions in millions of homes. Licensed copies of videotapes were rented and sold in national chains such as Blockbuster and a few mom-and-pop operations for less than two decades before they were rendered technologically obsolete by compact discs and DVD players. Video stores also rented computer games introduced for household use a decade earlier. Those consumers who acquired a console from a company such as Nintendo could rent or buy the new generation of electronic games. For many young people, the city and its problems were known to them mainly through the electronic games they played. It was easier to become an urban crime fighter when the weapon of choice was a joystick rather than a real gun.

During the 1980s, television remained one of the most powerful shapers of urban images. During the heyday of the evening soap opera, *Dallas*, starring Larry Hagman, attracted a large number of fans. The first episode of *Dallas* aired in 1978 and by 1980 it was the top-rated show in the United States. Viewers were presented with a version of life in a Sun Belt city on the rise, thanks in part to the unscrupulousness and double-dealing ways of oilman J. R. Ewing (Hagman) and his family and friends. Record-sized audiences tuned in on November 21, 1980, to learn the identity of the person who shot J. R. (an ex-mistress). The popular show spawned similar prime-time soaps, including *Dynasty* and *Falcon Crest*, before it was canceled in 1991. These successful shows collectively suggested that those in the know—those who were going places—lived in Sun Belt cities in Texas, Arizona, or California, not in gritty, crime-ridden New York City or Chicago.

The rising political and economic importance of ascendant southern cities was also underscored in another wildly popular 1984–1990 television show, *Miami Vice*. Not-so-undercover cops played by Don Johnson and Philip Michael Thomas pursued murderers, drug and arms dealers, robbers, and other criminals and used hot sports cars, fast boats, attractive women, and piles of cash as bait. The influence of the show was perhaps best seen in the fashion trends it encouraged. Soon, men all over the country were wearing casual, light-colored suit coats over T-shirts and allowing a little facial stubble to grow to contrast with their carefully maintained hair. The glamour and glitz surrounding Miami's famous television law enforcement duo provided a sharp contrast with the more cerebral Emmy Award–winning *Hill Street Blues*. Producer Steven Bochco shot the series in a manner that gave it a sense of realism then unmatched by other shows. In the Hill Street precinct, clearly located in a declining big-city neighborhood, police detectives struggled with their own personal problems and at the same time performed their incredibly demanding and often dangerous jobs. Bochco also produced *LA Law*, an Emmy Award–winning drama that offered a behind-the-scenes look at the inner workings of a high-profile Los Angeles law firm known for its criminal defense work. The chaste relationship between early television's Perry Mason and loyal secretary Della Street was replaced on *LA Law* by a new code of sexual ethics and behavior that often presented ethical dilemmas for the attorneys and their staff.

During the 1980s, the softer side of the city was presented in the Emmy Award–winning show *Cheers*. For the employees and the regular patrons, the

Boston neighborhood bar provided a surrogate home, a place where "every-one knows your name." *Cheers* was wildly popular at a time when Boston and many other cities were undergoing dramatic growth and redevelopment after years of economic stagnation. Immigrants from Asia, the Middle East, and Central and South America were changing city neighborhoods that had been abandoned by earlier immigrant and migrant groups. The show suggested that some of the good things about the city had not changed and that it was still possible for every person to find someone with whom they could relate.

Evidence of shifting urban demographics was underscored by the rise of rap music and an accompanying "gangsta" culture that was actively promoted by cable television's MTV and the Black Entertainment Network. People of color had been rapping, "toasting," or speaking in a rhythmic style for centu-ries, but it was not until the 1970s disco craze that deejays such as Grandmas-ter Flash and Kool D.J., who played in the South Bronx, Harlem, and West Coast black and Latino dance clubs, began to record routines spoken over dance music. "Rapper's Delight," recorded in 1979 by the Sugar Hill Gang, became the first rap tune to make the pop charts. By 1984, MTV watchers and radio listeners had brought megastardom to Run DMC, and they and other top rap artists received contracts from major record companies and movie producers. Just as rock and roll had been condemned for its socially corrosive effects, critics faulted rap artists (of all colors and backgrounds) for glamoriz-ing gun violence, drug and alcohol abuse, and sexual exploitation. By the early 1990s, rappers such as Queen Latifah were urging women of color to stand up for themselves and their children and take pride in their communities.

Although rock's influence began to wane in the 1980s, some rock musicians continued to use their influence to agitate for economic and social change. Three singers who commented on the decline of American cities as manufac-turing hubs and the loss of economic opportunity for wage earners were John Mellencamp, Bruce Springsteen, and Billy Joel. In his hit song "Allentown," Joel bemoaned the loss of the employment opportunities enjoyed by earlier genera-tions of urban dwellers. He and his fellow baby boomers were "waiting here in Allentown for the Pennsylvania we never found." As the 1980s progressed, it was becoming clear that the music video, the inexpensive video camera and DVD player, and gaming technology were infrequently employed to raise politi-cal or social awareness of urban inequities, pollution, and other problems or to find solutions to their declining economic and social fortunes.

## THE 1990s: CITY.COM

During the 1990s, the Internet brought a whole new means of transmitting images of the city. By the close of the decade, cities large and small had created websites largely to encourage tourism and business investment. Many metropolitan leaders hoped their cities could become like Boston and the suburbs along Massachusetts Route 128 (America's Technology Highway) and California's Silicon Valley, located between Palo Alto and San Jose, and become a center for high-tech research and manufacturing or e-commerce. Internet provider America Online (AOL) grew so profitable during the 1990s that it purchased media giant Time Warner Inc. for $16.5 billion in January 2000.

The city—or images of it—became further known to millions of people through a new generation of highly sophisticated computer games. Some games allowed players to engage in virtual urban warfare and to destroy popular landmarks in leading American cities. The promises and pitfalls of urban life were also presented by television talk shows. As a genre, the programs had existed for decades, but during the 1990s their influence reached new heights largely because of the popularity of Chicago-based Oprah Winfrey. From the time of her first program in 1986, Winfrey took on issues that affected Americans across the nation. Geraldo Rivera, an attorney turned talk show host who worked out of Los Angeles, adopted a more confrontational style that also won a huge viewership.

On March 3, 1991, Americans were confronted with evidence of the racism they heard described by Oprah and Geraldo. The beating of an unemployed African American construction worker, Rodney King, by Los Angeles police officers after he resisted arrest would probably have attracted little attention had not the entire incident been recorded on video by a bystander. The tape, which clearly showed a defenseless King being kicked and struck by police, was released to the press. President George H. W. Bush expressed the views of millions of Americans: "What I saw made me sick." Still, he and Congress failed to respond to the tragic incident as a sign of a much larger problem involving the lack of economic and social opportunities for advancement in Los Angeles and other cities across the United States. This public policy failure contributed to the situation that arose following the acquittal of three of the four officers accused in the King beating. When Los Angeles residents outraged by the King verdict rioted in 1992, a second videotape gained fame. This tape showed Reginald Denny, a white truck driver, being pulled from his cab and beaten. The videos showing the police beating King and the Denny assault provided convincing evidence that the politicians who sought election in 1992 needed to do more to make America's cities more equitable and less violent places.

The presidential election of 1992 became a three-way contest between incumbent President George H. W. Bush, a Republican; William Jefferson Clinton, the Democratic former Arkansas governor; and H. Ross Perot, an Independent. Perot cultivated his folksy image and familiarized television viewers with his squeaky voice during his "infomercials." He and other candidates appeared on "America's new political theater," CNN's *Larry King Live!* show.[5] When candidate Bill Clinton played the saxophone on the *Arsenio Hall Show* and appeared as a guest on *Saturday Night Live*, he projected an image of someone who had come far since his humble boyhood in Hope, Arkansas, and had developed an easy familiarity with urban popular culture. Even President Bush, who cultivated a homespun image when cutting brush on his Texas ranch attired in boots and jeans, also found it necessary to appear to be city savvy—as indicated by his appearance on MTV. During the 1990s, this cable television network played an activist role in the campaign by focusing its message on getting eligible youth registered to cast a vote that really could make a difference.

Following Clinton's 1992 victory, popular media outlets did not remain politicized for long. The focus on urban problems and issues during the election gave way to the more traditional and popular view of the city as a place of opportunity where it was still possible to escape poverty and discrimination and advance economically and socially. Los Angeles was presented as a place where dreams could still come true in the popular film *Pretty Woman*. A prostitute (played by Julia Roberts) finds love, happiness, and fortune and leaves her unsavory past behind when the successful Mr. Right (Richard Gere) comes along. When the extraordinary intellect of a young Cambridge, Massachusetts, janitor played by Matt Damon employed by the Massachusetts Institute of Technology was inadvertently discovered, the possibility of social and economic class mobility was offered in the award-winning film *Good Will Hunting*.

*Terminator 2*, released in 1991, was the most expensive movie ever produced up until that time. Star Arnold Schwarzenegger wreaked havoc in cities as the Terminator, but once he left Hollywood for Sacramento in 2003 to take his place as governor, he realized that the cities of the Golden State needed billions of dollars of infrastructure improvements at the very time when federal and state revenue was diminishing. Fans of the *Terminator* films and others of that genre, which relied on special computer effects to simulate urban doomsday scenarios, seemed to look forward to the day when cities would be destroyed for harboring evildoers. By contrast, other films of the 1990s depicted city dwellers as capable of great compassion. Real-life city problems included the need for treatment and social services for those suffering from the disease known as AIDS, which was the topic of a 1993 movie *Philadelphia* starring Tom Hanks and Denzel Washington. Rock star Bruce Springsteen received an Oscar for the theme song he wrote and recorded for the movie.

Popular television shows such as *Murphy Brown, Seinfeld,* and *Friends* portrayed a lifestyle among urban professionals that glossed over the economic and social realities they faced as more and more companies automated or outsourced their employment. In 1992, approximately 38 million Americans watched the episode of *Murphy Brown* where the title character, played by Candice Bergen, gave birth to a child out of wedlock. Speaking in San Francisco, Vice President Dan Quayle argued that the show was indicative of the moral decay in the United States that contributed to the Los Angeles riots. The vice president's remarks rekindled the old debate about the corrosive moral effects of electronic media—and the city.

Images of Beverly Hills and Los Angeles became familiar to television viewers who followed the news stories surrounding the arrest and the 1995 trial of O. J. Simpson, a widely admired former professional football star and media spokesman. Simpson was accused of the stabbing death of his former wife, Nicole Brown Simpson, and her companion, Ronald Goldman. After revelations of police tampering with the evidence, the jury acquitted Simpson. Shortly afterward, he lost in a civil suit brought against him by the Goldman family. The televised criminal trial revealed the strength and persistence of the color line in the United States. A decade later, Simpson was convicted and imprisoned of assault following an incident in Las Vegas that arose over the sale of memorabilia relating to his sports career.

Urban problems were among the issues that were treated with humor on one of the most popular television shows of the decade, *The Simpsons,* created by Matt Groening. When it first aired in December 1989 on the Fox network, some critics questioned the appeal of an animated show about a dysfunctional

American family. The show soon proved to be a hit, particularly among youth who identified with the rebellious "tween" Bart. Ironically, the Simpsons reside in "Springfield," the same city featured in the 1950s hit series *Father Knows Best*. In this later television family, father Homer, a nuclear plant worker with a beer belly, seldom knows what course of action to take when confronted with family problems.

By contrast, images of the city as a place where color and class consciousness ran high were presented in movies such as the 1991 *Boyz in the Hood*, produced by John Singleton, an African American filmmaker who studied at the University of Southern California. In the South-Central Los Angeles neighborhood where Singleton grew up, injury or death from gun violence and beatings was common. Lacking education and skills, most adolescents were effectively barred from participation in the regular economy and turned to the underground economy of drugs and crime as the only source of "advancement." Film director Spike Lee's award-winning 1989 film *Do the Right Thing* sensitively examined tensions between Italian Americans and blacks in a Brooklyn neighborhood undergoing racial transformation. His *Jungle Fever* (1992) detailed how an African American architect ruined his marriage when he crossed color and class lines and became briefly involved with his Italian American secretary, who was from a working-class community where class and racial bias combined with sexism.

Urban crime continued to be a favorite subject in television shows, movies, and novels. The television show *NYPD Blue*, premiering in 1993, depicted New York City police investigators as overworked, underpaid, and underappreciated. Although each of the characters had his or her own individual faults and weaknesses, most did their best to give everyone a fair shake. So-called investigative crime shows typically utilized urban settings for the violent crimes they investigated, further contributing to the myth that somehow crime was concentrated in the cities and had not migrated to the suburbs along with everything else.

During the early 1990s, the political and social influence of rock and roll continued to decline. Alternative rock bands, such as Smashing Pumpkins, Pearl Jam, and Soul Asylum, recorded songs with an antiestablishment and anticorporate flavor reminiscent of the San Francisco–area bands of the 1960s. When Pearl Jam issued its second album, *Vs.*, in October 1993, it sold more records in the first week than any prior release in popular music history. The

Seattle-based band Nirvana sold over 7 million records in 1992. The band's popularity reached new heights with the drug-related death of singer-guitarist Kurt Cobain in Seattle in April 1994. Ironically, these counterculture bands and the grunge style they popularized came to the forefront at a time when the Pacific Northwest was undergoing tremendous urban and suburban growth and city skylines were being reshaped by a multinational corporate presence.

As mainstream rock and roll lost its potency in the 1990s, white wage earners contributed to the growing popularity of country music. Although many male country artists wore cowboy hats and string ties, those who dominated the country charts during this time were hardly off the farm or ranch. Garth Brooks, for example, was raised in an Oklahoma City suburb and as a college student played in the bars near the Oklahoma State University campus. Knowing neither city nor rural life firsthand, they sought to anchor themselves to an unchanging world where it still remained possible to discern right from wrong.

The hip-hop artists of the 1990s were the antithesis of the rope-swinging, special effects–loving Brooks. Overtly urban, they both celebrated and condemned the cityscape and what it took to maneuver the obstacles of race and class. On his 1993 hit album *Lethal Injection*, the rapper Ice Cube offered profane commentary on police violence and racism within the criminal justice system. Two years earlier, rappers N.W.A. (Niggas with Attitude) attracted national attention with a best-selling record that endorsed violence against women, including those of color, undermining their more serious messages. In July 2000, Kim Mathers, the wife of rap star Eminem, attempted suicide. The Detroit hip-hop celebrity had previously recorded a song expressing his wish to murder his spouse and dump her body in a lake. National debate took place over the violence and sexism expressed in popular music, while the publicity further enriched Eminem and other recording artists. Later, Eminem had achieved enough mainstream acceptance to be featured along with a black gospel group in a Chrysler Corporation advertisement aired during the telecast of the 2011 Super Bowl. The advertisement depicted the Motor City not as the broken victim of corporate disinvestment but as a dynamic arts and culture center with great architecture and sex appeal.

On New Year's Eve 1999, many anxiously awaited what would happen to international computer networks when 2000 began. Would they crash as a result of damage done by the Y2K computer bug? In cities throughout the

United States, residents hoarded water, food, cash, and even fuel out of fear that these items would be unavailable if mass computer system failure took place. Nothing happened.

## THE 2000s: THE HANDHELD CITY

In 2000, the World Wide Web went wireless. The city and city life soon became known to millions of people primarily through the images communicated from handheld devices, such as cellular telephones. The introduction of so-called smart telephones made it possible for users to access the Internet anywhere. The first BlackBerry smart phone appeared on the market in March 2002. Thousands of Apple customers waited in line eagerly to snap up the long-awaited iPhone for somewhere between $500 and $600. Between June 29 and September 10, 2007, the company sold more than 1 million of the devices. High-quality still and motion picture images, text, and music could be sent and received via the phone with the cost of mobile service offered by a number of different corporate providers.

By the close of the decade, there was an explosion in the demand for "apps"—applications that could be downloaded on a smart phone and used, for example, in a phone with a Global Positioning System (GPS) to help a hungry group of conventioneers leaving a cocktail reception on the National Mall in Washington, D.C., to locate the nearest Thai restaurant, access the menu, read a few brief reviews, check on the availability of a table, and obtain directions and estimated travel time. The appeal of handheld devices was so great by 2010 that it became common to see men, women, and children walking down the street; traveling in a car, bus, train, ferry, or plane; and shopping, dining, and engaging in other activities while consulting a small iPod or iPad screen. The city also became known to millions of people as a result of the rise of blogging and postings on Myspace.com launched in August 2003, YouTube (purchased by Google for $1.65 billion in 2006), and social media networks such as Facebook, MySpace, and Twitter. In 2005, U.S. cell phone users sent an estimated 45 billion text messages, and the number was expected to continue to increase. Would electronic communications ultimately end or vastly curtail traditional mail delivery service?

For many people, a visit to a city attraction such as the Las Vegas Strip or the USS *Constitution* in Boston would not be complete without taking a picture with their cell phone, sending it directly to a relative or friend, or posting it on a social media network site. The most prominent of these, Facebook, was launched on February 4, 2004, in Cambridge, Massachusetts by Mark Zuckerman and a group of fellow Harvard University students. Hollywood's version of their story was told in an awarding-wining motion picture called *The Social Network*. The growing sophistication and affordability of handheld devices contributed to the marked changes in the music production business. Record stores that thrived as teen hangouts for two and three generations disappeared from downtown shopping districts and suburban malls as music lovers now visited websites and paid a fee to download their favorite songs legally. In February 2005, Apple announced that it had sold its billionth song through iTunes. The sale of digital music increased from $183.4 million in 2004 to more than $2 billion in 2009, and CD sales fell by more than 50 percent between 2004 and 2009.

During the 2000s, electronic games became so popular that they outsold movie tickets. Between 1996 and 2004, game sales doubled to $7.3 billion. The Xbox 360, a gaming console, was released by Microsoft in November 2005 and scored an immediate sales hit. Regardless of whether they were played on a smart phone or console, electronic games presented a range of differing notions or views of the city. Sim City made it possible for players (including university faculty who used the game as a teaching tool in architecture and city planning classes) to simulate being a city manager of a city. A very different image of the city was presented by other games, including Grand Theft Auto, which made it possible for a player to become virtually a member of an urban gang that steals luxury and other hot cars and tries to elude police and rival gang members. When Grand Theft Auto IV was released on April 29, 2008, more than 6 million copies were sold in the first week. The decade also saw greater overlap and convergence between video games and movies. Many of the action figures or sequences created for movies or television also appeared in electronic games, and characters from video games became the protagonists of action films.

The impact of the increased use of handheld devices on cities and city life continues to be assessed. By contrast, the Segway Human Transporter, a personal transportation device introduced by inventor Dean Kamen in December 2001, proved to be a flop within a short time. Promoters optimistically predicted that the Segway would bring about a transportation revolution and help reduce greenhouse gas emissions in cities clogged with cars, but sales of the vehicle have proved to be insignificant.

Television now competes with other forms of electronic media for consumer attention but still provides an important portal through which viewers come to know or think they know urban life. The characters in television dramas of the 2000s, such as *Sex in the City* and two movies by the same name, presented a version of urban life where the search for sexual satisfaction or titillation trumped all else. Are the *Desperate Housewives* desperate because they live in suburbia and seek urban sex and excitement? Taken together, these movies and television shows portrayed city professionals as self-absorbed people who lived to satisfy, realize, and indulge their individual needs and desires. Unlike the characters in earlier shows, such as the 1970s hit *All in the Family,* they did not discuss unemployment, poverty, or U.S. military action abroad. Film and television characters in many of the shows that depicted urban life in the 2000s often lacked the kind of familial, ethnic, religious, and neighborhood identity or consciousness that determined the choices weighed by many television characters of earlier generations. Perhaps the most important exception was *The Sopranos,* produced by HBO, which presented an image of Italian Americans, organized crime, and city life that differed little from those established by the 1970s movie *The Godfather* and the 1990s hit movie *Goodfellas. The Sopranos* ran from 1999 to 2007 and won its first Emmy Award in 2004.

HBO's 2002–2008 series *The Wire* was more than a crime and police drama set in Baltimore. Series creator David Simon, who had previously worked for the Baltimore *Sun* as a staff member and had published several nonfiction works on cities, produced the show in collaboration with an impressive team of well-known writers, detectives, and crime experts. The final year of the series was an electronic exposé of the media and its largely unrealized potential for helping solve urban problems. The quality of the commentary offered on *The Wire* has prompted the creation of at least one university course that uses the program as a class resource. Other television shows that presented U.S. cities as centers of vice and crime were *Law and Order,* which began in 1993; *NYPD Blue,* which ran from 1993 to 2005; and *Crime Scene Investigation (CSI),* based in Las Vegas, which began in 2000 and produced spin-off series set in New York City and Miami. *CSI* personnel battled their own personal demons as they utilized the latest technology to help solve cases in international terrorism, intellectual property and identity theft, and other cybercrimes, as well as murder, blackmail, and theft. It was the most highly rated show in 2002–2005.

The collective impression created by these urban crime dramas seemed to be that private wealth did not trickle down to the urban masses. They further suggested that the political programs created to help the jobless and impoverished during the 1960s and early 1970s had failed to eradicate these problems. Poverty, crime, and despair continued to lurk in every corner of the city. The persistence of these maladies was not cause for the punishment or destruction of U.S. cities but rather suggested that the optimism of earlier decades when reformers believed it possible to "fix" the city had given way to grim acceptance that they would persist indefinitely.

In 2002, American narcissism reached new heights with the popularity of the television show, *American Idol*. The show, similar in format to *The Original Amateur Hour* and *Star Search* from earlier eras, underscored the lengths to which Americans were willing to go to achieve fame and fortune. With two versions running on different nights, it was the top-ranked show in the nation for five consecutive seasons beginning in 2005. The rise of social networking in the late 2000s was among the factors that explained the declining popularity of talk-back and reality television. In 2010, Oprah Winfrey announced her plans for retirement from the Chicago-based show that had made her world famous and vastly wealthy and launched her own network in 2011.

Movies that helped shape urban impressions in the twenty-first century included *Mystic River*, based on a crime novel by Dennis Lehane. The 2003 film starring Kevin Bacon, Sean Penn, and Tim Robbins, set in a tough Boston-area neighborhood, examined how a childhood case of sexual molestation affected the victim and his friends both in childhood and as adults. *Crash*, a loosely-linked drama about the chance meetings that took place between the victims of a Los Angeles automobile accident and the investigating public safety officials, won an Academy Award in 2005. *The Departed*, an award-winning 2006 film by Martin Scorsese set in contemporary Boston, was a gritty tale of corruption among criminals and cops who had grown up in the same neighborhoods. The underside of life in Lowell, Massachusetts, revealed in the 2010 film *The Fighter*, was based on the true story of local members of the struggling working class. Actor Mark Wahlberg, a native of Dorchester, Massachusetts, played boxer Micky Ward, whose exploits in the ring followed the aborted comeback effort of his half brother, Dicky Eklund (played by Christian Bale), a washed-up boxer who became an alcoholic and crack cocaine addict. The film received several 2010 Academy Award nominations.

Hip-hop music further reinforced conflicting urban images, accounting for 13 percent of music and music video sales between 2000 and 2005. About one-quarter of all music and music video sales during the same period fell into the rock category; country and rhythm and blues each contributed about 10 percent of record sales. In 2000, rapper Sean ("Puff Daddy") Combs launched a clothing line marketed as "Ghetto Fabulous," a unisex style that incorporated trademark and other status symbols. To complete the look, Motorola offered a diamond-encrusted $25,000 mobile telephone. To Combs and other rappers, the city was a place for self-indulgence and not a canvas for collective action to address the dynamics of class and culture.

The Americans who migrated to the suburbs in the decades after World War II found that by the 1980s, the suburbs themselves had become the landing point for many newly arrived migrants and immigrants. For these new Americans and generations of others, the city was best known through an electronic image. The occasional foray into the city—to see a sports event or a concert, attend a museum, or consult a specialist in law or medicine, for example—could not substitute for the knowledge and insight that came with living and working in the city. As a result, as time went by and more and more Americans lived in the suburbs, television, rock and roll, disco, MTV, the Internet, and handheld electronic communication devices offered the most powerful images of post–World War II urban America. Together, they have reinforced a deeply conflicting dual image of the city as a place of danger and opportunity presented in pre–World War II movies, art, music, and literature. Will electronic media help to erode further the distinctions between urban, suburban, and rural America? Will the day come when Americans will be ready to admit or even take pride in the fact that "Cities R US"?

# 2

# Shaping the Postwar City: 1945–1960

In 1945, U.S. cities were crowded, gritty, and polluted, offering a grim home-coming to American soldiers returning from abroad. Within roughly fifteen years, the process of rebuilding the city around the automobile that had been disrupted by the Great Depression and World War II was nearly complete. Between 1945 and 1960, the city went from the place where most people lived, worked, shopped, and had fun to the place where the more affluent were found on the urban fringe. The automobile, suburbanization, dein-dustrialization, blighted housing, new consumption patterns, and racial and demographic change made the city of 1960 a much different place than it had been in 1945. Urban life increasingly revolved around the suburbs.

## THE AMERICAN CITY, 1945
World War II had reindustrialized urban America. During the 1930s, econo-mists had speculated about the end of urban manufacturing, but the war instantly revitalized aging, superannuated plants. In the year 1941 alone, Washington poured $131 million into Philadelphia's moribund shipbuilding, textile, and metal manufacturing facilities. Mobilization catalyzed Detroit, the Depression-beleaguered Motor City. Suburban Pontiac turned out artil-lery pieces, and Ford with federal dollars built the gigantic Willow Run plant to manufacture thousands of B17 bombers. Oakland, California, boomed as a shipbuilding center, and Los Angeles thrived in aircraft production, as did

New York City with its nearby Long Island aircraft plant facilities. The war even affected small cities such as Portland, Maine, where immigrant laborers packed the city's Greek Revival tenements working "around the clock" to turn out hundreds of Liberty Ships and to support the North Atlantic Fleet stationed in Casco Bay. The war left American cities with far greater industrial infrastructure than was needed to fulfill consumer demands.

While postwar demobilization cost jobs, the shift from a hot to a cold war and federal economic planning softened the economic thud and prevented the feared postwar recession. American cities remained manufacturing centers in the 1945–1950 era. In 1950, manufacturing accounted for almost 30 percent of nonagricultural urban employment, while financial, real estate, and insurance services made up just 26 percent. In the Chicago region, 667,000 of the area's 885,000 manufacturing jobs (78 percent) remained inside the Windy City. Sixty-two percent of the Philadelphia area's manufacturing resided in the city's aging industrial North and South Philadelphia neighborhoods. Despite competition from suburban Willow Run and Dearborn, Detroit itself retained the bulk of automobile manufacturing in 1950.

After losing population in the 1930s, cities grew during the 1940s as a result of the war—some modestly, some considerably. With its aircraft factories and refineries, Los Angeles surpassed Chicago as the nation's second-largest city, increasing 31 percent from a population of over 1,504,000 in 1940 to one of almost 2 million in 1950. Detroit grew 14 percent from 1,623,452 in 1940 to almost 1,850,000 in 1950. Most cities, like New York, Chicago, Boston, and Philadelphia, grew at least modestly between 4 and 7 percent.

Despite the hurried construction of some federally funded defense and wartime housing, the year 1945 found American cities still facing a severe housing shortage. The collapse of the construction industry during the Great Depression and the lack of private building during World War II left the housing stock in American cities grossly inadequate. By 1947, experts estimated that cities faced a housing deficit pegged at 3.2 million units. For example, between 1940 and 1947, Oakland's population rose by 100,000, but the city built only 14,000 units of new housing. Newly married veterans lived in trailers or doubled up with parents in small houses. In the housing-starved Pittsburgh area, a handful of veterans found shelter in nearby abandoned coke ovens.

The shortage of housing resulted from the continued arrival of rural migrants as well as the number of returning veterans. Black immigrants from

Mississippi, the Carolinas, Alabama, Arkansas, and Virginia accounted for a sizable part of this wartime and postwar migration to urban America. By 1950, Philadelphia's black population, close to 10 percent in 1940, exceeded 18 percent. Detroit's African American population topped 16 percent in 1950. In Los Angeles, almost 9 percent of the city's 1950 population was black and in New York approximately 10 percent. Enduring official and unofficial discrimination, black urbanites found the housing shortage especially severe. Blacks made up two-thirds of Detroit's 150,000 wartime population growth, yet during the war, only 1,895 units of public housing and a mere 200 units of private housing served the city's burgeoning black population. Like their counterparts in other U.S. cities, Detroit blacks found crude shelter in stables, attics, and a former church carved into tiny apartments.

## THE MEAN STREETS OF THE POSTWAR CITY

More congested but still industrialized, urban America in 1945 presented a tired, tattered, but essentially familiar visage to the world. The ethnic neighborhoods that formed in the late nineteenth century as millions of immigrants came to American cities from Europe and Asia—the Little Italys, Polish Hills, Deutschtowns, and Chinatowns—survived largely intact. Each neighborhood prided itself on its own little shopping section with a Woolworth's or Kresge's (the predecessors of today's dollar stores), a hardware store, millenary and other specialty shops, ethnic food stores, and a local bar or tavern with separate entrances for men and women. And there still existed a bustling downtown, the heart of what historian Robert Fishman called the Metropolitan Tradition.[1] The downtown functioned as the epicenter of the metropolitan region, the focus of a complex rail system of trains, trolleys, and subways and the core of the city's primary retail shopping district, including its leading department stores, Jordan Marsh (Boston), Wanamaker's (Philadelphia), Halle Brothers (Cleveland), Marshall Field (Chicago), Gimbels (New York), and Neiman-Marcus (Dallas). Here too were the theaters, restaurants, concert halls, museums, hospitals, colleges, and universities.

Between 1945 and 1950, the downtown largely retained its magnetism. Millions of businessmen, city workers, warehouse and factory employees, lawyers, doctors, clerical staff, and women shoppers thronged to the city center daily. By 1945, however, it was a downtown under increasing duress. City streets were traffic congested, often unlit, unrepaired, littered, and unwashed. Commuters jostled each other in cavernous, dank, foul, and ill-illuminated subway stations. Trolley passengers jam-packed rickety, poorly heated, twenty-year-old streetcars. Moldering coal-heated city halls, libraries, and school buildings sat unkempt and outdated. Cities exuded a gas-lit, nineteenth-century ambience at the dawn of the post–Great Depression, postwar era when Americans disdained the gritty past and embraced modernism.

## CATALYSTS OF POSTWAR URBAN CHANGE

Those grumbling trolley car riders in 1945, newspapers tucked under their arms, shoving their way through a people-stuffed car to clutch a reachable strap, and steadying themselves on the jarring, uncomfortable commute to work, barely realized the multiple postwar forces at work shaping their urban world. Postwar reliance on the automobile, suburbanization, heightened consumerism, and federal housing polices all unleashed an unprecedented pattern of urban decentralization that restructured urban form. Of no less significance, technology and other economic forces inexorably undermined traditional urban industrialization and the work–residence nexus that had molded nineteenth- and early twentieth-century cities. After 1945, the shipyards and steel, ball-bearing, carpet, and textile mills, along with breweries, machine shops, and other employers, either migrated to the suburbs, relocated west or south to the Sun Belt, or simply vanished. Industry had anchored urban community; decentralization fragmented and distended urban social and ethnic ties and dissolved the mosaic of little worlds that made up the nineteenth- and early twentieth-century city. Finally, federal postwar housing and urban development policies abetted racism and hardened emerging prewar urban segregation patterns so that by 1960 in city after city that weave of small, often fairly ethnically and racially diverse communities had been transformed and a seething black ghetto had emerged.

Meanwhile, suburbs burgeoned in postwar America. Federal support for state highway building and low-interest, no-down-payment, twenty- to thirty-year Federal Housing Administration (FHA) and Veteran's Administration (VA) mortgages helped subsidize the growth of the suburbs. The application of mass production techniques for home building used by firms such as William Levitt and Sons also helped remake the belts of small towns and rural villages into modern suburbia. Before 1942, two-thirds of American homes had been built either by owners or by small contractors who erected fewer than five homes per year. By the 1950s, large contractors like Levitt built two-thirds of new homes. Historian Dolores Hayden called Levitt and Sons the "General Motors of Housing Production." The corporate builders vertically integrated home building, owning lumberyards and forests and structuring production on an assembly-line basis.

In 1947, American suburbs were growing four times faster than central cities. New York's suburban population of 5,426,000 in 1950 grew to almost 10 million by 1970; Philadelphia's 1,598,000 suburban population in 1950 rose to almost 3 million by 1970; St. Louis's suburbs—about a million in 1950—almost doubled; and Milwaukee's 293,000 in 1950 more than doubled.

## THE POSTWAR LURE OF SUBURBIA

Veterans, especially those who before World War II had completed high school or who had a few years of college under their belt, joined that great postwar exodus to suburbia. Indeed, 28 percent of World War II veterans took advantage of VA home loans. But more than just the lure of low-interest VA and FHA mortgage loans swelled the tide of postwar suburbanization. Suburbia, as wartime *Life* magazine articles tirelessly told the very popular publication's national readership, epitomized the American Dream of owning the model home with modern bathrooms and an appliance-rich kitchen and fronting a grassy lawn on a tree-lined sidewalk. Here was the verdant space and modern living absent in the Philadelphia or Baltimore row house or in the New England's triple-decker or even the Chicago bungalow, all crammed on narrow city lots.

More important, to seal the bargain, FHA and VA mortgages made buying in a suburban Levitt-built suburb more affordable than renting in the city. In 1950, a Cape Cod–style, free-standing house, situated in 1,400-acre Levittown, Long Island, sold for the low price of $7,900—cheaper, claimed Levitt, than renting, especially if you negotiated a 30-year mortgage and paid only 5 percent down. In 1949, housing starts surpassed 1.4 million, and the next year they neared 2 million, effectively ending the postwar housing crisis for middle-class home buyers. World War II vindicated economist John Maynard Keynes's theory that underconsumption had triggered the Great Depression of the 1930s and massive wartime spending had resuscitated the American economy. In the postwar era, however, the suburban housing market kept the economy well lubricated in the form of heightened demand for building materials, home furnishings, stoves, washers, dryers, and vacuum cleaners. These 1950s suburban dream homes were not only split-level Colonial Revivals but often all-electric, poorly insulated dwellings, with hastily installed backyard septic systems. In short, they were ecologically disastrous. Moreover, not all of these suburbs on the "Crabgrass Frontier" housed the affluent, middle-class families of men wearing gray-flannel suits. Sociologist Herbert Gans's study of Levittown, Pennsylvania, described a youthful community of more modest teachers, clerks, and small businessmen. Bennett Berger, another sociologist, reported on life in a Pennsylvania suburb occupied largely by steelworker families. His 1960 study found that suburbia little affected the working-class lifestyle of these steelworkers, who continued to share a blue-collar culture.[2]

Working-class or middle-class postwar suburbs were mainly white. FHA policies, which since the 1930s steered mortgage money and home repair loans away from black or even potentially black neighborhoods, acted to make suburbia an essentially all-white enclave. Some African Americans moved from inner cities to suburbs in the late 1940s and 1950s, but significant black suburbanization awaited the civil rights legislative breakthroughs of the 1960s. Even after the 1948 Supreme Court decision of *Shelley v. Kraemer*, which made racially restrictive covenants unenforceable, the FHA deliberately avoided insuring mortgage loans in black or racially mixed central city neighborhoods in favor of white suburbs. Not only did VA and FHA policies favor suburbs, but during the Korean War (1950–1953), government contracts for war material helped expand armament suppliers in suburban and Sun Belt locations, thus accelerating the decentralization of industry and further unhinging the already fragile opportunity structure left behind in the central city. For example, during the Korean War and as part of Department of Defense policy, Chrysler shifted its tank engine production facilities from Detroit to the area outside New Orleans and its tank production to Newark, Delaware. While the white suburbs blossomed, inner cities grew blacker and poorer.

Suburban homes became the quintessential mass consumption commodity. Here in "mass suburbia," regardless of their background or education, steelworkers, lawyers, and business executives shared a common bourgeois ethic of consumption best symbolized in the suburban shopping center. Early in the postwar era, shopping strips opened on the periphery of new suburban developments where land was cheap and strip malls typically featured a small supermarket, a dry cleaner, a hairdresser, a hardware store, and plentiful parking. Local malls, such as the one constructed in Cherry Hill, New Jersey, were soon eclipsed by large regional shopping malls (anchored by several major department stores and acres of parking) that dotted the landscape. Historian Richard Longstreth identified the first such regional mall as Crenshaw Center, which opened in late 1947 in southwest Los Angeles. Others followed, such as the planner-architect Victor Gruen–designed Northland Mall in Detroit, Seattle's Northgate, Boston's Shopper's World, and New York City's Cross County Center. Soon, as another ominous sign for the historic "downtown," corporate office complexes gravitated to the regional mall. In the case of Boston, insurance offices, laboratories, and ultimately the first computer firms lined suburban Route 128, an early circumferential highway belting the city.[3]

## DEINDUSTRIALIZATION

As residential and commercial development decentralized, so too did industry. Philadelphia graphically illustrated the trend. A 1946 *Franklin Industrial Atlas* identified 101 industrial firms located within the orbit of the central city, the vast majority within a three- to four-mile radius of the Philadelphia City Hall. These bellwethers of the local economy included Westinghouse, the Electric Storage Battery, Nabisco and Tastycake bakeries, Hardwick and Magee carpets, Stetson hats, E. I. DuPont, Sharp and Dohme Pharmaceuticals, National Lead and Sherwin Williams paints, and the Curtis Publishing Company. Any observer in 1946 would have discovered similar industrial clusters in Chicago, Baltimore, Pittsburgh, Buffalo, Birmingham, Seattle, Oakland, and Providence. By 1960, most of these plants had abandoned the Philadelphia core, taking with them their needed tax revenues and job opportunities. Moreover, thanks to technology and urban renewal, the last vestiges of the industrial city, the scattered coal yards, icehouses, and junkyards, also vanished. The *Philadelphia Inquirer* that year published a special section titled "Delaware Valley, U.S.A." featuring a story, "Industrial Parks Spread," whose opening line noted that "twenty years ago the word 'industrial park' would have seemed paradoxical." A map accompanying the story showed Philadelphia encircled by twenty-seven industrial parks accessed by a network of superhighways, such as the Pennsylvania Turnpike and the Schuylkill Expressway.

## RACE AND THE POSTWAR CITY

In city after city, people of color disproportionately bore the economic and social burden of the deindustrialization of urban America. The process bequeathed to blacks a city shorn of what had once been the immigrant opportunity structure wherein each neighborhood sat in the shadow of a familiar mill complex, such as Chicago's stockyards, Detroit's automobile industry, or Philadelphia's shipyards and woolen and carpet mills. These factories provided avenues for upward mobility, even for those who lacked much education or marketable skills.

For many large American cities, race—like suburbanization and deindustrialization—reshaped the contours of the postwar metropolis North and South. Even smaller cities, such as Providence, Rhode Island, and Lancaster, Pennsylvania, had sizable black populations by the 1950s. The tide of postwar black rural–urban migration flowed mainly toward large northern cities, however, with New York, Chicago, Philadelphia, Detroit, Cleveland, and Pittsburgh receiving the most newcomers. A mere 8 percent of the black population lived in these northern cities in 1916; by 1940, 48 percent of all African Americans now lived there. That population continued to grow. Just 9 percent of Detroit's population in 1940, African Americans made up 30 percent of the Motor City's population in 1960. In 1940, a pattern of racial segregation had already emerged in Detroit's Paradise Valley and Eight Mile Wyoming neighborhoods; by 1960, abetted by discriminatory bank lending and real estate practices, as well as by segregationist FHA and Public Housing Administration policies, Detroit had emerged as an increasingly poor and ghettoized black city steeped in inequality. African Americans occupied the lowest tier of employment in a city whose economic base (as in other cities) had steadily withered. Thus, postwar racial discrimination produced black cities and white suburbs. It was as true in Greater Philadelphia as in Chicago and Detroit—as well as in Oakland, where federal government housing policies, local builders, and white home owners were complicit in shaping suburban East Oakland as an industrial garden and downtown West Oakland as a festering black slum.

White suburbs flourished, while black inner-city slums, eroded by inequality, deteriorated—despite the 1948 *Shelley* decision that ruled racially restrictive covenants unenforceable. White home owners freely resorted to violence in enforcing their "right" to protect home values from black "invasion."

Angry whites rioted in Levittown, Pennsylvania, in 1957 when the family of a black World War II veteran moved into a Levitt-built home on Green Springs Road. Other postwar riots occurred in Cicero, Illinois, in 1951 and in the Trumbull Park area of Chicago in 1953 when black home buyers met resistance from white residents determined to maintain the homogeneity of their neighborhoods. These white home owners were convinced that the mere presence of families of color would diminish the value of their real estate and negate the struggle they had undertaken to acquire their own homes.

Deindustrialization, federally sanctioned racial discrimination, and embedded inequality produced impoverished, blacker, and poorer cities. A 1956 Philadelphia "Environmental Survey" of one black North Philadelphia region reported that 37 percent of the heads of household there were jobless and that 42 percent worked only irregularly in domestic service or as common laborers. By 1960, 32 percent of Philadelphia's black families lived on annual incomes under $2,000. Meanwhile, in Philadelphia, as in Chicago, Oakland, and Providence, postwar code enforcement and slum clearance activity demolished thousands of housing units, aggravating the housing shortage for increasingly ghettoized urban black families. In 1950, Chicago reported a housing vacancy rate of merely .08. Over 79,000 married couples in the Windy City, most black, lived doubled up with kin and other families. Officials called South Side Chicago flats rat-infested "fire traps."[4] A 1953 study of housing in Providence's black neighborhoods found 50.2 percent of the housing in South Providence to be "substandard"; the number stood at 68 percent in the city's Fox Point neighborhood and 66 percent in Lippitt Hill.

## THE THREATENED DOWNTOWN

From the vantage point of urban civic and business leaders and the professional architects, planners, and social workers who together comprised a sizable segment of the so-called postwar pro-growth coalition, white flight, suburban decentralization, and the rise of a despairing black ghetto undermined the metropolitan tradition and threatened the viability of the downtown. By 1952, Chicago had already reported fewer people entering its downtown shopping district than in any year since 1926. Central-city property values either appreciated very slowly or, in the case of San Francisco, actually fell. Some experts feared that the downtown might actually be abandoned. Adding to the city's woes was the view of organizations such as the city chambers of commerce, which encouraged suburban relocation of retail establishments. Architect Victor Gruen charged that the aging downtown with its traffic congestion "repulses shoppers," especially white middle-class women, considered the gold-standard clientele. Downtowns, contended Gruen, suffered terminal obsolescence and begged to be modernized. Hired by planning commissions in Fort Worth, Texas, and Kalamazoo, Michigan, Gruen offered both cities the same recipe to save their downtown shopping district—construction of a series of roads and parking structures to ring the downtown and convert the principal streets into pedestrian malls. Kalamazoo city fathers opted against the ring roads but built the pedestrian mall. Even if they had implemented the original Gruen plan, it is unlikely that it would have arrested the departure of retail establishments and more affluent families to so-called white-flight suburbs.

## THE CRUSADE AGAINST BLIGHT

The word most used by mayors, planners, businessmen, and other civic elites to describe the malaise and obsolescence overwhelming the central city in the 1950s was "blight." During the war, city after city either created or resuscitated its planning commission and promptly put the crusade against blight at the top of its postwar "to-do list." Pushed by chambers of commerce that saw blight removal as part of a general and critically needed urban "face lifting," the campaign by 1947 became part of a larger movement for cities to purge the old, the ugly, and the outdated and to rebuild cities in a modern, streamlined mode, a towering, park-lined form able to compete with suburbia. An article from a 1950s *St. Louis Post Dispatch* newspaper titled "St. Louis Must Choose" complained that the city was ailing, its office buildings old and dingy, and its center "encircled by a rotting ring of slums." Yet, emphasized the newspaper, "the downtown is not dying. It is still the center, the core, the heart that pumps the blood of commerce through the area's arteries. . . . Without a vigorous Downtown, St. Louis loses its chief economic reasons for existence." The article could have appeared in any urban newspaper, from Seattle to Chicago to Atlanta.[5]

Planners, businessmen, and city officials alike imagined a modern city, purged of its old warehouses, junkyards, and excrescent slums districts. In their place would arise a gleaming, deslummed city of glass skyscrapers, verdant greenways, and historically preserved, upscale residential districts anchored by glitzy apartment towers. Sweeping and looping superhighways and expressways would give easy access to a shopper-friendly city thoroughly cleansed of its gritty industrial past.

City planners often shared a belief in modernism deeply rooted in Harvard's Graduate School of Design (GSD) and in the ideas of the *Congres Internationaux d'Architecture Moderne* (CIAM). CIAM's philosophy, espoused by the GSD's Joseph Hudnut, Walter Gropius, Werner Hegemann, G. Holmes Perkins, and others, broke with the historicism of the neoclassical Beaux Arts tradition that had strongly influenced American architecture since the late nineteenth century. Instead, it stressed clarity, continuity, functionality, and objectivity in design. In postwar planning, CIAM urged the rational restructuring of cities. Clear away the fetid slums and use zoning and land use ordinances to purge ugliness and to isolate industry and other nonconforming uses on the urban periphery. Modernist postwar planning also included the rational redistribution of the urban population into healthy, affordable planned communities located on the less costly urban edge. But modernists like Le Corbusier also envisioned an urban population living downtown in sleek tower residences situated in parklike settings.[6]

Regionalists such as Catherine Bauer Wurster and Lewis Mumford clung to the communitarian Garden City version of the modernist scripture that originated in Great Britain and became popular in the United States in the early twentieth century. They argued that the rehousing of low- and moderate-income families in planned communities located on more spacious and less expensive suburban land naturally and effectively decongested slums without engaging in painful slum clearance. Postwar, pro-growth advocates rebuffed communitarians, however, embracing instead CIAM's modernist vision of the postindustrial city purged of its industrial detritus and shimmering with the clarity and objectivity of office and residential towers aligned on wide, uncluttered urban arterials—the famous vision of the European International–Style architect Le Corbusier.

Ridding the twentieth-century city of its inheritance of the industrial past required not only imagination but also enormous fiscal and political resources. It required, moreover, a partnership of political entrepreneurs and downtown civic and business leaders, bankers, lawyers, educators, public health officials, social welfare luminaries, and economists who, faced with the prospect of a doomed downtown, saw in the public–private coalition the opportunity to make city rebuilding the basis for Democratic Party success. In other words, government largess sustained both urban growth and political loyalty.

Smokey Pittsburgh provided the corporate model. In the 1940s, the scion of a banking, petroleum, and metals fortune, Richard King Mellon, joined with Democratic Mayor David Lawrence to produce the famed Pittsburgh Renaissance. Building on an established tradition of planning in Pittsburgh, Mellon in 1943 assembled a cadre of prominent business and civic leaders into the Allegheny Conference on Community Development. Mellon and his civic partners convinced the State of Pennsylvania to turn an ugly rail yard located at the confluence of the Allegheny, Ohio, and Monongahela rivers into Point State Park and then in 1947 persuaded New York's Equitable Life Assurance Society to underwrite the gleaming Gateway Center office complex nearby.

Likewise in Philadelphia in 1943, a band of "Young Turks" formed the Citizens Council on City Planning, which proceeded to revitalize the city's moribund planning commission. Between 1947 and 1958 in city after city, downtown business, civic, and political elites fashioned the mechanism for downtown renaissance. Business and civic elites in Baltimore in 1954 formed the Greater Baltimore Committee. In Chicago, they created the Metropolitan Housing and Planning Council, and in Boston, a 1944 Boston College City Seminar (on city revitalization) became the pro-growth "Vault." Indianapolis named its 1955 pro-growth body the Civic Progress Association. Oakland formed the Metropolitan Oakland Area Program, whose early emphasis on a suburbanized industrial garden drew more from Catherine Bauer Wurster's, Lewis Mumford's, and Clarence Stein's regionalism than from the Le Corbusier modernists.

## LAUNCHING POSTWAR URBAN REDEVELOPMENT

Immediately after World War II, challenged by blight, the fear of joblessness, and the specter of decline, cities launched a host of anti–smoke pollution, water, sewer, street, parking, and other urban improvement projects. Street improvements invariably involved not only street widening but also, as in Los Angeles, removing trolley tracks and replacing streetcars with buses. Philadelphia, St. Louis, Pittsburgh, and Cincinnati all enacted tough smoke control ordinances. To overcome the city's reputation for its odiferous and barely potable water, Philadelphia undertook twelve costly major waterworks improvement projects between 1947 and 1958 that increased the city's water supply by 30 percent. Likewise, Cleveland, Chicago, and New York all invested heavily in new sewage treatment plants.

Except for federal monies for airport expansion and for new hospitals (the latter funded under the 1946 federal Hill-Burton legislation), money for these massive and costly housekeeping projects came mainly not from Washington but from leveraging the city's enhanced wartime fiscal status to issue bonds. Cities also relied on their ability to capture revenue from the suburbs in the form of city wage taxes. But while smoke removal, street widening, park building, and water and sewer improvements became important goals, they shrank next to the importance cities assigned to slum clearance, solving the problem of traffic congestion, and bettering traffic flow.

Historians have observed that, despite the huge expenditures on the federal interstate highway program, cities got little in return in the way of tangible benefits. Guided by a highway engineer mentality, the federal Bureau of Public Roads (BPR), according to one historian, "laid down expressways without regard for [either] their effect on the urban landscape" or their damage to the urban quality of life. The BPR's influential 1939 study "Toll Roads and Free Roads" envisioned an interregional system of defense highways linking American cities. After World War II, highway boosters imagined this interregional highway system decongesting, recentralizing, and revitalizing urban life. Enthralled by the General Motors–sponsored "Futurama" exhibit at the 1939 World's Fair in New York City, which portrayed a fantasia of looping, diving, and spiraling multilaned express highways where automobiles traveled at speeds of 100 miles per hour, young postwar city and state planners and civil engineers used highway building to control the monstrous traffic that threatened to suffocate the central city. Both the $500,000,000 Federal Aid Highway Act of 1944 and President Dwight D. Eisenhower's 1956 Federal Aid Highway Act unveiled a spoke-and-radial highway system that, in conjunction with strategically located parking garages, sought to regulate traffic flow and breathe life back into the tired arteries of the city. Between 1946 and 1955, federal expenditures for urban highways totaled $1.09 billion. The 1956 act that created the Highway Trust Fund committed the federal government to pay 90 percent of the cost of the interstate system and by 1960 poured a billion dollars annually into urban expressway building. Philadelphia's Schuylkill Expressway opened for traffic in 1958 and within hours was congested.

Similarly, via the 1946 Federal Airport Aid Act, Washington, D.C., funded the rapid postwar growth of urban airports and air traffic. Together, highway and airport building doomed passenger rail transportation and promoted suburbanization—not the intended recentralization of cities. Express and radial highways attracted malls and condemned the large fancy downtown department store to certain oblivion. Moreover, by 1960 in many central cities, the large architecturally striking union or grand central railroad stations steadily deteriorated, stood empty, or awaited demolition. Meanwhile, airports such as Chicago's Midway and O'Hare, New York's LaGuardia, Baltimore's Friendship, and Boston's Logan boomed. Such big-city airports were to be reached by automobile; despite the large subway systems in New York and Boston, neither city offered riders direct access to the airports. Increasingly, port and regional authorities—not the city—managed these busy and growing airports, focusing their efforts on improving interstate highway access for airline passengers.

Next to unsnarling traffic via new freeways, beltways, and parking lots, blight removal topped the postwar redevelopment agenda. On Chicago's West Side, the dreaded "contagion" of blight riveted postwar city officials. Many believed that blight possessed an "organic qualit[y] capable of spreading and infecting neighboring properties," including the revered downtown itself. During the 1940s, one state after another enacted legislation authorizing cities to create redevelopment authorities armed with the power of eminent domain and enabling them to seize private property for private redevelopment. Every court challenge upheld the right of the state under its police power to condemn property and resell it for renewal purposes. Philadelphia, Pittsburgh, Minneapolis, Chicago, Boston, New Haven, Lancaster, Pennsylvania, and Portland, Maine, among many other postwar cities large and small, joined Baltimore in establishing redevelopment authorities. These eminent domain powers notwithstanding, the staggering cost of downtown slum removal discouraged most cities, even those with stellar bond ratings. It was this prospect of interminable delay in urban rebuilding that, after four years of wrangling, compelled Congress in 1949 to pass at last the Taft-Ellender-Wagner (TEW) housing legislation that funded costly slum demolition and raised expectations of large-scale urban redevelopment.

## THE POLITICS OF URBAN RENEWAL

Before downtown bankers, lawyers, and department store tycoons could forge coalitions with city mayors and Washington, D.C., officials, just as in the earlier Progressive Era, reformers had first to expunge the aura of municipal corruption and convince insurance companies and developers that efficiency and not the "old politics as usual" of cronyism and bossism prevailed.

Representing Old Guard establishments in many cities, mayors in the 1940s typically ruled politically exhausted regimes often steeped in scandal. A Philadelphia "Committee of Fifteen" in 1949 uncovered $152 million in graft payments to city officials, leading to a grand jury hearing and several suicides. The spirit of reform, brewing as early as 1943, blossomed at war's end. Business-led reform organizations challenged the status quo of the Old Guard. Chicago in 1947 ousted the corrupt regime of Mayor Ed Kelly for reformer Martin Kennelly, who appointed the housing reformer Elizabeth Wood to head the city's corrupt Chicago Housing Authority. In Boston, John Hynes replaced the notorious Boss James Michael Curley. In 1951, Philadelphia's aristocratic Knight in Shining Armor, Joseph S. Clark, replaced the embattled party hack Bernard Samuels, while in Baltimore in 1947 a pro-growth politician, Thomas D'Alesandro, became mayor, and in Cleveland anti-boss, pro–slum clearance Anthony Celebrezze won the mayor's office in 1953.

The so-called new-breed mayors often lacked ties to local political machines. They tended to be well educated and in possession of strong credentials in business or the legal profession. The new-breed mayors presented themselves as disinterested managers uniquely qualified to administer municipal affairs. Often, as in Philadelphia, they entered office empowered by new "home-rule" city charters that created a business-like government. These new charters established strong executive branches that withdrew from city councils administrative duties now vested in the mayor's office. They awarded the mayor power to appoint and remove department heads. City councils retained power over the budget, but in a number of cities, expert administrators (i.e., managing directors) were ensconced in the mayor's office to oversee the efficient operation of city services.[7]

Postwar demographic change and political reform had replaced Old Guard Republican politicos with reformist Democratic Party rule that won the kudos of the business and civic leaders. Democratic reformers often worked closely with the corporate executives who orchestrated the political coups and funded the advertising campaigns for the new city charters and the bond issues that would translate political victory into physical revitalization. Although the new-breed mayors may still have attended Sons of Italy dinners and walked in St. Patrick's Day parades, they also maintained a strong presence in local business communities. The renaissance mayors simultaneously cultivated the support of the neighborhood political organizations, powerful corporations, real estate interests, and Washington bureaucracies that dispensed aid to cities.

## HOUSING AND THE FEDERAL GOVERNMENT

Anticipating a postwar housing shortage and determined to combat urban blight, New York Senator Robert Wagner led the congressional effort to draft a new housing and urban redevelopment bill. The legislation drafted in 1943 provided federal grants to local urban redevelopment authorities to purchase and clear slums; however, in light of a predictable postwar housing shortage and thanks to pro-housing pressure, the proposed legislation evolved a "primarily residential" purpose that called for public housing to be built "equivalent" to those slum units demolished. The legislation also propounded the national goal of "a decent home in a decent environment for every American."

From its introduction in 1944, the housing legislation that eventually passed Congress in 1949 proved controversial mainly because of its generous provision for public housing. The TEW Housing Act generated fierce opposition from a determined group of adversaries. While many downtown businessmen found the idea of the federal government underwriting massive slum clearance and urban redevelopment appealing, powerful organizations, such as the National Association of Real Estate Boards (NAREB), the United States Savings and Loan League, the American Bankers Association, and the U.S. Chamber of Commerce, vehemently opposed the revival of public housing. NAREB and the Urban Land Institute called public housing "socialism." One spokesperson for these groups protested that if "I had to choose between seeing every old city in the country as an ash heap and seeing the government become a landlord to its citizens, I should prefer to see the ash heap."[8]

On the other side stood the pro-growth forces, the U.S. Conference of Mayors, the White House, labor unions, social workers, city planners, lawyers, downtown department store owners, and city developers who saw the Title I clause of the TEW bill (which underwrote the cost of buying, clearing, and disposing of slum property) as capable of revitalizing the grim downtown and boosting city revenues. Planners and social workers viewed slum clearance and public housing as a chance to transform socially dysfunctional and physically unsafe urban neighborhoods into healthy, modern urban communities. Not all housing reformers cheered the legislation's slum clearance and housing emphasis, however. Catherine Bauer Wurster, who saw cheap suburban land as ideal for low-cost community building, blasted the law, writing that "in the name of saving cities it is proposed to bail out with federal subsidies the owners of slums and blighted property—not in order to re-house their present tenants properly, but to stimulate another wave of speculative overbuilding for [the] well-to-do."[9]

In the wake of President Harry S. Truman's surprising 1948 victory over Republican Thomas Dewey, housing reformers pressed forward with renewed vigor. With the solid backing of big-city mayors, organized labor, and the local pro-growth coalitions, the TEW Housing Act of 1949 became law despite the staunch opposition of Michigan Representative Jesse P. Wolcott and the red-baiting of Wisconsin Senator Joseph P. McCarthy. As Wurster, who ultimately if reluctantly supported the law, observed about the diversity of the constituency finally backing its passage, "Seldom has such a variegated crew of would-be angels tried to sit on the same pin at the same time."

Title I of the new housing and redevelopment law of 1949 enabled cities to purchase and clear blighted urban land. Congress budgeted $500 million in capital grants and $1 billion in loans over five years to provide private development firms with capital. These grants and loans aided redevelopment authorities to clear and sell or lease improved urban land in designated redevelopment areas to private developers or public agencies (such as housing authorities) at below-market rates. But, in deference to Senator Robert Taft (Republican, Ohio), Title I limited federal aid to slums and blighted areas that were "primarily residential or would be redeveloped for primarily residential purposes." As a boon to planning, slum-cleared areas would have to be redeveloped in accordance with a city master plan, and to placate housing reformers, uprooted families would have to be re-housed in "safe and sanitary dwellings."[10] Title I did not specify how slums and blighted areas would be selected for redevelopment sites; the decision was left to local redevelopment agencies, which, in the words of one urban scholar, "tended to choose areas that were run down enough to justify demolition, but not so run down as to scare off developers."[11]

The TEW Housing Act of 1949 profoundly shaped the postwar city, clearing thousands of acres of urban land and in doing so displacing thousands of families. In the hands of modernist architects and aggressive developers, redevelopment launched the rebuilding of urban America in a modern, postindustrial form. But, as many urban historians have observed, in its early phase redevelopment was usually privately and locally funded. Local and private ventures, not Title I federal projects, led the way and made the headlines in urban redevelopment initially. While Congress financed municipal airports and the cost of new city hospital centers, prior to the late 1950s relatively little federal cash underwrote urban development plans. Pittsburgh's pathbreaking Gateway Center, Philadelphia's Penn Center, Boston's Prudential Center, Chicago's Lake Meadows, and Baltimore's Charles Center were all financed by corporate investment or giant insurance companies such as the Equitable Life Assurance Company. Philadelphia undertook its acclaimed Penn Center redevelopment after the Pennsylvania Railroad announced plans to demolish the city's forbidding downtown "Chinese Wall," a huge railroad viaduct that broached the heart of the city.

Although undeniably important for the history of the postwar city, the TEW bill failed to unleash the expected bonanza of renewal activity immediately. Several points explain the delay in robust federal participation in postwar urban revitalization. First, the Korean War cut into redevelopment by limiting the public housing funding necessary under the law to rehouse families displaced by urban redevelopment action. To conserve building materials, President Truman in July 1950 directed the Housing and Home Finance Agency (HHFA) to reduce FHA credit and slash authorizations for public housing under the 1949 act from 135,000 units annually to only 30,000. The war also fueled Joseph McCarthy's anticommunist crusade that portrayed public housing as "socialistic."

Second, in almost every city, the redevelopment law's provision for using federal funds to seize property for resale to private parties at below-market rates had to be tested in the courts and found constitutional. These court decisions frequently took several years. Meanwhile, during the 1940s and early 1950s, states endowed locally created redevelopment authorities with the power of eminent domain enabling them without federal help to undertake cleanup campaigns, to launch housing and sanitary code enforcement campaigns, and in other ways to engage in citywide deslumming crusades. States and municipalities enthusiastically accepted the federal funds that eventually became available but, as in the notable case of New York City, launched projects of their own in the meantime.

But making progress in urban redevelopment proved difficult, and during these early years victories over blight often proved either temporary or disappointingly limited. Mindful of the serious postwar housing crisis across urban America, much of the early redevelopment activity, with or without Title I help, stressed housing. During the 1950s, Baltimore pioneered the use of code enforcement to improve housing. The so-called Baltimore Plan began in East Baltimore as a demonstration project that employed a privately financed "Fight Blight Fund" to assist home owners in city code enforcement and housing rehabilitation. Baltimore created a Housing Bureau Advisory Council headed by James Rouse, who later chaired the Greater Baltimore Committee, and the Baltimore Plan became a model for similar neighborhood conservation work in Detroit, St. Louis, and other cities. In 1953, Boston Mayor John Hynes set up an Advisory Committee on Rehabilitation and Conservation to spur neighborhood rebuilding; that same year, Chicago's Metropolitan Housing and Planning Council launched its program of slum clearance, slum prevention, and housing conservation. Philadelphia rivaled Baltimore in its housing conservation approach to early redevelopment. The city in the early 1950s opposed the "project" approach to redevelopment that they identified with New York's Robert Moses. Instead, planners in Philadelphia adopted what they called the "penicillin" approach to attack blight in downtown neighborhoods.

## PRO-GROWTH COALITIONS IN THE 1950S

While critics praised Baltimore's code enforcement approach, Pittsburgh's public–private Renaissance, and Philadelphia's innovative Penn Town, by 1952 a consensus had emerged that urban redevelopment merely lumbered along, languidly, rather than surging forward to meet crises. Some disappointed citizens described redevelopment as lying in the dumps. Potential developers feared to invest in risky, blighted neighborhoods. In many cities, acres of slum-cleared land sat idle, the large, rubble-strewn sites, often two or five city square blocks in size, visibly marked off by white fences. In response, pro-growth forces endeavored to steer redevelopment away from the Robert Moses–style, project-oriented, "bulldozer" approach while at the same time whetting the appetite of private developers for inner-city redevelopment. They urged Washington to reconsider the "primarily residential" clause of the 1949 law, which city officials had seen as hamstringing urban development.

In response, President Dwight D. Eisenhower, a fiscal conservative yet sympathetic to some aspects of the New Deal, in 1953 assembled a twenty-three-member, largely business/banker-oriented Advisory Committee on Government Housing Policies and Programs chaired by HHFA chief Albert Cole. The pro-growth committee included among its members Miles Colean, author of the influential book *Renewing Our Cities,* and the banker and developer James Rouse, a firm disciple of the Baltimore Plan. The 1954 law that emerged from the deliberations of the Colean–Rouse committee bore the deep imprint of both individuals and, as intended, clearly refocused postwar urban rebuilding from housing to downtown development. Some 10 percent of Title I funds, formerly earmarked for "primarily residential" projects, could be used for building urban hospitals, universities, stadiums, and office towers. Significantly, following the reasoning of Colean and Rouse, the 1954 law replaced the phrase "urban redevelopment" with the comprehensive term "urban renewal," which stressed citywide neighborhood revitalization, code enforcement, and housing rehabilitation. Moreover, urban renewal was intended to emphasize planning and citizen participation. The new law also included funds for hiring professional planners, required citizens' advisory committees, and demanded that qualifying cities submit "workable plans" for HHFA approval.[12]

Between 1955 and the early 1960s, the 1954 renewal law did, as hoped, trigger urban development, although some of it—especially Robert Moses's Columbia Circle, Lincoln Center, and New York University–Bellevue projects—remained very much still in the federal bulldozer mode. Other projects—such as the massive Oak Street and Church Street projects in New Haven, Connecticut, launched under Mayor Richard C. Lee and his urban renewal czar, Edward C. Logue—won accolades from HHFA administrator Albert M. Cole as a "model for urban renewal." In 1956, Boston unveiled plans for the sixty-one-acre Government Center to replace a mélange of seedy single-room-occupancy hotels, tattoo parlors, and bars. Two years later, officials in Boston broke ground for the forty-eight-acre West End development to replace a graying, Italian working-class community with a posh, 240-unit high-rise, upper-middle-class housing development. Increasingly, redevelopment targeted the "blight that's right"—that is, redevelopment not in the most depressed areas but in areas deemed attractive for investment, where land write-downs and tax abatements would attract investment in the city.

Some cities effectively used the housing rehabilitation features of the 1954 law to dabble in historical preservation. Philadelphia, for example, turned a seedy eighteenth-century neighborhood, Society Hill, into an upscale residential showplace and tourist attraction crowned by architect I. M. Pei's Society Hill Towers. In 1958, Minneapolis demolished its Lower Loop neighborhood for upscale apartment complexes and the Sheraton Ritz Hotel. All this development—whether in Philadelphia's Society Hill, St. Louis's Plaza Square, or Boston's West End—displaced thousands of poor, often nonwhite families. In a famous article titled "Grieving for a Lost Home," psychologist Marc Fried publicized the emotional grief and agony of the Italian families uprooted from Boston's West End renewal area. In Detroit, Birmingham, Atlanta, St. Louis, Oakland, Philadelphia, Chicago, and many other cities, most of the residents removed were African Americans.[13]

## RACE, RENEWAL, AND REMOVAL

As mechanized cotton picking and the rise of postwar agribusiness rendered tenant farming less productive and less viable, the tide of black urban migration northward grew in the 1950s and 1960s. Philadelphia's black population, measured at 18.2 percent in 1950, rose to 33.6 percent by 1970. Baltimore's black population, 23.7 percent in 1950, reached 46.4 percent in 1970. Chicago's black population, 13.6 percent in 1950, climbed to 33 percent in 1970. Detroit's black population, 16.2 percent in 1950, rose to almost 44 percent in 1970. Coupled with white suburbanization, discriminatory real estate practices, and federal housing and redevelopment policies, these cities became more and more segregated. According to sociologists Douglas S. Massey and Nancy A. Denton, racial segregation became a permanent spatial feature of American cities in the years after World War II. By 1960, for Philadelphia to achieve a "balanced," nonsegregated population distribution, 87.1 percent of the "brotherly city's" black population would have had to move to all-white blocks. In Baltimore, the number was 91 percent; in Chicago, 92.6 percent; and in St. Louis, 90.5 percent.

In 1955, Philadelphia's white reformer mayor, Joseph S. Clark, recognized the ghettoization pattern but was unable to stop it from spreading further. Clark espied the emergence of an invidious, donut-shaped urban form, a hypersegregated poor black inner city surrounded by prosperous white suburban neighborhoods. Private banking and real estate practices, plus federal highway building and FHA mortgage insurance policies, helped carve these patterns. Notwithstanding the landmark *Shelley v. Kraemer* decision rendering restrictive covenants unenforceable in federal courts, many real estate agents and federal officials still tacitly honored these covenants in the 1950s and after. While as historian Amy Hillier insists, FHA "redlining" policies did not cause segregation or neighborhood deterioration, the FHA's notorious "security maps" designating safe as opposed to unsafe loans reflected and reinforced popular assumptions and prejudices concerning what constituted a good neighborhood and what made neighborhoods bad. White residents banded together to defend those "good" neighborhoods against black encroachment—with violence if necessary.[14]

Public housing played an important role in shaping the new racial lineaments and the skylines of the postwar city. In St. Louis, as in other cities, public housing "tightened the noose woven by restrictive covenants, private realty, and the FHA."[15] To comply with the 1954 law that families uprooted by urban renewal and other public action (such as code enforcement) must be rehoused in "safe and sanitary" dwellings, city officials—ignoring the outcry of housing reformers such as Catherine Bauer Wurster or Chicago's Elizabeth Wood—turned to high-rise, elevator buildings. In effect, public housing officials adopted the "radiant city," or "towers in the park," concept elucidated by Le Corbusier and seemingly successfully adapted to both the low- and middle-income needs of New York City's Manhattan. In the 1950s, urban housing authorities nationwide erected one modernist, slablike high-rise public housing tower after another. The Chicago Housing Authority (CHA) in 1956 built the dreary, industrial-looking Harold Ickes Homes, the Henry Horner Homes in 1957, and the grim Stateway Gardens in 1958. Four years later, the CHA opened the 4,400-unit Robert Taylor Homes, twenty-eight sixteen-story modernist buildings abutting the Dan Ryan Expressway. That same year, Chicago unveiled the 1,400-unit Washington Park Homes and the 1,000-unit William Green Homes addition to the Cabrini Green housing project. All these projects were racially segregated.

Few cities outdid St. Louis in utilizing public housing to warehouse uprooted black families. Just as Chicago housing officials proclaimed the newly opened Stateway Gardens in 1958 as "beautiful to behold," St. Louis's Mayor Joseph Darst regarded that city's spanking new Pruitt-Igoe project in 1956 as utopian. Mayor Darst loved New York's skyscraper housing. Like Corbusier, he believed that modernist tower housing could help reverse the spread of blight and promote the revitalization of the city's downtown. St. Louis in 1955 had cleared away the 180-acre De Soto slum that adjoined the downtown, and to rehouse those uprooted families efficiently and creatively, Darst consulted with the architect of New York City's World Trade Center, Minoru Yamasaki. To solve St. Louis's rehousing problem, Yamasaki designed thirty-three eleven-story towers: the Pruitt towers for blacks and the Igoe complex for whites. Skip-stop elevators served every third floor. On each level, open cyclone-fenced galleries provided room for drying wash as well as play space for children. By 1960, the projects, later vilified by social psychologist Oscar Newman as "indefensible space," suffered a 16 percent vacancy rate. Sociologist Lee Rainwater decried them as high-rise ghettoes where gangs with impunity roamed the bleak, graffiti-scarred halls.

Increasingly, in every city, these segregated towers housed the poorest and most broken families. While many black female-headed families struggled heroically to develop effective social and political strategies for surviving in socially segregated, economically impoverished environments, housing officials worried about the high percentage of public housing tenant families headed by women and the increasing number of tenant families living on welfare payments.

## A CHORUS OF URBAN CRITICS

As President John F. Kennedy prepared to take the oath of office in 1961, many Americans—especially suburbanites—anticipated happy days and new affluence. At the same time, others despaired at the unfolding urban landscape of poverty, boarded-up industrial buildings, vacant houses, and grim high-rise public housing projects. While the nation's slick, modern freeways and expressways opened a new middle-class world of residential suburbs, shopping malls, and industrial parks, that same trend had rendered historic downtowns bereft of department stores, more blighted, and more racially segregated. Indeed, by the 1960s, white flight had severely eroded urban populations. The 1960 census underscored the losses. Boston, St. Louis, and Pittsburgh all dropped 10 percent or more of their populations during the previous decade. Detroit, Buffalo, and Minneapolis fell over 7 percent, while Cleveland, Philadelphia, New York City, Baltimore, and Cincinnati declined 5 percent.

At the heart of America's declining cities sat not only the shuttered department stores but also the new towers and other monuments to early urban renewal: the gleaming modern, glass and stainless-steel International Style office buildings; upscale apartments; stadiums; archways; and, of course, the rows of antiseptic, slablike, modernistic public housing projects. Catherine

Bauer Wurster found this specter of high-rise public housing especially depressing. Writing in *Architectural Forum* in 1957, Wurster—once the loudest proponent of public housing—turned her back on the experiment. She condemned what she now called "the Dreary Deadlock of Public Housing" and confessed that these high-rise warehouses crowding inner cities are simply "not the way most American families want to live."[16]

Wurster hardly stood alone in her denunciation of the handiwork of 1950s city rebuilders. One year after Wurster's diatribe, the editors of *Fortune Magazine* published *The Exploding Metropolis*, where, among others, William H. Whyte, Daniel Seligman, and Jane Jacobs vented their anxieties and despair about the fate of America's cities, especially the failure of urban renewal. Seligman assailed "the enduring slum," where "some 17,000,000 Americans [still] live in dwellings that are beyond rehabilitation . . . decaying, rat infested without decent heat or plumbing." The critics spewed their strongest venom on what they viewed as the socially destructive wages of modernist city planning. Jacobs decried the elements of the modern postindustrial city unfolding before her in the late 1950s. "From city to city," she wrote, "the architect [sketches conjure up] the same dreary scene; here is not hint of individual whim or surprise, no hint of that there is a city with a tradition and flair of its own." Jacobs disdained "renaissance" projects hailed in Pittsburgh, Cleveland, Nashville, and San Francisco, predicting that they "will not revitalize downtown; they will deaden it." She called modernism "anti-city." The International Style, the Corbusian towers, replaced the density, diversity, and dynamism of the urban neighborhood with an antiseptic homogeneity.[17] They shattered the safety and creativity of the sidewalk community. By 1960, the Wursters, Whytes, Seligmans, and Jacobses had compiled a scathing critique of American cities that foreshadowed the depiction of the "Other America" by social critics Dwight McDonald and Michael Harrington. Although McDonald and Harrington commented primarily about the existence of stark poverty in the countryside, their muckraking descriptions of the Other America paid particular attention to the impoverished, "invisible," disproportionately black populations of the cities.[18] During his short time in office, President Kennedy challenged Americans to contribute to a national effort to conquer space, the "next frontier." It would be the work of his successor, Lyndon B. Johnson, to inaugurate a national campaign to reclaim America's ailing cities.

# 3

# Federal Policy and the American City

By the close of the 1950s, the future of America's largest cities looked peril-ous. Worsening conditions in the inner cities mirrored the rise of suburbia, as people, jobs, retail outlets, and tax dollars fled the urban core for the crabgrass frontier. In Rust Belt cities scattered across the Northeast and Midwest from Boston to Chicago, manufacturing bases withered in the face of technological revolutions; urban decline followed the falling productivity and rising unem-ployment plaguing the steel mills in Pittsburgh and Gary, automobile plants in Detroit and Flint, and tire factories in Akron. At the same time, Sun Belt cities from Miami to Los Angeles enjoyed a period of remarkable population and economic growth. Burgeoning military-defense budgets, the development of petrochemicals industries, the nation's inexorable conversion to an infor-mation-based economy, and the rapid growth of retirement communities in warm-weather sites transformed sleepy southern and southwestern communi-ties into boomtowns. Local efforts to fashion an urban renaissance in Rust Belt cities, launched after World War II by a new breed of reform-minded mayors allied with corporate executives, produced some striking successes but not in sufficient quantity to offset the overall downward trajectory. The construction of massive highway networks and urban renewal projects in the postwar years funded largely in Washington, D.C., similarly offered hope, but the scope of federal commitment appeared inadequate to the task of saving the cities. Demo-crats blamed the do-nothing policies of President Dwight D. Eisenhower for the worsening condition of urban America; Republicans countered that the demographic changes of the 1950s simply reflected the natural flow of population and wealth in a free society with government appropriately restrained. In the 1960s, John F. Kennedy's New Frontier and Lyndon B. Johnson's Great Society sought to aid the distressed cities by enhancing the federal government's presence in local affairs. Their liberal activism constituted the high-water mark of government involvement in post–World War II urban America but failed to arrest the decline of inner-city neighborhoods. The best efforts of the liberal Democratic administrations notwithstanding, urban America continued to divide into cities of affluence and cities of poverty.

## JOHN F. KENNEDY AND URBAN AMERICA

The public perception of urban decay provided the backdrop for the 1960 presidential election. During the campaign, Democrats cited President Eisenhower's inattention to urban affairs during the preceding eight years as a good example of how his detached leadership style had held the nation back from achieving its full potential. Eisenhower's do-nothing conservatism allowed a number of the nation's critical domestic problems to worsen, the opposition charged, the decline of urban America being a prime example. Identifying the septuagenarian Eisenhower's age and recurring health problems as the principal reasons for the alarming inactivity in the White House during the 1950s, the Democrats cheerfully pointed to their presidential candidate, Senator John F. Kennedy of Massachusetts, as a strong antidote to the recent torpor in Washington, D.C. Youthfully handsome and vigorous, the forty-three-year-old Kennedy promised in his campaign that year to quicken the pace of change and get the country moving again after the eight-year hibernation of the Eisenhower years. In Kennedy, critics of purported Republican indifference to the cities could not have found a better candidate. The grandson of a Boston mayor, congressman from an urban district, and senator from the nation's most urbanized state, Kennedy had a thorough and intuitive knowledge of the problems plaguing the cities. Indeed, if elected, he would become the nation's first president born and raised in an urban environment.

The fate of urban America never became the centerpiece of the 1960 presidential campaign as both candidates understandably devoted most of their attention to U.S. interests abroad, developments in the Cold War, and a sluggish economy. The Republican nominee, Richard M. Nixon, talked about housing on several occasions at the outset of the campaign but increasingly avoided the issues that he believed the Democrats had skillfully co-opted. The Democratic Party could not be beaten on domestic issues, Nixon told the journalist Theodore H. White, so his campaign concentrated on foreign policy matters. The subject of housing came up only once in the famous televised presidential debates, engaging the two candidates briefly before giving way to other topics. With the enthusiastic support of the big-city mayors and the major urban lobbies and confident of securing comfortable electoral margins in the inner cities, Kennedy campaigned frequently in the suburbs to offset expected Republican majorities. In one of the closest presidential contests in history, the urban vote proved to be crucial for the Democrats, as Kennedy carried twenty-seven of the forty largest cities. Thanks no doubt to his tireless courting of suburban voters, he also made a respectable showing among what had been predicted to be a constituency solidly in the Nixon column; he managed to increase the Democratic suburban vote in the nation's major metropolitan areas from 38 percent in 1956 to 49 percent in 1960. Kennedy fared poorly in the Great Plains, the Far West, and the smaller communities of the South where anti-Catholicism and the burgeoning civil rights movement drove many voters to the Republican candidate, but his success in the great metropolitan regions proved essential to the Democratic victory. Looking at the electoral returns, New Haven Mayor Richard Lee exulted, "Kennedy is more than anything else the president of the cities."[1]

## DEPRESSED AREAS

Kennedy's transition team appointed an unprecedented twenty-nine task forces in the weeks before his inauguration, two of which explored pressing urban problems in significant ways. Along with groups to recommend policy directions in such areas as education, defense, economics, and the space program, the president-elect created on December 5, 1960, a twenty-three-member task force chaired by Senator Paul H. Douglas (Democrat, Illinois) to study the problem of depressed areas. Having spent considerable time during the campaign in strategically important West Virginia, Kennedy had become interested in the grinding poverty endured by the residents of the Appalachian Mountains and had originally intended the task force to concentrate exclusively on that region. A product of Chicago's vital reform community who had been a champion of the urban poor harkening back to his association with Jane Addams and others at Hull House early in the twentieth century, Douglas became a passionate spokesman for the ailing cities of the Northeast and Midwest. He argued that area redevelopment legislation should especially aid the poor in communities with high unemployment caused by the introduction of new technology and stiff competition from low-wage regions such as the South. He persuaded the president-elect to broaden the scope of the investigation beyond the hills and hollows of Appalachia. The task force conducted hearings in Washington, D.C., as well as in Charleston, West Virginia, before formulating a program with a decidedly urban flavor.

Kennedy identified area redevelopment as his first legislative priority, and on January 5, 1961, Douglas introduced a bill drafted with the aid of White House staffers and cosponsored by forty-three other senators. The measure sought to attract private industry into areas with high and protracted unemployment rates by providing government incentives, allocating $300 million for loans in three separate funds of $100 million each for industrial areas, rural areas, and public facilities. Unlike earlier versions introduced by Douglas during the Eisenhower years, the bill encountered very little opposition in Congress and passed both houses by lopsided margins. The Area Redevelopment Act, which Kennedy signed on May 1, 1961, did not cure the nation's unemployment problem or bring massive changes to great numbers of declining inner-city neighborhoods, but it eased deplorable situations in a few chronically depressed sites. The Area Redevelopment Agency, which was replaced by the Economic Development Administration in 1965, served as a precursor to many Great Society programs initiated later in the decade.

## LEGISLATIVE SUCCESSES AND FAILURES

The Task Force on Housing and Urban Affairs, created on December 6, 1960, spoke more directly to the problems of the nation's major metropolises. In addition to calling for the creation of a new cabinet department for urban affairs, the task force recommended additional federal funding for low-income housing, urban renewal, and mass transit. On March 9, 1961, Kennedy delivered a special message to Congress that summarized the housing bill he was sending to Capitol Hill. Believing the urban task force report to have been essentially useless as a legislative blueprint, administration officials crafted housing legislation that offered no pathbreaking innovations but rather prescribed the revitalization of traditional programs that had been allowed to atrophy during the Eisenhower era. The omnibus measure called for the completion of the 100,000 units of public housing authorized but never completed by the Taft-Ellender-Wagner Act of 1949 while seeking additional housing for the elderly, college students, and farm families. Attributing urban renewal's shortcomings to faulty conception and constrictive operating regulations, the bill increased funding for nonresidential uses, allowed developers additional freedom to craft more ambitious projects, and proposed a startling $2.5 billion for urban renewal over the next four years. Emphasizing the desirability of comprehensive solutions to address complex metropolitan problems, the bill repeatedly urged systematic research and regional planning. With just a few exceptions, the Kennedy administration's proposal increased funding for existing agencies and programs.

The Democrats retained slender majorities in both houses of Congress after the 1960 election, having lost twenty seats in the House and one in the Senate, so passing legislation depended to a great extent on the administration's ability to maintain the loyalty of the party's sizable stable of southern conservatives. Fortunately for the fate of the Housing Act of 1961, a pair of Alabama Democrats friendly to housing reform occupied the chairmanships of the key Banking and Currency Committees in the Senate and the House. Senator John Sparkman and Congressman Albert Rains had lost numerous battles for increased federal support of housing during the Eisenhower years, and both men welcomed the opportunity to support the new president's bill. In the Senate, Sparkman and other housing partisans defeated a series of crippling amendments offered by such conservative Republicans as Homer Capehart of Indiana and Everett Dirksen of Illinois. In the House, where opponents of housing legislation enjoyed a long record of success, Rains ruthlessly pushed the measure through committee hearings in what one outraged bystander called "the worst railroad job I've ever seen." The bill's proponents acceded to the charges of fiscal irresponsibility by reducing the requested $2.5 billion for urban renewal by $500 million. When the representatives of suburbs and small towns objected during floor debates to the monopoly on government largess that the big cities would enjoy if the bill passed, Rains quickly offered an amendment that added $500 million for gas, water, and sewage improvements that appealed particularly to developing communities with incomplete infrastructures. Such extemporaneous horse trading paid off, and the bill passed by comfortable margins of 235 to 178 in the House and 64 to 25 in the Senate. Kennedy signed the bill into law on June 30, 1961.[2]

The 87th Congress passed the Housing Act of 1961 with remarkable dispatch, elevating the hopes of its supporters in urban America, but long-term results proved to be mixed. Kennedy loyalists immediately called the housing law the most significant since the 1949 measure, but enthusiasm for its passage dissipated quickly. An economic recession inherited from the Eisenhower administration persisted, delaying home construction until 1962 when conditions began to improve in the suburbs but inner cities continued to suffer. The amount of government-subsidized housing for the elderly increased substantially during the Kennedy years, but overall low-income housing construction never exceeded the rate achieved in the last year of the Eisenhower administration. The law's innovative attempts to increase federal support for moderate-income housing foundered, according to the National Commission on Urban Problems, because builders balked at the excessive red tape necessary to acquire loans and local Federal Housing Administration (FHA) field officers refused to embrace the program's social welfare goals. The Housing Act of 1961 specified appropriations only for the next few years, its supporters anticipating that the White House would submit a comprehensive housing bill during the presidential election year of 1964—an eventuality negated by the president's assassination in 1963. In fact, the Housing Act of 1961 ended up being the most significant piece of urban legislation passed during the Kennedy years.

While Congress considered housing legislation in 1961, officials at the Housing and Home Finance Administration (HHFA) under the direction of Robert Weaver proceeded with their plans to reform the nation's public housing program. A Harvard-educated economist who had worked in various capacities in the federal government's subsidized housing programs in the 1930s and in wartime production agencies in the 1940s, Weaver had championed the cause of poor and minority public housing tenants during his tenure as vice chairman of the New York City Housing and Redevelopment Board during the 1950s. Working with Public Housing Administration Commissioner Marie McGuire, the former executive director of the San Antonio Housing Authority, Weaver as head of the HHFA granted local housing authorities greater autonomy in the design and construction of public housing projects and in the use of federally subsidized, privately built low-income units. Weaver and McGuire, who had pioneered in the provision of public housing for the elderly in San Antonio, made low-income housing for senior citizens a priority of the federal government. The Housing Act of 1961 allocated one-half of new public housing units to older people, establishing a precedent that housing officials followed in subsequent decades. Catering to the potential political power of the growing number of superannuated voters in the American electorate and sensitive to the poor public image of family public housing by the early 1960s, members of Congress thought that older tenants would cause fewer problems than did low-income families. The federal government devoted steadily increasing proportions of its subsidized housing to the elderly, so much so that in later years it became the centerpiece of public housing.

After passage of the 1961 Housing Act, members of the administration interested in urban affairs turned their attention to two policy goals—the establishment of a cabinet department for cities and the eradication of residential segregation—that proved exceedingly difficult to reach. Kennedy had repeatedly endorsed both measures during the 1960 campaign. He had been especially critical of Eisenhower for condoning racial segregation in housing underwritten by the federal government, lamenting the fact that his predecessor had not taken any action to address what Kennedy portrayed as a straightforward problem. Matter-of-factly commenting that federally assisted housing could be "desegregated by the stroke of a presidential pen," Kennedy strongly suggested that he would issue such an executive order if elected president. When months went by after his inauguration without the new president fulfilling his promise, civil rights leaders who had avidly supported Kennedy grew restive. The White House feared that alienating the large and powerful contingent of southern Democrats in Congress by issuing the controversial executive order on desegregation would jeopardize chances of obtaining additional liberal legislation, a concern reinforced by the recognition that the Housing Act of 1961 would never have passed without the backing of John Sparkman, Albert Rains, and other influential Dixie legislators. Although many policymakers in the administration considered passing the housing discrimination bill more important, the president first sent the cabinet department bill to Congress on April 19, 1961. According to presidential aide and speechwriter Theodore Sorensen, Kennedy gambled that he could get the cabinet department bill through Congress that year and then issue the executive order after the close of the legislative session when it would cause less of a stir; if the bill failed to pass, the housing order could still be issued at a later time.[3]

The idea of a cabinet department for the cities, variously called the "Department of Municipalities," the "Department of Urbiculture," the "Department of Urban Affairs," and, in its most recent incarnation, the "Department of Urban Affairs and Housing," had been around for decades. Kennedy contended that the elevation of the HHFA to cabinet rank would create "an awareness" of urban issues and provide "coordinated leadership" to federal programs for the cities. Perhaps most important, he argued, its creation would be symbolic recognition of the importance of metropolitan issues in an America where 125 million people resided in urban and suburban areas and only 13 million on farms or in small towns. Senator Joseph S. Clark (Democrat, Pennsylvania), who introduced the administration's bill in the Senate, praised the idea because it would give urban America "an equal voice" in Washington for the first time and warned that the cities would be "doomed" without increased aid from the federal government. As expected, such organizations as the United States Conference of Mayors, the National Housing Conference, the National Association of Housing and Redevelopment Officials, the American Veterans Committee, and the American Federation of Labor–Congress of Industrial Organizations enthusiastically supported the initiative. Representatives from the American Institute of Planners and the American Institute of Architects suggested that a cabinet department would give greater unity to the traditional hodgepodge of urban programs. Legislators from heavily urbanized states and metropolitan districts, along with the mayors of the largest cities, testified in Congress in favor of the bill.[4]

A bipartisan coalition of conservatives in the Senate, which had already scotched the administration's Medicare and federal-aid-to-education bills, eagerly joined in the effort to stymie what they perceived to be yet another ill-considered liberal measure. Influential Senators John McClellan (Democrat, Arkansas), Sam Ervin (Democrat, North Carolina), Karl Mundt (Republican, South Dakota), and Carl Curtis (Republican, Nebraska) joined with Minority Leader Everett Dirksen in railing against the creation of a new federal agency that they feared would ally with corrupt big-city political machines. Additional opposition to the bill came from a group of southern legislators who would not vote for the new agency as long as HHFA administrator Robert Weaver stood to become the first African American cabinet member. Although Kennedy had made no promises, saying only that Weaver would be a "logical contender" for the cabinet post, the HHFA administrator believed that the president had given him sufficient encouragement to believe that he would be appointed. In 1961, increased civil rights agitation raised the level of anxiety among southern legislators about an African American at the head of an executive department who could use his authority to foster desegregation by tampering with federal programs and to expand the reach of federal power in other ways. As much as Kennedy felt obligated to appoint Weaver to repay northern black voters, he encountered a solid roadblock of congressional barons dedicated to preserving segregation in the Jim Crow South.[5]

As Congress conducted hearings on the bill, Kennedy urged Weaver to maintain a low profile. When questioned about the prospects of becoming a cabinet secretary, the HHFA administrator declined to comment and studiously avoided making any remarks that drew attention to his situation. No amount of care could airbrush Weaver out of the picture seen by southern legislators, who had provided the necessary votes to pass the Housing Act of 1961, and even the region's moderates fell in line behind the unreconstructed racists. Failing to extract a private guarantee from the president that Weaver would not be appointed secretary, the estimable John Sparkman reneged on an earlier statement in support of the bill and deserted the administration camp. The defeat became official on January 24, 1962, when the House Rules Committee, comprised mostly of Republicans and southern Democrats, killed the bill. Frustrated and angry, Kennedy tried an end run around Capitol Hill by invoking an obscure 1949 government reorganization statute that allowed the president to create cabinet posts by executive order unless either chamber of Congress voted negatively within sixty days. Not surprisingly, the House rejected the reorganization order on February 20 by a vote of 246 to 150.

After the months-long struggle to create the Department of Urban Affairs and Housing collapsed so ignominiously, the press called the failure the worst legislative embarrassment of the Kennedy administration. *Newsweek* sniffed that White House operatives "maneuvered with all of the finesse of third-rate precinct captains." The president admitted as much in his own analysis of the debacle, saying, "I played it too cute. It was so obvious it made [Congress] mad." Kennedy spoke of the inevitability of an urban cabinet department and predicted that the growing importance of the cities guaranteed success for urban forces sometime in the near future but discontinued efforts for the balance of his time in the White House. Public recognition of the worsening urban situation remained too slight and southern resistance to any measure

associated with the burgeoning civil rights movement too strong for the creation of an urban cabinet department in the early 1960s.[6]

The issue of discrimination in housing, which Kennedy had deferred repeatedly since taking office, resurfaced in the spring and summer of 1962 as
that year's congressional elections approached. Civil rights activists mailed
the president pens as a reminder of his 1960 pledge to end the practice with
a stroke of the presidential pen, and picketers assembled outside the White
House to shame the administration into action. Before reaching any conclusions about how best to handle the combustible issue, Kennedy waited for
a report on housing from the Civil Rights Commission and conferred with
a variety of advisers. Presidential confidante Theodore Sorensen later explained that the crux of the matter became how best to respond to a series
of questions regarding coverage: Would an executive order cover all or just
some of the various housing activities subsidized by the federal government?
Would it apply to housing in which government was involved only through
mortgage guarantees? Would the order be retroactive? And potentially most
troublesome of all, would the government become involved in housing built
exclusively with bank loans? In other words, how deeply should Washington
intrude into the affairs of the private housing industry to ensure compliance
with an antidiscrimination directive? Sorensen recalled that the Federal Home
Loan Bank Board, which supervised the activities of savings banks and savings
and loan institutions, expressed a willingness to go along with the executive
order; the Federal Deposit Insurance Corporation did not.

Waiting until after the election, Kennedy signed Executive Order 11063,
which mandated an end to discrimination in housing provided wholly or partially with federal assistance, on November 10, 1962. His order applied only
to new public housing and guaranteed federal loans, however, and exempted
all low-income units built or planned before November 20, 1962. Although
in many respects a noteworthy breakthrough on the path to racial equality,
the executive order fell short of its potential impact by severely limiting the
scope of the federal government's influence in the private housing market. In
its decision to restrict government involvement to federally financed housing and not to supervise transactions involving banks and savings and loan
associations, the administration gave free rein to private builders and lenders
in most of the housing constructed in the nation; the guidelines mandated
by the presidential directive applied to less than 1 percent of the nation's

housing units. Closely monitoring developments thereafter, officials at the HHFA—and its successor, the Department of Housing and Urban Development (HUD)—assessed the impact of Executive Order 11063 and found compliance erratic. Local housing authorities continued to perpetuate racial segregation through their site-selection practices, and private lending institutions awarded mortgages in customary fashion. In fact, as historians of the civil rights movement have noted, Kennedy's much-anticipated executive order altered racial patterns in housing imperceptibly if at all. Local ordinances, public attitudes, and the great disparity in income between blacks and whites combined to curtail the residential mobility of racial minorities.

The Kennedy administration's record on increasing federal aid to mass transit likewise proved to be mixed. The Federal-Aid Highway Act of 1962, which the president signed on October 23, authorized the use of federal funds for relocation assistance payments to individuals and businesses displaced by highway construction in cities. The allocation of federal dollars for that purpose broke new ground but required approval by state governments while limiting outlays to $200 for individuals and $3,000 for businesses. The law also required that all federally aided highway projects in metropolitan areas approved after July 1, 1965, be based on comprehensive planning conducted cooperatively by state and local governments. In 1962 and 1963, the White House also introduced legislation for a federal matching-grant program to help states and municipalities improve mass transit systems. Both measures died in the House, where Republicans and conservative Democrats argued that the costly measures would dangerously inflate the federal budget. Besides, the conservatives argued, transportation problems in urban areas should appropriately be handled at the state or local level.

Defeats for mass transit legislation in 1962 and 1963, the failure to create the Department of Urban Affairs and Housing, and the belated issuance of the executive order on housing discrimination, all of which the press portrayed as sharp setbacks for the administration, led to the president's growing inattention to urban matters. Diverted by Cold War crises in Cuba, Germany, Laos, and Vietnam, Kennedy concentrated increasingly on foreign affairs—a development reflected in the budgets submitted to Congress that earmarked the preponderance of federal funds for the armed forces, military research and development, and the nascent space program. Concerned mayors and other city boosters voiced their concerns, urging the president to redeem the promises he had made in 1960 about giving the cities their due. In January 1963, a mayoral delegation urged Kennedy to convene a White House conference to assess the state of the cities after two years of his leadership. The White House announced that such a conference, emblematic of renewed attention to the cities, would be held in December.

## KENNEDY'S MARK ON THE CITIES

The assassination of President Kennedy on November 22, 1963, rendered moot any speculation about future directions the administration may have taken in urban affairs, leaving only a record compiled over 1,000 days to consider. As in all efforts to evaluate the Kennedy presidency after its abrupt termination, any assessment of the administration's urban policies must evoke such terms as "brevity" and "incompleteness" more than "success" or failure." In the beginning, Kennedy spoke boldly about increased attention to festering urban problems and thereby excited the imaginations of local officials, planners, and others who cared deeply about cities. Troubled relations with an essentially conservative Congress produced uneven results, however, the early and surprisingly easy passage of the Housing Act of 1961 being offset by later reverses as an alliance of southern Democrats and conservative Republicans gained the upper hand on Capitol Hill. The administration's inability to breathe life into the proposed Department of Urban Affairs and Housing symbolized the disjuncture between the executive and legislative branches in Washington during the early 1960s. A Democratic president working with unreliable Democratic majorities in the Senate and the House compiled a paltry record of urban legislation.

Consistently thwarted on Capitol Hill, Kennedy's New Frontier reform program affected urban America chiefly through its unprecedented attention to urban problems. His presidency consumed by Cold War crises and by the struggle to revive a balky economy, Kennedy achieved less in urban America than he would have liked or than his liberal supporters had hoped. He left a copious list of issues plaguing the nation's cities to his successor, involving low- and moderate-income housing, urban renewal, residential segregation, mass transit, crime, juvenile delinquency, and other problems that by the mid-1960s were said to constitute an "urban crisis." Much of the Great Society legislation that followed originated in embryonic Kennedy programs that failed to mobilize public opinion, fell short of obtaining legislative majorities, or languished at first before coming to fruition later in the 1960s. A few months after the martyred president's death, a political scientist observed, "Kennedy will be remembered for many things, but in the long run, it may well be that he will be best remembered as the first President to understand the implications of the metropolitan revolution in the United States and as the first to try to do something about it." The federal government became the great benefactor of the cities not under Kennedy but under his successor, Lyndon Johnson, a politician who seemed at the time to be an unlikely friend of urban America.[7]

## LYNDON B. JOHNSON AND THE CITIES

Unlike Kennedy, a cosmopolite from the bustling northeastern megalopolis who was thoroughly conversant with big-city habits and issues, Lyndon B. Johnson hailed from an isolated small town on the cusp of the American South and Southwest. Raised in a community of fewer than 1,000 residents in the rugged hills of central Texas, Johnson spent his formative years in a poor rural environment that he later acknowledged seemed a world apart from the big cities he encountered after going to Washington, D.C., as a young New Dealer in the 1930s. Growing up, he recoiled at the destitution that surrounded him in the Texas hill country and vowed to aid the impoverished settlers and townsfolk who strove to make ends meet in a harsh land; that empathy resurfaced when he later observed the dire poverty of the urban slums and ghettos. If the teeming cities seemed alien to Johnson, the needs and hopes of the struggling masses seemed all too familiar. An early and dedicated advocate of low-income housing, he worked feverishly as a freshman U.S. congressman in 1937 to secure a public housing project for Austin, the largest city in his legislative district. In the 1950s, as a Democratic Senate majority leader whose cautious conservatism often rankled his more progressive colleagues, he frequently joined the small but influential bloc of southerners who voted for low-income housing and other measures to aid the urban poor. Johnson met frequently with delegations of big-city mayors during his tenure as majority leader and won high praise from them for his openness, accessibility, and willingness to learn about urban problems. His painstaking leadership proved instrumental in passing the Civil Rights Acts of 1957 and 1960, two modest pieces of legislation noteworthy more for having laid the foundation for future successes than for any substantive reforms achieved in race relations. Yet, although some liberals rued his moderating influence on the civil rights measures in 1957 and 1960, the fact that a southerner would work for such legislation in any form seemed remarkable at the time. The loss of Kennedy appeared at first to be a terrible setback to those who championed urban causes, but these examples from Johnson's congressional career suggested that the new president might not be wholly indifferent to the plight of the millions of people living in America's beleaguered cities.

## THE WAR ON POVERTY

The new president's great interest in the nation's cities figured prominently in his administration's declaration of war on poverty. The Kennedy White House had already embraced the idea of submitting a large-scale antipoverty bill to Congress in 1964, and the secretaries of Health, Education, and Welfare (HEW); Agriculture; Commerce; and Labor—along with the director of the budget and the HHFA administrator—were hurriedly preparing legislation at the time of Kennedy's death in November 1963. Asked immediately after Kennedy's assassination whether the cabinet members should continue this work, Johnson replied affirmatively. This is "my kind of undertaking," he enthused. "I'm interested. I'm sympathetic. Go ahead. Give it the highest priority. Push ahead full tilt." Previous federal efforts at combating poverty, including a host of categorical and grant programs that provided aid for relief, housing, education, and job programs, operated independently and lacked a common purpose and effective coordination. Recalling the impressive scale of the federal initiatives created by Franklin D. Roosevelt during the Great Depression, Johnson sought a massive program for the 1960s that could rival and even surpass the New Deal. Averse to increasing federal spending on welfare, the president wanted government to wage a war on poverty by enhancing economic opportunity for the American people. Forswearing tax increases, Johnson asked officials in his administration to create a program of education and job training that would allow the people to better their skills and improve their lot in life—government would offer, in the Johnson administration's formulation, a "hand up, not a handout."[8]

At his January 8, 1964, State of the Union Address, the president declared passionately, "This administration, today, here and now, declares unconditional war on poverty." On March 16, he sent to Congress the Economic

Opportunity Act (EOA) and requested an appropriation of $962 million to fund the ambitious program. Title I of the law consisted of the Job Corps, an employment program targeting impoverished males between the ages of sixteen and twenty-one, and other work training and work-study initiatives. Title II created the Community Action Program (CAP), which would encourage the "maximum feasible participation" of poverty area residents and be administered by local agencies representative of their communities. Additional titles requested funding for such programs as Volunteers in Service to America (VISTA), aid to migrant workers, training for unemployed heads of households on welfare, and a federally financed loan program for businesses that would hire the hard-core unemployed. Title VI of the EOA provided for the creation of a new agency, the Office of Economic Opportunity (OEO), to administer the legislation's disparate components. In his message to Congress introducing the bill, the president spoke in general terms, avoided specifics about the operation of the various titles, and essentially limited his remarks to a broad discussion of government's role in increasing opportunity for the nation's poor. After the Senate passed the bill 61 to 34 and the House followed suit by a vote of 226 to 185, Johnson signed the bill into law on August 20. The bill authorized $947 million for the first year's antipoverty programs, just $15 million less than the amount requested by the president.[9]

Even after the passage of the EOA in the summer of 1964, the substance of the war on poverty remained murky to many people inside and outside the Johnson administration. Never entirely conversant with the intricacies of the law, Johnson vaguely hoped that the OEO's varied programs would reduce poverty levels, but he still remained indifferent about how the programs would actually work. Sargent Shriver, whom the president coerced into accepting the OEO directorship, found himself in charge of a puzzling concatenation of programs that included an urban Job Corps, VISTA, and the ill-defined community action initiative. Social scientists disagreed about the effectiveness of the legislative package approved by Congress, a reflection of the lack of consensus among poverty experts at the time about how best to raise income levels. Daniel Patrick Moynihan, who had served on the task force that proposed the antipoverty program, concluded, "This is the essential fact: The government did not know what it was doing."[10] A leading historian seconded Moynihan's assessment twenty years later, saying,

When the Economic Opportunity Act was enacted, neither the President who sponsored it, the director-designate who would administer it, nor the congressmen who passed it really knew what they had done. Indeed, a history of the legislation might well be entitled . . . "How Not to Fight Poverty."[11]

In the generally muddled picture of the antipoverty crusade after the passage of the EOA, the role of community action seemed especially unclear. The CAP, which originated with a modest program conceived during the Kennedy administration to address rising levels of juvenile delinquency in the cities, propounded community empowerment but offered little detail about how city halls and local activists would share power. For the most part, members of Congress gave scant attention to the matter in their discussions of the legislation. Chicago Mayor Richard J. Daley's congressional testimony warning that community action threatened a loss of control for city halls went largely unheeded. Although he prided himself on being a master of legislative detail who intuitively grasped the political implications of all congressional actions, Johnson failed to appreciate the potential divisiveness of Title II. In the rush to launch the war on poverty, he apparently did not foresee how community action could pit mayors and city councils against neighborhood interests, whites against blacks, and the rich against the poor—in other words, the entrenched urban elites against the groups newly empowered by the EOA. Apart from a coterie of policy experts, few people in Washington understood the radical implications of the community action idea for the nation's cities. The war on poverty affected urban America in ways that were not altogether clear in 1964.

## THE GREAT SOCIETY

In the preparation of legislation drafted specifically to address urban issues, Johnson at first closely followed the path of his predecessor. In a December 4, 1963, meeting with Princeton University historian Eric F. Goldman, the president speculated about the domestic issues he would be confronting in the upcoming years. When Goldman suggested that "our cities, now heading for such disarray, appeared certain to be a prime problem," Johnson nodded affirmatively. "'The cities, yes,' he murmured. 'They are something I am going to have to learn a lot about.'" On January 27, 1964, just nineteen days after delivering his State of the Union Address, Johnson gave his first speech to Congress on a single topic—housing. The president noted often during his talk the centrality of the housing program to the administration's war on poverty, which he had dramatically proclaimed in his January 8 State of the Union Address. His initial foray into housing followed closely the contours of previous Kennedy legislation, primarily adding flesh and sinew to the legislative skeleton already prepared by the HHFA for the 1964 legislative session. The Housing Act of 1964, which Johnson signed on September 2, authorized the expenditure of $1.13 billion for new and existing housing and urban renewal programs through September 1965 and allocated federal grants totaling $350 million for mass transportation improvements in metropolitan areas. The Urban Mass Transportation Act of 1964, another bill originally conceived in the Kennedy years, authorized the expenditure of $375 million over three years to help state and local governments improve existing transit systems and construct new facilities. The law mandated that federal grants and loans be awarded for comprehensive urban transportation systems in the planned development of metropolitan regions and that the awards be approved jointly by the HHFA administrator and the secretary of commerce; it also provided funding for research and for demonstration projects.[12]

While Johnson staffers labored for housing and mass transit bills on Capitol Hill in 1964, work proceeded to tie urban policy into the sweeping reform program the new administration was formulating. The president struggled for a pithy phrase to label the grandiose legislative package taking shape, briefly considering the "Better Deal" a possible choice because of his reverence for Roosevelt's New Deal. He eventually settled on the Great Society, a slogan that historian Eric F. Goldman and speechwriter Richard Goodwin had adapted from Walter Lippmann's 1937 book *The Good Society*. Johnson formally unveiled the Great Society program in his May 22, 1964, commencement address at the University of Michigan. A bold statement of national purpose that summoned Americans already blessed with plenty to strive for true greatness, the speech challenged an affluent populace to share its bounty with the less fortunate and reiterated the president's earlier call for a full-scale war on poverty. Moreover, Johnson's impassioned speech made clear the centrality of the cities to any attempt at constructing the Great Society. He said,

> In the remainder of the century, urban population will double, city land will
> double, and we will have to build homes, highways, and facilities equal to all

those built since this country was first settled. So in the next forty years we must rebuild the entire urban United States. . . . Our society will never be great until our cities are great.[13]

Following his landslide election over Republican Barry Goldwater in November 1964, Johnson set out to translate his soaring rhetoric into a coherent legislative program. (Democrats enjoyed huge majorities in both houses of Congress after the election—68 to 32 in the Senate and 295 to 140 in the House). The Housing Act of 1965, one of the first measures the White House sent to the heavily Democratic 89th Congress, advanced the federal government's role in housing far beyond the standards set by the comparatively modest law passed the year before. The colossal bill sent to Capitol Hill that spring proposed the construction of 240,000 new units of low-income housing over four years; designated $2.9 billion for urban renewal; increased housing allocations for the elderly, veterans, college students, and the physically handicapped; funded the construction of experimental new towns; and included a modest rent supplement program for moderate-income families. Section 23 authorized persons of low income to lease existing units from private landlords with government subsidies provided by local housing authorities. The bill also provided for "turnkey" housing, by which a developer acquired land and contracted with the local housing authority to construct public housing according to its specifications; after completion of the project, the developer "turned the key" over to the city agency for rent to low-income families. Stunning in its scope and complexity, the measure thrilled liberal supporters of the Great Society and alarmed the traditional opponents of housing reform who feared a vast expansion of government authority in the private housing market.

The most controversial aspect of the housing bill proved to be rent supplements. Beginning in the 1950s, as disenchantment with public housing mounted, some reformers had suggested that government provide the poor with rent certificates that could be used in lieu of cash as an alternative means of providing low-income housing. In the mid-1960s, HHFA administrator Robert Weaver supported the innovation as a method by which the federal government could underwrite moderate-income housing. As proposed in the legislation sent to Congress in March 1965, just $150 million would be allotted for rent supplements between 1965 and 1968. Only new or renovated buildings developed by nonprofit or limited-dividend companies receiving federally insured financing would be eligible to receive rent supplements. However narrowly conceived, rent supplements generated a firestorm of criticism from Republicans in Congress who railed against the government encroachment into the free market and from liberal Democrats who feared that increased subsidies for moderate-income families would divert resources away from public housing. In the spring and summer of 1965, paralleling the rising tension between inner cities and suburbs nationally, race became an important subtext in the intensifying congressional debate over rent supplements. Newspaper accounts describing the assault on civil rights demonstrators in Selma, Alabama, the struggle for voting rights legislation in Congress, and battles in northern communities over public school desegregation provided an uneasy backdrop to the discussion of federally aided housing. After six days of rioting in the Watts area of Los Angeles, local officials counted thirty-four dead and 1,032 injured with more than 600 buildings damaged by arson and looting and property losses exceeding $40 million. When liberals suggested that lowering the eligibility standards of the rent supplement program could allow poor families to escape the barriers confining them to distressed central cities, conservatives inveighed against the possible invasion of the suburbs by unwanted minorities. Although Senator John Tower of Texas and other southern legislators denied that race figured in their opposition to rent supplements, their fulminations against forced integration left little doubt about what they feared.

Fully engaged in the effort to push the voting rights and Medicare acts through the 89th Congress—and poised to submit the next batch of Great Society laws, including measures to reform immigration policy and abrogate right-to-work legislation—the administration found its housing measure stalled by a decidedly minor component of the massive bill, the relatively innocuous rent supplement provision. As a concession to the liberals whose expected support had not materialized, Senator Edmund Muskie (Democrat, Maine) introduced an amendment to lower the eligibility standards for rent supplements below the ceiling allowable for public housing. Johnson signed the bill with Muskie's key amendment on August 10, calling it the most important housing legislation since the landmark 1949 law. The final version of the Housing Act of 1965 retained the rent supplement provision but only for people who qualified for low-income housing; thus, an odd alliance of conservatives and liberals had subverted the original aim of the new program, as conceived by Johnson and Weaver, to address the housing issues of middle-income families.

## HUD

The other major urban initiative that the president had identified for 1965, the creation of a cabinet department for the cities, finally seemed attainable in ways that it had not in previous years. Johnson declined to tackle the issue during his first year in the White House, but the huge majorities the Democrats enjoyed in both houses of Congress after the November 1964 election left the political landscape considerably more inviting to such a proposal. The president believed that the bill submitted to the 89th Congress, which was virtually identical to the versions presented to the 87th and 88th Congresses, required only a few cosmetic changes to gain the necessary votes for passage. Trying to anticipate any possible roadblocks, the administration changed the name of the proposed cabinet department from "Urban Affairs and Housing" to "Housing and Urban Development." Giving housing top billing in the title would reassure the construction and banking industries that their interests remained paramount in the presidential cabinet. The choice of "urban development," with its implied emphasis on the physical environment of the urban landscape, allayed concerns that the more nebulous "urban affairs" might encompass any and all topics remotely related to metropolitan life. The parsing of language in such fine detail mattered in the attempt to assuage the concerns of legislators poised to add another big piece of bureaucracy to a federal government already considered bloated and ponderous in some quarters. Determined to avoid the kind of controversy that helped to derail Kennedy's earlier efforts, Johnson denied that any decision had been made to appoint Robert Weaver the new department's first secretary. The Civil Rights Act of 1964 and the impending passage of the voting rights bill may have signaled that southern obstructionists no longer could use the race issue with the same effectiveness, but Johnson was taking no chances.

Reflecting the sense of inevitability about the new cabinet department, consideration of the administration's bill proceeded perfunctorily through Congress. Republicans argued that such legislation would relegate state and local governments to subordinate roles but, resigned to the certainty of the federal government devoting greater attention to urban affairs, offered little resistance. The law passed by comfortable margins in the House and the Senate, and the president signed the law creating HUD on September 9, 1965. Although Johnson had declined to designate Weaver as the first secretary of HUD prior to the legislation's passage, Washington pundits considered the HHFA administrator the best-qualified candidate for the position and fully expected him to be appointed. So did Weaver. Johnson delayed for months, however, while he considered several possible appointees. In the end, after all the major civil rights leaders endorsed the HHFA administrator, Johnson followed their recommendation. On January 13, 1966, with little fanfare, the president appointed Weaver the first HUD secretary at a small White House ceremony arranged at the last moment. The Senate Banking Committee approved after a hearing that lasted barely an hour, and the full Senate unanimously consented to the appointment later that day. The president's lack of enthusiasm and the muted nature of the historic appointment raised questions about Weaver's ability to chart a clear course of action for the new agency. Would HUD be simply a glorified housing agency, or would it fashion a broader urban vision under Weaver's leadership? The future of HUD as the principal voice of the cities in the federal government remained very much in doubt in 1965.

## THE ACHIEVEMENTS OF 1965

The Johnson administration also sought to pass legislation in 1965 to improve education in urban America. As the members of the huge baby-boom generation inundated the nation's public schools in the 1950s and 1960s, local school districts, city halls, and state governments struggled to pay the bills. Studies of inner-city schools found rickety buildings, overcrowded classrooms, inadequate supplies, underpaid and demoralized teachers, and outmoded curricula. Only about one-third of public elementary schools contained libraries, and many schools averaged fewer than one book per pupil. A task force on education commissioned by Kennedy recommended unprecedented levels of federal aid for education, with the bulk of funding targeted for poor states and ghetto schools in big cities; a task force appointed several years later by Johnson echoed the call for a significant increase in federal support of public education in inner-city schools. Reflecting the Johnson administration's determination to make education an important part of the war on poverty, early drafts of the EOA contained programs to improve social conditions in inner cities through the wholesale revision of public school curricula. Although education lost its prominent position in the antipoverty legislation passed by Congress in 1964, Johnson remained dedicated to improving the nation's underperforming public schools—especially in the cities.

The Elementary and Secondary Education Act (ESEA) deviated from traditional education legislation that had allocated funds across the board for school construction and teacher salary increases. Instead, intent on improving education in poor inner cities, the ESEA provided more specialized types of aid for school districts serving large numbers of children from low-income families. Johnson pointed out that cities spent only about two-thirds as much as suburbs on education and that nearly two-thirds of tenth graders from poor neighborhoods in the nation's fifteen largest cities dropped out before receiving a high school diploma. As framed by Education Commissioner Francis Keppel, the ESEA roughly doubled federal expenditures on public education with the bulk of the new funds targeting poor children in order to break the cycle of poverty prevailing in urban America. Title I, the heart of the law, provided federal grants to the states on the basis of the following formula: the number of children from low-income families (under $2,000 a year) multiplied times 50 percent of each state's average expenditure per pupil. The U.S. Conference of Mayors unanimously endorsed the measure, which sailed through Congress in a mere three months. The president signed the bill in the presence of seventy-two-year-old Kate Deadrich Loney, who had been his first teacher, outside the dilapidated one-room schoolhouse he had attended as a four-year-old decades before.

The legislative bounty of 1965, the year that constituted the pinnacle of the Great Society, also included measures to protect the environment. Contrary to the view of Johnson as a loyal servant of Texas oil interests who would never advocate laws to protect the environment, the president frequently invoked the example of Theodore Roosevelt in seeking to conserve natural resources in the wilderness—and superseded Roosevelt's example by championing environmental reform in urban settings as well. Johnson inveighed against industrial miscreants that dumped their toxic waste indiscriminately, polluted the water, and befouled the air. The Water Quality Act of 1965, which the president signed on October 2, 1965, required the states to enforce water quality standards; the Clean Water Reclamation Act, which Johnson signed on November 3, 1966, provided matching grants for the construction of sewage treatment plants. Enforcement of these laws proved problematic, requiring additional amendments in later years to guarantee the quality of drinking water in the cities. The report of the President's Task Force on Environmental Pollution documented the damage to the air by emissions from coal-burning factories and automobile exhaust, especially the air pollutants that fell back to earth as "acid rain." Public concern about air pollution grew after an ecological disaster in New York City on Thanksgiving Day in 1965, when an air inversion trapped lethal levels of soot in the atmosphere, suffocating eighty people and leaving hundreds hospitalized. Johnson signed the Air Quality Act of 1967 on November 21, establishing stricter standards for automobile emissions and industrial pollution. Incomplete and underfunded, the Great Society's environmental legislation nonetheless constituted the federal government's initial steps to protect the urban masses from water- and airborne pollutants.

Passage in 1965 of a related environmental bill, the Highway Beautification Act, owed largely to the indefatigable work of the First Lady. At Lady Bird Johnson's request, the president in 1964 convened the Task Force on the Preservation of Natural Beauty to extend the earlier work on wilderness beautification to more populated areas. Using Washington, D.C., as a test case, the First Lady, the National Park Service, and private donors refurbished Pennsylvania Avenue between the White House and the Capitol and landscaped a series of parks throughout the city. Arguing that crumbling buildings, open sewage, and rabid rats presented greater threats to urban life than unsightly billboards and a dearth of green space, critics dismissed Mrs. Johnson and others interested in city beautification as effete members of the "daffodil-and-dogwood" set. The president informed Congress that he fully supported his wife's crusade, calling city beautification good for business and an important step in reviving the nation's flagging tourism industry. The final bill passed by Congress restricted the use of billboards except in designated industrial areas and mandated the erection of fences around junkyards and other eyesores adjacent to highways.[14]

By the end of 1965, onlookers marveled at Johnson's success in assembling the framework of his Great Society reform program. Driven by the insatiable taskmaster in the White House, the 89th Congress achieved a breathtaking record of accomplishment. Building on an impressive start in 1964 and abetted by that year's elections that returned hefty Democratic majorities to Capitol Hill, the administration in 1965 secured the Medicare and Medicaid health care programs for the aged and indigent, unprecedented amounts of government loans for college students, a landmark voting rights law, immigration reform, environmental legislation, protection for consumers, and the creation of the National Endowment for the Humanities and the National Endowment for the Arts as well as several lesser laws. Legislation directly targeting the cities included a major housing bill, aid for inner-city schools, and the creation of a cabinet department for urban affairs. Determined to confront rising urban unrest that seemed to worsen with each summer of his administration, however, the president felt the need to do more for the nation's beleaguered cities. With HUD finally created and its secretary firmly ensconced, Johnson demanded in 1966 a daring new program that would combine the resources of the federal government's many agencies in a massive campaign to save America's declining inner cities.

## MODEL CITIES

The president had been intrigued by a May 15, 1965, memorandum from Walter Reuther, president of the United Auto Workers, proposing a "Marshall Plan for the Cities." Rather than devising a generic program that awarded grants wholesale to American cities, as had been done routinely in the past, Reuther proposed "a bold restructuring in six selected American cities of full and complete organic neighborhoods for 50,000 people." He suggested that six cities—Detroit, Chicago, Philadelphia, Los Angeles, Houston, and Washington, D.C.—serve as test cases for an innovative federal program that could be replicated on a much larger scale if successful. In Reuther's design, the federal government would mobilize such varied elements as business, labor, local government, and community organizations into a powerful alliance to improve all aspects of urban life—housing, jobs, education, health care, recreation, transportation, and public safety. Johnson liked the audacity of the ambitious plan, thought that it could be incorporated effectively into the existing Great Society apparatus, and believed that federal involvement must go beyond housing to make a difference in the aging central cities. He appointed a task force, chaired by HUD Undersecretary Robert C. Wood, charged with effectuating Reuther's design for "demonstration cities."[15]

In the course of its meetings in the fall of 1965, the task force significantly reworked Reuther's original plan for six demonstration cities. Believing that political support would grow if a greater number of congressmen could vote for a measure that directly benefited their constituents, the task force increased the number of demonstration cities to sixty-six. The final bill that the president sent to Congress outlined a program for six large cities (population exceeding 500,000), ten medium-sized cities (population 250,000 to 500,000), and fifty small cities (population less than 250,000). The sixty-six communities selected for participation by a special presidential commission would be expected to avail themselves of the full panoply of federal programs already in existence so that this effort would dovetail, not compete, with the Job Corps, CAP, and other Great Society creations. The task force affixed a $2.3 billion price tag over six years on demonstration cities, the federal government paying 80 percent ($1.9 billion) and local authorities assuming responsibility for the remaining 20 percent. HUD would serve as the lead agency to administer the program.

With the threat of more racial violence in the cities looming in the spring and summer of 1966, the battle over the program became one of the bitterest experienced in the Johnson years. Congressional conservatives took aim at the appellation "demonstration cities," suggesting that the president had succumbed to the antics of rioting African Americans and antiwar demonstrators in the cities; administration supporters soon adopted the less suggestive term "model cities." Still, a number of legislators on both sides of the aisle grumbled about passing legislation simply to appease ghetto rioters. Debate on the bill reflected the national preoccupation with race in the summer and fall of 1966—involving what the Model Cities program would mean for the racial desegregation of white neighborhoods, the location of public housing in homogeneous suburbs, busing to achieve racial integration, and indeed how the nation would react to yet another summer of racial discord in the cities. As Congressman Henry B. Gonzalez (Democrat, Texas), an avid supporter of the measure, proudly proclaimed, "The Demonstration Cities and Metropolitan Act of 1966 is the real antiriot bill of the 89th Congress." Johnson finally signed the bill on November 3, 1966, and proudly proclaimed his high hopes for what he judged to be the administration's signal effort on behalf of the cities.[16]

Almost from the beginning, however, Model Cities suffered a series of setbacks that vitiated the president's optimism. Because Congress failed to appropriate the funds specified in the legislation and HUD processed the necessary paperwork at a glacial pace, the program sputtered in its infancy. HUD finally approved the first city for full funding on December 23, 1968, less than one month prior to the inauguration of a new president. Only nine cities received any Model Cities funding during the Johnson administration. Allegations surfaced about politics permeating the selection process as awards went to communities in states where Democratic congressmen had strongly supported the legislation, and critics labeled Model Cities just another pork-barrel project depositing funds into the coffers of the administration's friends at the expense of slum-ridden cities that continued to suffer without federal aid. Controversy also arose over the handling of Model Cities awards at the local level where mayors and other city officials rejected federal supervision and sought autonomy in the dissemination of the largess. In Chicago, for example, HUD ignored the protests of citizen groups representing the neighborhoods designated for Model Cities funding for fear of alienating Mayor Richard J. Daley, a powerful Democrat and strong supporter of the president's domestic and foreign policies. This tension between HUD and Model Cities grant recipients, duplicated in communities throughout the nation, contributed further to the declining fortunes of what the president had hoped would be the crown jewel of his design to aid the cities.

## FINAL ATTEMPTS AT REFORM

The Johnson administration allied with many of the local groups and neighborhood associations energized by Model Cities to preserve historic properties, many of which were being razed under the auspices of federal programs ostensibly designed to benefit cities. Clearing land for the construction of massive expressways and the implementation of urban renewal programs often meant destroying stately buildings of historical importance. A federal report endorsed by the First Lady detailed the harmful effects of urban renewal and called for legislation to sustain a community's heritage by safeguarding designated structures. President Johnson signed the National Historic Preservation Act (NHPA) on October 15, 1966, which required federal agencies to evaluate the impact of federally funded projects on historic properties and created several institutions to protect the heritage of the nation's built environment. The Advisory Council on Historic Preservation, consisting of twenty members drawn from government and the private sector, would advise the president and Congress on historic preservation issues. The State Historic Preservation Offices in each of the states nominated properties for preservation according to a rigorous set of criteria, the worthy districts, sites, buildings, and structures being listed on the National Register of Historic

Places. Later amendments, such as the National Environmental Policy Act of 1969, expanded the area protected by the NHPA by including the environment surrounding historic sites.

In the last years of his presidency, Johnson still yearned to help the cities, but the growing cost of American military involvement in Southeast Asia reduced the resources available for domestic spending. The president's hope of maintaining support for Great Society initiatives while waging a costly war—the quest for both guns and butter—faded as the number of U.S. troops in Vietnam reached 525,000 in 1968 and the cost of underwriting the expeditionary force exceeded $28 billion. In seeking to make social progress without investing billions of dollars, the administration opted for the issue of fair housing building on Kennedy's Executive Order 11063 to combat racial discrimination in urban neighborhoods and suburbs. The idea of federal support for open occupancy proved to be anathema to many white home owners, and legislation introduced by the administration in 1966 encountered the full opposition of a bipartisan coalition in Congress that had lost battles over civil rights bills in 1964 and 1965 but remained a formidable opponent. Presidential aide Joseph Califano remembered that the issue "prompted some of the most vicious mail LBJ received on any subject and the only death threats I ever received as a White House assistant." The bill's supporters failed to muster the votes to break a filibuster mounted in the Senate by southerners, and support for open housing became a lethal issue for liberal Democrats seeking reelection in 1966 against Republicans who opposed the measure; Paul H. Douglas, who served as Senate floor leader for the bill, lost to Charles Percy in Illinois, and Governor Edmund "Pat" Brown lost to Ronald Reagan in California. Although willing to accept the antidiscrimination provisions of the 1964 Civil Rights Act and the broadening of the franchise by the 1965 Voting Rights Act, many whites in the North as well as in the South balked at the prospect of residential desegregation.[17]

The administration persisted, submitting fair housing legislation in 1967 and again in 1968. Discussing the inadequacy of the Kennedy executive order, Secretary Weaver testified before Congress that existing federal nondiscrimination provisions still applied to only 4 percent of the nation's housing stock. Citing evidence that residential segregation was actually increasing, Johnson urged passage of sweeping legislation that would bar discrimination in the sale and rental of all housing in the nation. The assassination of Martin Luther

King Jr. on April 4, 1968, which sparked another series of racial conflagrations in the cities, added a sense of urgency to the passage of legislation prohibiting racial segregation. The president made an unabashed appeal to Congress to approve the fair housing bill as a testament to the principles for which the martyred civil rights leader had stood. "What more can [you] do to achieve brotherhood and equality among all Americans?" Johnson asked in an open letter to congressional leaders. The most meaningful response legislators could make, he answered, was to "enact [fair housing] legislation so long delayed and so close to fulfillment." Congress complied, and the president signed the bill on April 11.[18]

The Civil Rights Act of 1968 declared equal housing opportunity the official policy of the U.S. government. When fully implemented in 1970, the law covered 80 percent of all private housing. Title VIII of the law made discrimination illegal in all houses and rental units, prohibiting real estate agents and brokers from refusing to sell or rent any dwelling on the basis of race, color, religion, or national origin. The law, which would be administered by the HUD secretary, outlawed blockbusting, panic peddling, and other unsavory real estate practices designed to maintain racial segregation. Any person who suspected foul play could file a grievance with HUD and, failing to receive satisfaction with the federal agency, could sue in federal court for injunctive relief. The U.S. attorney general could bring a civil suit where a pattern of discrimination existed. The law also contained a series of antiriot provisions, part of the price the administration paid for passage.

Along with the open housing measure, Johnson also proposed an omnibus housing bill in 1968 that would increase significantly the amount of low- and moderate-income housing available to the public. In a special message to Congress on February 22 devoted exclusively to the problems of metropolitan America, the president spoke movingly of how solving the urban crisis depended on the provision of better housing. Like the Civil Rights Act of 1968, the housing bill no doubt benefited from the increased interest in ameliorative urban legislation in the wake of the King assassination that year. The Housing and Urban Development Act of 1968, which Johnson signed on August 1, established an ambitious goal of constructing or rehabilitating 26 million housing units, 6 million for low- and moderate-income families; in the first three years, $5.3 billion would be spent for 1.7 million units of low-income housing. The law called for 300,000 housing starts in Fiscal Year 1969, an allocation of $230 million for Fiscal Year 1970 so that cities could plan for mass transit improvements, a HUD guarantee of $250 million of bonds for the planning and construction of new communities by private developers, and expansion of such existing programs as rent supplements and Model Cities. Following the examples of the Section 23 and turnkey programs created by the Housing Act of 1965, the measure sought to increase the privatization of low-income housing. Section 235 of the 1968 law, which provided federal subsidies for home purchases, and Section 236, which was designated for rental housing, employed FHA and Federal National Mortgage Administration instruments such as the below-market interest rate and accelerated depreciation allowance to induce builders to supply decent and affordable housing for low- and moderate-income families.

Title IV of the Housing and Urban Development Act of 1968 constituted the federal government's most significant attempt yet to encourage the creation of new communities, continuing a halting effort begun earlier in the decade. Title VII of the Housing Act of 1961 and Section 702 of the Housing and Urban Development Act of 1965 had provided federal aid for the construction of public facilities within new towns; Title IV of the Demonstration Cities and Metropolitan Development Act of 1966 had established a mortgage insurance program for that purpose. The 1968 law authorized a revolving fund for loan guarantees to provide capital to developers of new communities who otherwise shied away from the considerable risk necessary in creating entire urban infrastructures for towns built from scratch. Weaver requested the cooperation of the secretaries of transportation, HEW, labor, commerce, interior, and agriculture in what administration officials assumed would be a collaborative effort. Because planners and developers would select sites for the new towns nearby existing metropolitan areas, Department of Transportation officials expected that they would play a large role in securing external access as well as establishing internal transit systems. Although a relatively minor part of the legislative package, the new towns proposal sparked considerable interest among planners, developers, and federal bureaucrats.

## THE FAILURE TO SAVE THE CITIES

As with so many other negative assessments of the Great Society, Johnson found by the close of his presidency widespread dissatisfaction with his considerable efforts at achieving reform for the cities—from conservatives who

condemned the urban programs as wasteful and wrongheaded and from liberals who repeatedly clamored for more programs and more funding. Federal
efforts to aid the cities came up short because of a lack of clarity in program
development, the ineffectiveness of government bureaucracies, and, perhaps
most often, a crippling shortage of funding. The urban education initiative foundered as the ESEA's Title I benefits went all too often to children
who did not need them. A HEW survey of elementary schools in 1967–1968
found that the program aided pupils from middle-class families rather than
disadvantaged children with much greater needs. CAP succeeded in raising
the consciousness of local activists and straining the relationship between
mayors and the Johnson administration while resulting in, as Daniel Patrick
Moynihan put it, "maximum feasible misunderstanding." Model Cities, the
putative centerpiece of the urban program, proved equally frustrating—and
downright confusing. A full year after Congress created the program, Vice
President Hubert Humphrey wrote a plaintive letter to a HUD official saying
that he had been unable during recent speeches to explain how Model Cities actually worked and asked for an explanation. "I want to get this for the
President and, indeed, for myself," he admitted. In response, a HUD official
told Humphrey that a community receiving a grant would not see any benefit
for at least five years—not soon enough for the administration to receive any
credit. Dividing inadequate sums of money among too many communities,
battling constantly to retain the support of reluctant federal administrators
who harbored serious reservations about the program, and awarding grants
at a snail's pace according to an arcane process that no one seemed to com-
prehend, Model Cities achieved little by the time that Johnson left office.[19]

Although many of the administration's urban initiatives fell short of the
expectations set by the president's soaring rhetoric, Johnson devoted more
attention to urban affairs than any other president in the twentieth century.
Furthermore, he could claim a number of substantive achievements by the
end of his tenure in the White House. The war on poverty failed to lift all the
urban poor into the middle class, but the combination of sustained economic
growth and antipoverty programs roughly halved the poverty rate between
1960 and 1973; the elderly and African Americans enjoyed the greatest economic gains during those years. The various housing acts of the Johnson years
substantially increased the number of new units and commenced a shift from
public housing construction to the creation and management of subsidized

housing by the private sector. The enforcement provisions of the 1968 Civil Rights Act proved wanting in later years, but the law nonetheless opened up the suburban housing market to blacks in ways that would have been impossible under Kennedy's limited 1962 executive order. The African American population in the suburbs increased nearly 50 percent in the 1970s, and by 1990 nearly one-fourth of black families resided in suburban locations. As Wendell Pritchett, Robert Weaver's biographer, has observed, "In terms of legislation Weaver's tenure oversaw the passage of more laws regarding the issues under his purview—housing production and antidiscrimination—than any period before or since."[20]

Regardless of the success or failure of the myriad urban programs, there could be little doubt that Kennedy and Johnson expanded the federal government's presence in the cities. Federal grants-in-aid to the cities rose from $7 billion in 1960 to $24 billion in 1970, most of the increase occurring between 1964 and 1969. Within its first three years of operation, HUD assumed responsibility for most of the federal activity. Weaver and his staff administered a disparate set of programs that included bellwethers such as public housing, urban renewal, and the FHA, along with new programs, such as Model Cities and New Towns. The agency presided over a diverse complex of housing programs, including Section 23, Section 235, Section 236, and turnkey housing, with an enhanced emphasis on providing moderate-income as well as low-income units. Under the auspices of the Civil Rights Act of 1968, HUD also applied a new set of fair housing rules that would potentially alter the racial makeup of metropolitan areas. Other agencies in Washington controlled federal programs with ties to urban America—mass transit, community action, education, and job training, for example—but HUD clearly bore the lion's share of the responsibility for the federal government's investment in the cities. By the close of 1968, with the war in Vietnam claiming the nation's resources at a stunning and accelerating rate, it seemed unclear whether the new cabinet department could manage so complex a task or whether future administrations would pursue policies to ameliorate conditions in the cities in the same manner that Kennedy and Johnson had done. Even as the decade's liberal presidents crafted programs and created government bureaucracies to aid the cities, incessant talk of an urban crisis in the 1960s underscored the degree to which urban America was continuing its steady decline.

# 4

# The Tarnished Face of the American City

Despite the best efforts of the federal government, which created numerous programs and spent unprecedented sums of money in the 1960s, urban America continued to suffer as a consequence of deindustrialization. The legislative achievements of the Kennedy and Johnson administrations provided some relief but failed to obviate the loss of people, jobs, and tax revenue that undermined the health of older municipalities. Cheap land and generous government subsidies made home ownership affordable in the suburbs, but low- and middle-income families struggled to find suitable lodging in the declining housing stocks of the inner cities. Unchecked expressway construction destroyed viable neighborhoods and became the greatest source of air pollution. Escalating homicide rates and the rising incidence of narcotic drug usage left many big-city residents concerned about their safety. Racial tension increased, resulting in a series of destructive riots that convulsed the cities annually during the decade in what came to be known as the red-hot summers. The intractable problems facing the cities led experts to bemoan the flagging quality of life there and to speak darkly of an "urban crisis." By the end of the decade, even as metropolitan decentralization continued apace, questions also arose about the environmental cost of unplanned and unregulated suburban sprawl. The optimism that pervaded postwar America dimmed as the prospects for the nation's cities failed to improve significantly in the 1960s.

## THE FAILURE OF URBAN RENEWAL

Along with other programs designed to revitalize the cities, urban renewal was proving not to be the panacea envisioned by so many well-intentioned groups in the postwar years. To be sure, the program scored a number of successes in declining inner-city neighborhoods with the construction of gleaming new structures that improved the faces of downtowns. The list of impressive urban renewal creations included the Lincoln Center for the Performing Arts in New York City, the Charles Center in Baltimore, and the Gateway Center in Minneapolis, to name just a few; such institutions of higher education as Fordham University in New York City and St. Louis University also used urban renewal largess to expand their campuses. Despite the completion of these glittering showplaces, however, a growing legion of skeptics questioned the value of urban renewal to the cities. By the early 1960s, both conservatives and liberals were assailing the program as a questionable enterprise that spent exorbitant amounts of tax dollars while exacting a terrible toll on the city's working and lower classes. Looking at the inner-city residents who consistently bore the brunt of the federal program, African American author James Baldwin charged that urban renewal basically amounted to "Negro removal." Rightwing critics opposed the federal government's extensive involvement in local affairs and rued the expense of urban redevelopment as a harmful deviation from sound financial practice. In his polemical *The Federal Bulldozer*, conservative policy analyst Martin Anderson of the Joint Center for Urban Studies formulated a comprehensive critique of the program and argued strenuously for its termination. He charged that the federal government's intrusive presence in cities disrupted the private housing market, wasted millions of taxpayers' dollars, and uprooted hundreds of small businesses in neighborhoods designated for redevelopment. The average length of time necessary to complete a project from inception to dedication ceremony, determined Anderson, totaled an astonishing twelve years. Moreover, he contended, urban renewal projects devoted only 62 percent of new construction dollars to housing, and over 90 percent of the replacement housing arranged by the government charged rents that proved unaffordable to displaced residents.

Many members of the liberal intelligentsia grew equally disillusioned with urban renewal, if for different reasons than did conservative commentators. Jane Jacobs cataloged the progressives' most trenchant criticisms in her romantic *The Death and Life of Great American Cities*. Outraged by the New

York City renewal agency's designs on the Greenwich Village neighborhood in which she lived, Jacobs composed a passionate defense of the well-worn portions of cities erroneously labeled slums by ravenous developers and Washington bureaucrats. Decrying wholesale neighborhood destruction, she praised dense populations, the preservation of old buildings, and mixed economic functions—in short, she extolled the heterogeneity and diversity that made metropolises vibrant and exciting places in which to reside. The toll of urban renewal on the housing stock she calculated as follows:

> Low-income projects that become worse centers of delinquency, vandalism, and general social hopelessness than the slums they were supposed to replace. Middle-income housing projects which are truly marvels of dullness and regimentation, sealed against any buoyancy or vitality of city life. Luxury housing projects that mitigate their inanity, or try to, with vapid vulgarity. . . . This is not the rebuilding of cities. This is the sacking of cities.[1]

The published attacks on urban renewal by Anderson, Jacobs, and others across the political spectrum resonated with much of the public because of the program's disappointing outcomes in city after city. In many instances, charged local activists, federal bulldozers destroyed vital communities while exacerbating housing shortages. Moreover, massive public housing projects proved no substitute for cohesive neighborhoods. In the celebrated case of Boston's West End, approximately 7,500 residents of a primarily Italian community singled out for removal vehemently objected and mounted a protracted grassroots protest. The demonstrators lost their battle with city hall, then helplessly stood by as wrecking balls pulverized their homes and developers erected luxury apartment buildings. Sociologist Herbert Gans's *The Urban Villagers* chronicled the Italian Americans' emotional attachment to their doomed Boston neighborhood, and the clinical psychologist Marc Fried wrote movingly about the grief experienced by the uprooted West Enders. The housing expert Chester Hartman contended that nearly one-half of these "slum dwellers" lived in perfectly good housing and reported that the median monthly rents for the 73 percent of dislodged people for whom the city found new housing subsequently rose from $41 to $71. Similar battles between local governments and grassroots organizations in Chicago, Philadelphia, Buffalo, Cleveland, and other big cities, all ending in the capitulation of protesters and the destruction of viable neighborhoods, further tainted urban renewal's reputation.

## THE EXPRESSWAY MENACE

While ordering the demolition of homes and businesses to make way for luxury housing, hospitals, expanding universities, convention centers, and high-end retail emporiums, city officials also uprooted thousands of inner-city residents to accommodate the construction of high-speed expressways. Designed to save core cities by providing workers and shoppers easier and quicker access to central business districts, the metropolitan freeways ironically increased the attractiveness of suburban living by extending the distances that commuters could traverse with reasonable ease each day. Exercising the right of eminent domain, local governments acquired the extensive parcels of land necessary for the construction of multilane roadways, entrance and exit ramps, and looping cloverleaf exchanges, razing entire neighborhoods and leaving gaping empty spaces alongside highways. Superhighway construction displaced an estimated 19,000 people in Cleveland by the early 1970s, for example, and 5,800 residents lost their homes to make way for a new expressway in Pittsburgh. In communities such as St. Louis, Baltimore, Indianapolis, and Milwaukee, bulldozers leveled acres of low-income housing to clear the way for new expressways. The final report of the National Commission on Urban Problems, issued in 1969, found that expressway construction had necessitated the demolition of at least 330,000 housing units in America's cities between 1957 and 1968. By 1969, the commission reported, federal highway construction was claiming 62,000 housing units annually and displacing perhaps as many as 200,000 people per year. According to the historian Mark I. Gelfand, "No federal venture spent more funds in urban areas and returned fewer dividends to central cities than the national highway program."[2]

Government bureaucrats, planners, and civil engineers usually chose to build highways through declining neighborhoods as the most efficient means of improving metropolitan automobile travel. Such routes allowed highway builders and urban planners to eliminate blighted areas of the city, acquire land relatively cheaply and easily, and foster economic development without disrupting the lives of the city's affluent residents. Robert Moses, who built New York City's extensive expressway network after World War II, defended the ruthless destruction of neighborhoods by saying, "When you operate in an overbuilt metropolis, you have to hack your way through with a meat ax." The residents forced to move, usually poor and nonwhite, seldom wielded political power in city halls and boasted little clout in state or local agencies.

The widespread devastation left in the wake of expressway construction led increasing numbers of urban residents to question their faith in the efficacy of the freeways in dozens of cities nationwide, and conservationists and civil rights activists joined residents and business owners in efforts to delay or deflect neighborhood destruction.[3]

The mounting dissatisfaction with big city expressways stemmed from a number of causes besides neighborhood destruction. Concerns about traffic safety mounted as the number of accidents and fatalities increased along with elevated speed limits on multilane, limited-access expressways. Indeed, so many accidents occurred on Philadelphia's Schuylkill Expressway that it became widely known as the "sure-kill." While eliminating stores and houses, superhighways also destroyed urban parks, including parts of Delaware Park in Buffalo, Fairmount Park in Philadelphia, and Forest Park in St. Louis; altogether, New York City lost more than 400 acres of parkland to the wrecker's ball by 1961. Environmentalists railed that the expressways robbed cities of precious greenery while the rising volume of automobile traffic dangerously increased air pollution levels in the cities. Having removed coal-burning railroads and eliminated soot as the leading downtown pollutant, cities were allowing skyrocketing carbon monoxide levels from automobiles to create an arguably more worrisome public health problem.

The freeway revolt, as it came to be known, began in the late 1950s and continued for more than a decade. The first battle erupted in San Francisco, where civil engineers drafted an elaborate plan for the completion of five new expressways in the city. Local activists and the press joined forces to oppose the extension of the two-tiered Embarcadero Freeway through Golden Gate Park and adjacent middle-class neighborhoods. Bowing to the weight of citizen protest in 1959, the San Francisco Board of Supervisors shelved plans for the entire freeway network and instead approved a design for the development of an extensive Bay Area mass transit system.

Citizen activism scored another notable triumph in overturning plans to build the Lower Manhattan Expressway in New York City. Robert Moses had lobbied the City Planning Commission since 1941 to construct an expressway across the southern part of the island, and in 1960 the Board of Estimate approved an east–west route connecting the Holland Tunnel to the Williamsburg and Manhattan Bridges. Beset by protesters determined to retain their homes and businesses in the path of the proposed highway, Mayor Robert F. Wagner

Jr. and the Board of Estimate refused to authorize condemnation proceedings on the targeted real estate. Demonstrators picketed city hall, threatening to vote Wagner and other city officials out of office, and even Eleanor Roosevelt weighed in on the side of the threatened residents. The Board of Estimate retreated from its earlier support of the project, and lower Manhattan remained safe from the designs of the highwaymen.

By the mid-1960s, uprisings against expressways had shattered the peace in dozens of communities across the country. In Washington, D.C., a biracial coalition of activists succeeded in derailing plans to construct thirty-eight miles of interstate highways through the city. Thirty-five neighborhood groups in Baltimore formed Movement Against Destruction, an organization that successfully resisted the plans of local officials and the business community to build expressways through the downtown waterfront area, African American neighborhoods, and a number of historic districts. Local activists in Memphis filed a series of lawsuits and ultimately prevailed in the U.S. Supreme Court, blocking extension of Interstate 40 through Overton Park, a beloved wilderness retreat in the city designed by the Olmsted landscape architecture firm that had designed New York City's Central Park. In the most widely publicized case, neighborhood groups and preservationists in New Orleans opposed construction of the elevated Riverfront Expressway designed to overlook the city's historic Vieux Carré. The guerilla warfare of local protesters against expressway construction, waged successfully in many noteworthy cases, led U.S. Secretary of Transportation Alan S. Boyd to recommend more citizen participation in the route selection of urban highways. Surprisingly, given the expense of delays, route alterations, and project cancellations, Boyd commented in 1967 that "the so-called freeway revolts around the country have been a good thing."[4]

## THE CURSE OF PUBLIC HOUSING

Public housing projects, in which low-income families increasingly resided after World War II, likewise fell into disfavor with the American public. Originally conceived as temporary way stations for respectable families laid low by the economic dislocations of the Great Depression, public housing became by the 1950s and 1960s permanent repositories for society's unfortunates. Decreasing numbers of residents promptly vacated their low-income units to move into other forms of housing, while a disturbing number of tenants remained in the projects and descended into a perpetual state of dependency. By 1963, half the families moving into public housing projects in St. Louis collected welfare benefits; 63 percent of Detroit families in government-subsidized housing were receiving public aid. Critics charged that the poor design and shoddy workmanship of the high-rise public housing projects built after World War II, in stark contrast with the attractive units built by the New Deal in the mid-1930s, contributed to the worsening quality of life experienced by the residents. Enthusiasm for the tower-in-the-park design widely adopted after the war, an accommodation to the prohibitive cost of land, labor, and construction materials, dissipated along with the chronic mechanical breakdowns, high incidence of vandalism, and rising vacancy rates that increasingly plagued the intimidating structures. Warehoused in sterile silos that loomed over barren cityscapes, concentrated in high-rise slums and isolated from healthier surrounding neighborhoods, families stuck in public housing complained about their treatment at the hands of paternalistic local housing authorities. With inadequate sums of money allocated for maintenance and security, the high-rises deteriorated quickly and became hotbeds of crime. Although some intrepid residents fought valiantly to make the best of a dreadful situation, most became disillusioned, surrendered their dreams of creating cohesive residential communities, and settled simply for day-to-day survival in a perilous environment.

In many big cities, local authorities used public housing to bolster existing patterns of racial segregation. Nonwhite families occupied 70 percent of low-income units nationwide by the end of the 1960s, as much as 95 percent in Atlanta and San Francisco's notorious Hunter Point project. In Chicago, where Mayor Richard J. Daley confined African Americans to low-income units in all-black neighborhoods, the city council approved the construction of forty-nine of fifty-one public housing project sites in the ghetto areas of the South, West, and Near North Sides. Chicago's Robert Taylor Homes, the largest public housing project in the world at the time of its opening in 1962, consisted of 4,415 units in twenty-eight identical sixteen-story buildings. Adjacent to Stateway Gardens, an austere high-rise project completed in 1957 that contained 1,684 units in two seventeen-story buildings, the Taylor Homes originally housed 27,000 people (of whom approximately 20,000 were children, all were poor, and almost all were black). For Daley and other big-city mayors concerned with the political fallout from rising black populations and white flight to the suburbs, public housing provided a means of preserving racial segregation and—as the historian Arnold Hirsch has shown for Chicago—fashioned "second ghettos."[5]

## THE PROLIFERATION OF GHETTOS AND SLUMS

As public housing projects fell into disrepair and the private housing stock deteriorated, ghettos and slums spread inexorably across cityscapes. Falling tax revenue led to the reduction of public workforces, in turn completing garbage collection, street repairs, and other routine maintenance tasks irregularly. Evicted renters and delinquent property owners carted off fixtures and other salvageable items when they deserted their apartments and houses. In blighted neighborhoods, well-maintained structures dwindled in number, surrounded by abandoned dwellings, burned-out shells of vacant apartment buildings, and weed-strewn empty lots. Observers compared declining inner-city neighborhoods such as New York City's South Bronx, Baltimore's West Side, North Philadelphia, and Cleveland's Hough area to German cities leveled by Allied bombing at the end of World War II.

Urban blight spread as factories shut down, and the staggering loss of manufacturing employment severely limited economic opportunity for the working class. Cities that made the United States the "arsenal of democracy" during World War II experienced an accelerating decline of industrial jobs in the postwar decades. Cognizant of the threat posed by the rising number of plant closings, municipalities devised elaborate and generously funded programs to retain local industries. Providing free land, tax abatements, and other attractive inducements to keep manufacturers from relocating elsewhere, aging industrial cities from New England to the Great Lakes managed to achieve modest employment gains in particular industries but overall continued to suffer disheartening net losses in jobs. The disappearance of factory jobs especially hurt the poorest workers with the least education and fewest skills, particularly blacks and other minorities who had during and immediately after the war found an inviting path to economic security and middle-class status through factory work.

The calamitous effects of deindustrialization showed dramatically in Detroit, which had been a bellwether of American manufacturing productivity in the early decades of the twentieth century. Its fortunes overwhelmingly dependent on the rise and fall of the automobile industry, the Motor City prospered when sales rose for the General Motors, Ford, and Chrysler corporations. In the postwar years, however, increased automation and heightened competition from automobile producers abroad brought assembly lines to a halt, resulting in forced retirements, layoffs, plant closings, and the wholesale loss of jobs on the shop floors. Factories moved first to suburbs in southeastern Michigan, then relocated to other states, and finally fled to other nations where much lower labor costs ensured greater profits. The city lost almost 130,000 manufacturing jobs between 1948 and 1967, and the trend continued in subsequent decades. Less than a generation after the end of World War II, vacant factories, abandoned shops, and deserted homes lined Detroit's quiet streets.

Inner-city decline and the loss of economic opportunity led to soaring crime rates, which accelerated flight to the suburbs and left the remaining residents of decaying neighborhoods apprehensive about their safety. With the largest cities leading the way, the nation's homicide rate doubled between 1962 and 1972; the robbery rate rose even faster, doubling between 1966 and 1970. A parallel increase occurred in narcotic drug use and addiction. Public health officials found an explosion in heroin use during the 1960s, and medical examiners reported dramatic increases in the number of drug overdoses during the decade. Addiction and destructive drug usage, which frequently led to an increase in robberies and related offenses, predominated among disadvantaged young males. In Washington, D.C., for example, 13 percent of males born in 1953 became heroin addicts; an estimated 25 percent did so in some especially desolate areas of the city. The public believed that urban America was becoming an increasingly hazardous place, leading liberals to demand a more effective war on poverty to improve the economic and social conditions that bred crime; conservatives and others dissatisfied with the immediate results of 1960s liberal reform demanded more repressive measures by law enforcement authorities, fewer procedural safeguards to protect the rights of criminals, heightened attention to the plight of victims, and stiffer penalties for offenders to preserve law and order. Nothing seemed to produce satisfactory results, and many residents purchased firearms to protect themselves and their property—an action encouraged in popular films of the time, such as *Dirty Harry* (1971) and *Death Wish* (1974), which celebrated vigilantism as a necessary last resort when law-abiding citizens felt unsafe in big cities.

## THE RED-HOT SUMMERS

Urban violence crested in a series of race riots that devastated the cities in the so-called red-hot summers of the 1960s. Despite the promise of the civil rights movement, which achieved its greatest victories in the middle of the decade, African Americans in the cities had grown impatient with the pace of change. In northern ghettos, the Reverend Martin Luther King Jr. and other leaders of mainstream civil rights organizations lost much of their cachet with a downtrodden population that remained confined to segregated neighborhoods and lacked economic opportunity. At the same time, a younger generation of activists rejected the gradualist tactics that had produced incremental progress, embraced Black Nationalism, and trumpeted the ill-defined goal of black power. Proud, angry, and unwilling to tolerate the sordid urban environments in which they were forced to live, militant blacks took to the streets no longer satisfied with the nonviolent protest that had won grudging legal victories since the mid-1950s. Even as Lyndon Johnson affirmed that minorities would be included in his administration's Great Society reform program, the hopelessness and rage that had been festering in African American ghettos for decades began to ignite.

The decade's first race riot erupted in the New York City neighborhood of Harlem, like so many that followed the result of an incident involving an altercation between a white policeman and black ghetto residents. On July 16, 1964, two weeks after Congress passed the landmark Civil Rights Act of 1964, a white police lieutenant shot and killed a fifteen-year-old African American during a routine arrest. After a protest demonstration degenerated into a battle between protesters and the police, African American mobs began attacking other whites and burning uptown Manhattan neighborhoods. The Harlem riot lasted for five days, after which disturbances broke out in another New York City ghetto, the impoverished Bedford-Stuyvesant area of Brooklyn. Immediately after policemen restored order in both neighborhoods, riots followed in Rochester, New York; the Chicago suburb of Dixmoor, Illinois; and the New Jersey communities of Jersey City, Elizabeth, and Paterson. Nearly a month later, violence ensued in Philadelphia when two white policemen arrested a black woman for a minor traffic violation. As the political rhetoric in that year's presidential election between Johnson and Republican Barry Goldwater intensified, the racial violence of the summer gave rise to heated discussions of a potential white backlash against the struggle for racial equality.

In 1965, minor racial disturbances flared in Chicago and San Diego, but that summer's most devastating riot occurred in the Los Angeles neighborhood of Watts. Even though most of the African Americans in the Pacific Coast's largest ghetto lived in detached, one- and two-story homes on tree-lined streets, the dire socioeconomic problems typical of Rust Belt slums prevailed in Watts. Lacking adequate transportation, confined to segregated schools, and suffering from an unemployment rate roughly twice the national average, adult black males seethed against a society that failed to deliver on the promise of opportunity. The resentment boiled over on August 11, 1965, when a California Highway Patrolman stopped a twenty-one-year-old black motorist for drunken driving. The motorist resisted arrest, and police reinforcements were soon battling an angry crowd hurling rocks and bottles and chanting, "Burn, baby, burn!" Marauding blacks fought with police, pummeled white newsmen, and pulled white motorists from their cars to beat them. Looters roamed through the Watts business district, breaking into storefronts and carting off groceries, liquor, appliances, and anything else easily carried away. Arsonists lit an estimated 1,000 fires in the city, and snipers shot at city firemen who attempted to put out the blazes. A carnival atmosphere prevailed as emboldened rioters paraded through the pulsating streets. A force of 13,900 National Guardsmen restored order after six days of upheaval, and local officials counted thirty-four dead and 1,032 injured; with more than 600 buildings damaged by arson and looting, property losses exceeded $40 million in the worst race riot since the East St. Louis uprising of 1917.[6]

In the wake of a ferocious civil uprising that left onlookers baffled, Governor Pat Brown of California appointed an investigative commission to study the cause and consequences of the Watts conflagration. The McCone Commission, named after its chairman, prominent industrialist and former CIA director John A. McCone, worked rapidly to prepare its report. The eight commission members heard testimony from seventy-nine witnesses, including Watts residents, local politicians, police administrators, black leaders, and civil libertarians; commission staff members interviewed hundreds of riot participants, including ninety who had been arrested. On December 2, 1965, the commission published its eighty-six-page report, *Violence in the City—an End or a Beginning?*, which pleased law-and-order conservatives by portraying the riot as a senseless spasm of violence perpetrated by an unrepresentative segment of the population and engineered by an irresponsible cadre of black agitators. Denying that Watts was a ghetto and dismissing the grievances of the rioters, the report blamed the disturbance on the "riffraff" who occupied the margins of society and sought to exploit volatile conditions for personal gain.[7]

Widespread dissatisfaction with the conclusions of the hastily prepared McCone Commission Report surfaced immediately as a number of follow-up studies of the Watts riot advanced very different interpretations. Groups such as the U.S. Civil Rights Commission, the U.S. Office of Economic Opportunity, and the President's Commission on Law Enforcement and Administration of Justice all released reports questioning the McCone Commission's methodology and challenging its findings. These later studies found, contrary to the McCone Commission's identification of a relatively small group of alienated African Americans as the principal troublemakers, broad community participation in the disturbances and widespread sympathy for the rioters among law-abiding bystanders. Documenting the rigid segregation and high unemployment in Watts, the later studies characterized the lawlessness as understandable protests against insufferable ghetto conditions—in short, legitimate grievances expressed that could not be dismissed as aberrations. The reports concluded that maintenance of civic order depended on fundamental changes to the conditions that allowed ghettos to exist in big cities and that additional outbreaks of violence would likely occur in the future.

Adding to the growing national concern with race and violence, the federal government released a report in August 1965 by Assistant Secretary of Labor Daniel Patrick Moynihan that linked family dissolution, high unemployment, and welfare dependency in the ghetto. Moynihan had completed *The Negro Family: The Case for National Action* in April of that year, and President Johnson had made the report the core of a major speech on race relations that he delivered at Howard University's commencement ceremonies in June. The Howard University address occasioned little comment, but the publication around the time of the Watts riot of what came to be called the Moynihan Report plunged the administration into bitter controversy. Arguing that the report had been laudatory of the civil rights movement's achievements and supportive of black aspirations in its call for national action, Moynihan expressed bewilderment at the negative reaction that *The Negro Family* engendered among many African Americans and white liberals. The report had carefully documented family breakdowns in black communities, which the author attributed to the debilitating heritage of slavery and rapid urbanization, and had empathetically detailed the preponderance of female-headed households, astronomical school dropout rates, and the youth crime that resulted. Moynihan employed phrases such as "tangle of pathology" to explain the deterioration of life in urban ghettos—an unfortunate choice of words that critics viewed as condescending if not racist. Civil rights leaders criticized Moynihan for misinterpreting statistics, for failing to recognize the resiliency of matriarchal black families, for minimizing the importance of white racism and the institutional impediments arrayed against hardworking African American strivers, and indeed for blaming the victim. Moynihan's attempt to analyze the outbreak of racial violence in the cities left policymakers and the public uncertain about the causes of the recurring strife; the furor surrounding his report clearly underscored the delicate state of race relations that continued to exist in the nation.

The red-hot summers resumed in 1966. Race riots erupted in thirty-eight cities that year, the most extensive in Cleveland, Chicago, and San Francisco. As before, confrontations between local police and angry black ghetto residents frequently escalated into pitched battles between large numbers of African Americans and a variety of law enforcement agencies, looting, and arson. In Cleveland's Hough neighborhood, for example, police intervention in a dispute between a white bartender and a black patron provided the spark igniting widespread violence. In the days that followed, thirty-eight fires blazed in the area, twelve policemen received medical treatment for injuries, and a stray bullet killed an innocent bystander observing the disturbance from an apartment window. In Chicago, where the Reverend Martin Luther King Jr. sought to conduct his initial civil rights campaign in a northern city, a stalemate between civil rights activists seeking open housing in all-white neighborhoods and Mayor Richard J. Daley's powerful Democratic machine elevated tensions during an intolerably hot summer. When local police refused to allow black children to seek relief from the 100-degree heat by following the time-honored practice of turning on fire hydrants, a scuffle between firemen and ghetto residents quickly degenerated into burning, looting, and sniping. The riot consumed several square miles on Chicago's West Side, as policemen trying to protect firemen traded gunfire with snipers. The arrival of 4,200 National Guardsmen restored order, but during the three-day battle, two African Americans died, more than eighty people suffered injuries, and police arrested 400 rioters. Property damage in the city's West Side ghetto exceeded $2 million. San Francisco's Hunter Point neighborhood erupted after a white policeman fatally shot a black teenager who refused to halt at the officer's command. Although local authorities reported no fatalities, the drama of prolonged vandalism, looting, and arson earned the San Francisco outbreak extensive media attention. In all, the 1966 disturbances claimed seven lives, led to 3,000 arrests, and totaled $5 million in property damage.

Racial turbulence in American cities peaked in 1967. Authorities counted 164 disturbances by the end of the summer that year; governors dispatched the state police to riot-torn cities on thirty-three occasions and summoned the National Guard eight times. The two biggest clashes—in Newark and Detroit—each lasted for more than a week and rivaled the 1965 Watts outbreak in intensity and destructiveness. In Newark, a crumbling industrial city where African Americans made up 52 percent of the population and the unemployment rate stood at four times the national average, an anachronistic, corrupt white political machine controlled local government and callously ignored the grievances of ghetto residents. The riot began on July 13 when rumors spread that white policemen, who regularly abused black residents, had arrested an African American taxi driver and beaten him to death in a jail cell. After police killed five rioters in two days of fighting and the disturbance seemed to be waning on the third day, the New Jersey governor called Newark "a city in open rebellion" and sent in the National Guard. Local police and National Guardsmen discharged over 13,000 rounds of ammunition in the ensuing days, killing twenty more blacks and wounding an additional 1,200 people. Arrests numbered more than 1,300 by the end of the week, and property losses reached $10 million.[8]

On July 23, 1967, the worst riot of the decade commenced in Detroit. Unlike Newark, where a venal and unresponsive government combined with catastrophic economic conditions and urban decay to create a perfect scenario for civil unrest, Detroit seemed to be a community where a large African American population enjoyed a striking level of prosperity and an enlightened, race-conscious local government was responding conscientiously to citizens' concerns. Unemployment rates remained low, and both skilled and unskilled black auto workers received comparatively generous wages and benefits packages. Mayor Jerome Cavanagh, who owed his election to the overwhelming support of African American voters, had proved deft at landing hundreds of millions of federal dollars for antipoverty programs and urban renewal projects. Yet violence boiled over in Detroit all the same. Again, a clash between white policemen and black residents—in this case, mass arrests at a nightclub selling alcohol in violation of the legal closing time—led to an orgy of violence. An estimated 4,000 fires incinerated 1,300 buildings, leaving 5,000 African Americans homeless and countless thousands jobless. Property damage stood at a quarter of a billion dollars. Police and National Guardsmen killed forty-three persons and wounded more than 1,000—in large measure, according to newspaper reporters and other observers, because frightened and undisciplined National Guardsmen discharged their weapons willy-nilly during the week. Both during and after the riot, President Johnson and Michigan's Republican governor, George Romney, quarreled over matters of jurisdiction and responsibility, each blaming the other for the failure to quell the violence more expeditiously. The tragedy of Detroit symbolized the collapse of civil order in 1967 as the fires of racial enmity consumed urban America.

The civil disturbances of that summer provided an uneasy backdrop for mayoral elections held in a number of large industrial cities in November. Race became the predominant issue in Boston where an embattled white population staunchly resisted integration in the schools and in the city's insular ethnic neighborhoods. Racial enmity rose in Boston, a community with only 80,000 African Americans, because of the sense of crisis caused by the rapid flight of the white middle class to the suburbs, a faltering economy, and a wretched public school system. The plight of the schools became the focus of racial tension as African Americans pushed hard for integration at the same time that the Harvard Graduate School of Education found the situation so dreadful that seventy-one of the city's 200 schools should be closed. Louise Day Hicks, a pugnacious lawyer who had been reelected to the Boston School Committee in 1965 by a huge margin on a platform of opposition to integrated schools, became one of the leading spokespersons in the nation against busing to achieve racial balance in public schools. In 1967, Hicks ran for mayor, aggressively representing the anti-integration sentiments of her constituents in predominantly Irish South Boston. Lacking money and a first-rate political organization, she nevertheless conducted a passionate grassroots campaign that attracted huge crowds and intense national media interest. Appealing to the class resentments and the tribalism of white blue-collar Bostonians, she dared suburbanites to accept busloads of inner-city black students into their schools and to build low-income housing for minority families. Hicks lost the mayoral election to Kevin White, but her surprisingly strong showing underscored the strength of the opposition to integration in Boston and elsewhere in urban America.

On November 7, 1967, the day that Hicks lost in Boston, the issue of race also dominated mayoral elections in Gary, Indiana, and Cleveland, Ohio, where voters elected African American mayors. Blacks had been elected mayor in medium-sized American communities before—in Flint, Michigan, in 1964, for instance—but never in large industrial cities. The historic breakthrough in American politics owed to the coalescence of several factors, including the remarkable growth of black populations in large cities, the concomitant loss of white populations to the suburbs, and the increase of black voter turnouts fueled by civil rights legislation passed by Congress in 1957, 1960, 1964, and 1965 (especially the Voting Rights Act of 1965). The civil rights activism of the 1950s and 1960s spilled over into politics as previously disengaged African Americans, emboldened by courtroom and legislative triumphs, began to believe that "black power" could be translated into meaningful political reform. Richard Hatcher won election in Gary, a gritty industrial city with a dwindling white population, promising to defuse racial tensions and create a "healthy, vital black nationalism." According to the historian James B. Lane, "Underlying Hatcher's political insurgency was the implied threat that Gary was on the verge of going up in flames." Carl Stokes, an African American who had lost the mayoral race in 1965, won the support of the business community in Cleveland two years later through his explicit assurances that he could prevent a repeat of the racial violence that had torn the city apart in 1966. Stokes carried 95 percent of the black vote in 1967 and captured just enough support from middle-class whites to win the election by a narrow margin. The victories by Hatcher and Stokes signaled a sea change in urban politics, and African American politicians enjoyed remarkable success in big-city mayoral elections during the remaining decades of the twentieth century.[9]

## THE KERNER COMMISSION

On July 27, 1967, as federal troops were regaining control of the Detroit streets, President Johnson addressed the nation on television to discuss the measures his administration would be implementing to address the racial violence pervading the nation's cities. First and foremost, he announced the formation of a bipartisan blue-ribbon commission on civil disorders with Otto Kerner, the Democratic governor of Illinois, and John Lindsay, the Republican mayor of New York City, serving as chairman and vice chairman, respectively. Johnson saw the creation of the National Advisory Commission on Civil Disorders (known popularly as the Kerner Commission) as a preemptive strike against the rumored congressional investigation that he assumed would provide a forum for conservatives to level charges of pampering lawbreakers and for liberals to decry the inadequacy of the administration's urban aid programs. Although he publicly asked for a disinterested examination of the problem and insisted that the commission would enjoy complete autonomy in conducting the investigation, the president anticipated a ringing endorsement of his Great Society programs as the only viable solution to urban unrest. He fully expected the commission to recommend heightened congressional funding for Model Cities, rent supplements, and other programs that he still felt held the greatest likelihood of relieving the despair in inner-city ghettos.

At the end of February 1968, the president received an advance copy of the report prepared by the National Advisory Commission on Civil Disorders. After conducting a seven-month investigation and compiling hundreds of interviews with mayors, rioters, ghetto residents, businessmen, law enforcement authorities, and witnesses in dozens of cities, the Kerner Commission concluded that the racial turmoil in America's cities stemmed from an endemic and pernicious racism. Its report concluded, "Our nation is moving toward two societies, one black, one white—separate and unequal." The commission railed against the doleful influence of the federal government, which it said had been complicit in the maintenance of ghettos, and prescribed the expenditure of vast amounts of money to improve housing, education, welfare, and job training. The estimated cost for these program enhancements in Fiscal Year 1969 approached $12 billion, more than doubling to $24.5 billion in Fiscal Year 1971; the president estimated the price tag to be an unrealistic $100 billion over the next several years. The preliminary report infuriated Johnson, who suspected that Mayor Lindsay and a few other liberals had gotten control of the commission and rammed through a series of outrageous proposals. He thought their demands for increased funding totally unrealistic but more fundamentally objected to the imputation that his administration bore considerable responsibility for the tragic events unfolding in the cities. Had he not done more than any other president to tackle urban decline and racism?

The president sent word of his displeasure through emissaries to commission members, prodding them to make more reasonable recommendations and to provide details about possible funding sources, and became even angrier when they failed to respond. He threatened to reject the report or simply ignore it but formally accepted the 513-page document on February 29, 1968. In subdued fashion the following month, he thanked the commission members for their efforts and expressed his fundamental agreement with their goals. The dubious criticisms of the Kerner Commission notwithstanding, he assured the nation, his administration would continue looking for solutions to the urban crisis.[10]

## PERSISTENT RACIAL VIOLENCE

Even as debate over the Kerner Commission Report continued, the race riots of summer commenced again in the wake of the Reverend Martin Luther King Jr.'s assassination on April 4, 1968. In cities across the country, local officials pleaded with ghetto residents to remain calm and refrain from arson and looting in honor of King's lifelong commitment to nonviolence—a plea echoed by President Johnson in a televised address calling for peaceful mourning as an appropriate tribute to the slain civil rights leader. The violence began almost immediately, however, eventually spreading to 130 cities across the nation. In Washington, D.C., nine rioters died in the rampage that began just hours after the news of King's death became known. The next day, as more than 700 fires raged in the smoldering city, army units in full combat gear established a defensive cordon around the White House and encircled the U.S. Capitol. In Chicago, firefighters gamely tried to keep up with arsonists who raced through the West Side ghetto igniting one blaze after another, but buildings in more than twenty blocks burned to the ground. Frustrated and angry at the destruction he had been unable to curtail, Mayor Daley ordered police to "shoot to kill any arsonist or anyone with a Molotov cocktail in his hand in Chicago because they're potential murderers and . . . to shoot to maim or cripple anyone looting any stores in our city." By the end of the harrowing week, despite the efforts of 21,000 U.S. Army troops and 34,000 National Guardsmen, property damage in the nation's ravaged cities totaled $45 million; human losses included forty-six fatalities and more than 3,000 injured.[11]

Although few full-scale civil disturbances ensued after the rash of outbreaks following the King assassination in April, a number of issues related to race relations continued to unsettle urban America throughout the summer of 1968. President Johnson had successfully invoked the martyrdom of King to push fair housing legislation through Congress, signing the Civil Rights Act of 1968 just one week after the assassination, which immediately provoked a white backlash that escalated in subsequent years. Embattled white home owners voiced their resentment at the activism of a federal government that they felt was succumbing to the lawlessness rampant in the cities. In their view, African American insurrectionists had run amok, destroyed their own neighborhoods, and been rewarded with generous benefits at the expense of a law-abiding white citizenry whose interests were overlooked by a misguided liberal government in Washington, D.C. White members of the working class, many of whom had invested their life's savings in modest homes that seemed in jeopardy of losing value, feared that racial equality would come at their expense. Unable or unwilling to leave their inner-city neighborhoods, angry whites often forcefully resisted black newcomers whose incursions seemed to threaten economic loss as well as social change. The backlash against desegregation surfaced in a swing rightward politically as disaffected whites, many of whose parents had been staunch New Deal Democrats, turned to conservative presidential candidates such as Republican Richard Nixon and segregationist Alabama Governor George Wallace in 1968 and 1972.

## RACE AND EDUCATION

In many large cities, racial hostilities flared over the issue of education. In communities such as Boston, where Louise Day Hicks had become a symbol for many Americans of resistance to governmental tyranny, white residents resisted court orders mandating the busing of their children to achieve racial balance in public schools. Dissidents invoked the hallowed tradition of neighborhood schools, argued that they had purchased their homes largely on the basis of school boundaries, and argued against their children (white or black) having to spend inordinate amounts of time each day on buses that conveyed them to distant schools in foreign environments. Having lost court battles, they frequently moved to the suburbs or enrolled their children in private schools. Opponents of busing often explained their actions in terms of cost, inconvenience, and degraded educational standards, but cynical African Americans attributed the defense of segregated schools to racism. "It's not the distance," charged a National Association for the Advancement of Colored

People Legal Defense Fund official, "It's the Niggers." Antagonists over busing squared off primarily in the courts and city halls, but violence also erupted
in the streets where angry whites overturned buses and pelted black students
with rocks and bricks.[12]

Racial discord also existed within the beleaguered inner-city public school
systems that struggled to provide excellent instruction in the face of declining
revenues, bureaucratic infighting, and conflict between minority families and
white teachers. In the polyglot New York City public school system, which
enrolled more than 1 million students in the late 1960s, African American
and Puerto Rican students still overwhelmingly attended segregated schools,
received paltry per capita funding, and scored decidedly lower than white
students on standardized tests. The public schools invariably employed white
teachers who had graduated from the city's public colleges, which boasted
97 percent white enrollments; only about 10 percent of public school fac-
ulties—and virtually no principals—were African American. Increasingly
dissatisfied with the poor educations that they felt their children were receiving and frustrated with the unresponsive public school bureaucracy, blacks
demanded greater control of neighborhood schools. In 1967, the city created
three experimental districts with autonomous neighborhood boards, a pilot
project that educators hoped would be a model for inner-city school districts
nationwide. The tempest that soon erupted in one of the districts located in
the Ocean Hill–Brownsville area of Brooklyn ratcheted up racial tensions in
New York City.

The black school board in Ocean Hill–Brownsville soon warred openly with
the district's white faculty, which was represented by the United Federation
of Teachers (UFT), and in the spring of 1968 terminated the employment of
thirteen teachers and six assistant principals. When the UFT called a strike to
protest the firings, the board dismissed all 350 teachers employed in Ocean
Hill–Brownsville schools. The New York City school superintendent rein-
stated the terminated teachers, who returned to work with police escorts for
protection against angry neighborhood residents. In the weeks that followed,
students and parents threatened and assaulted teachers; hate literature distributed to teachers, many of whom were Jewish, contained anti-Semitic language.
As many as 1,000 policemen patrolled the schools to maintain order at the
height of the crisis. The union called a citywide strike in support of the Ocean
Hill–Brownsville teachers, and racial tensions increased throughout the polar-

ized city. A negotiated settlement finally allowed classes to resume, although tensions remained high for the remainder of the 1968–1969 academic year. A commission appointed by Mayor John Lindsay to investigate the Ocean Hill–Brownsville contretemps concluded, "Over and over again we found evidence of vicious anti-white attitudes on the part of some black people, and vicious anti-black attitudes on the part of some white people." No riot occurred in Brooklyn in 1968, but the clash over schools in Ocean Hill–Brownsville offered little hope that the cities were any closer to achieving racial amity.[13]

## THE DOUGLAS COMMISSION

The concatenation of problems in the cities led President Johnson to activate the National Commission on Urban Problems, which had been authorized under the auspices of Section 301 of the Housing and Urban Development Act of 1965. Johnson selected to chair the commission Paul H. Douglas, a liberal Democrat who had played a major role in fashioning federal urban policy during his three terms in the U.S. Senate from 1949 to 1967. For nearly two years, Douglas and the other fifteen members of the commission conducted a far-ranging investigation of urban life, assembling data at its temporary quarters in Washington, D.C., and receiving testimony from approximately 350 witnesses in twenty-two cities around the country, most notably in Boston, New Haven, Pittsburgh, Detroit, East St. Louis, and Los Angeles. Much of the testimony dwelled on the shortcomings—not just the good intentions—of federal programs created by the Johnson administration.

Indeed, the commissioners heard from a steady stream of disgruntled public housing residents, community organizers, civil rights activists, and others who lambasted the Department of Housing and Urban Development as a remote, ineffective government bureaucracy that had constructed low-income housing at a snail's pace, maintained the public housing projects fitfully, and then responded indifferently to tenants' complaints. Witnesses further excoriated urban renewal for its wholesale destruction of housing in respectable neighborhoods and for its woefully inadequate construction of replacement units. Municipal officials predictably defended the federal government's efforts, but the majority of witnesses—especially unscheduled speakers who took the opportunity afforded by the visiting commission to speak extemporaneously—painted a dispiriting picture of government indifference and lassitude.

The commission provided a plethora of recommendations, many of which could be described as excessively ambitious. First, the commission called for construction of 2.0 million–2.5 million housing units annually—including 500,000 units devoted to the low- and moderate-income families unable to secure satisfactory lodging in the private housing market. In addition, the commission report recommended the construction of low-rise public housing only and outlined a series of steps to be taken to improve the quality of life for residents of extant high-rise projects. Most provocatively, the commission urged that, if state and local housing authorities failed to make satisfactory progress in meeting the housing needs of low- and moderate-income families, the federal government should assume control and become the builder of last resort—in effect, prescribing a return to the practice of the mid-1930s when the Public Works Administration directly built public housing. In all, the recommendations constituted a ringing endorsement of the liberal vision for improving urban America by calling for a larger role by the federal government and the investment of increasing amounts of the nation's resources in the fight to save the declining cities. Angry at the criticism of his administration, Johnson refused to meet the commission and repudiated the report.

The furor surrounding the report of the National Commission on Urban Problems seems in retrospect altogether predictable. The White House had, after all, given an equally frosty reception several months earlier to the Report of the National Commission on Civil Disorders. Johnson could not abide the accusation that so little progress had been made under his leadership in the quest to aid the cities. He had followed the recommendations of numerous task forces that called for increased federal involvement in the cities and increased his efforts as a response to the rising violence in urban America. With considerable justification, the president contended that he had pushed more legislation through Congress to benefit urban America than had any of his predecessors in the White House. Still, the results of unprecedented levels of federal generosity remained disappointing. Conditions in the nation's largest cities continued to worsen, racial violence persisted summer after summer during the 1960s, and the gulf between whites and blacks over such issues as housing and education continued to widen throughout the decade.

## THE SIREN SONG OF SUBURBIA

The demise of inner cities fed the corresponding growth and development of the suburbs, which accounted for the lion's share of the expansion in the nation's metropolitan areas in the post–World War II years. By 1970, for the first time in the nation's history, more Americans lived in suburbs than in cities or on farms. Despite all the attention lavished in the 1960s on the shrinking core cities by policymakers and the press, America could justly be described as a suburban nation. The chaos in declining industrial cities, where aging infrastructures went wanting for repairs and minorities competed with a shrinking white population for precious space and resources, contrasted sharply with the abundance of available land and economic promise on the urban rim. In the popular imagination, images of urban life featuring pinched row houses, triple-deckers, and small bungalows on postage-stamp lawns suffered in comparison with the tree-lined streets, ranch-style homes with double garages on cul-de-sacs, and cavernous shopping malls of suburbia. Seeking better lives for themselves and their families in an era of widespread prosperity, Americans of varied backgrounds, races, ethnicities, and eco-nomic circumstances eagerly departed inner cities for inviting communities that existed on the metropolitan fringe.

Along with the whites who left inner cities, African Americans joined the suburban exodus in unprecedented numbers after 1960. Black residents had been settling in suburbs and unincorporated areas in the metropolitan hin-terlands harkening back to the nineteenth century, but the pace of decentral-ization quickened significantly in the 1960s and 1970s. Improved economic circumstances and the enhanced opportunity available for upward mobility afforded by the successes of the civil rights movement led to the expansion of the black middle class, the members of which sought to move into inner suburbs that were losing white populations to more distant communities. In addition, deindustrialization took its toll on the African American working class; rampant unemployment led to rising rates of poverty, crime, and social dislocation; and members of the black middle class sought the safety and security no longer offered by their big-city neighborhoods. In both instances, the lure of "a decent house in a decent neighborhood" proved as compelling to black families as to their white counterparts. Between 1960 and 1980, the rate of African American suburbanization exceeded that of whites, and the number of blacks residing in suburban communities doubled during those twenty years.[14]

Just as whites fiercely resisted black incursions into their inner-city neighborhoods, the contests for living space between the races proved no less heated in suburban locations. Redoubling their efforts in the face of open housing legislation, real estate agents, lending institutions, landlords, and sympathetic local officials cooperated with individuals and home owners associations to circumvent laws barring racial discrimination. Opponents of open housing continued to employ tools such as zoning and restrictive covenants, the enforcement of which had been outlawed by the U.S. Supreme Court decision in *Shelley v. Kraemer* (1948), as a means of retarding black suburbanization. In California, a leading battleground in the struggle over suburban desegregation, the leading association of real estate brokers spearheaded the drive for a referendum, Proposition 14, in favor of a state constitutional amendment guaranteeing property owners the right not to sell or rent to anyone they chose. In November 1964, California voters approved Proposition 14 by a two-to-one margin, but the state supreme court later declared the amendment unconstitutional. Undeterred, California Governor Ronald Reagan continued to endorse racial discrimination in the sale of housing as a "basic human right." Looking to the example set in California, real estate associations challenged fair housing statutes in other states across the nation.[15]

When legal subterfuges failed, whites in suburban communities often relied on intimidation and violence to deter African Americans from crossing residential color lines. Blacks attempting to move into homes in all-white communities frequently confronted vandalism and petty harassment before their antagonists finally resorted to brute force. In the most benign cases, white hooligans tormented unwanted black home owners by dumping garbage on their lawns, playing music loudly throughout the night, and yelling racial slurs from passing automobiles. When such understated methods of persuasion failed to unnerve the newcomers, hostile whites threw pipe bombs at houses and fought in the streets with fair housing demonstrators. Blacks won access to better homes and schools only after protracted struggle and not surprisingly often settled in suburban black belts reminiscent of segregated inner-city neighborhoods. As in the industrial cities, spatial segregation remained the norm throughout metropolitan America.

The majority of African Americans who left inner cities during the 1960s and 1970s relocated nearby in older inner-ring suburbs. In effect, because of expanding minority populations and the disappearance of suitable housing, expanding black inner-city neighborhoods eventually reached city limits and "spilled over" into adjacent suburbs. In St. Louis, for example, black families left the city's West End in the 1960s and relocated in Wellston, Pine Lawn, University City, and Northwoods. Outside Washington, D.C., several communities in Prince George's County, Maryland, became preferred locations for the black middle class seeking to escape inner-city overcrowding, rising property taxes, and worsening public services. African Americans living in Chicago's sprawling South Side ghetto moved farther south into such suburbs as Markham, Robbins, Harvey, and Chicago Heights. These older interior suburbs often exhibited the same wear and tear that afflicted core cities, however, and new residents encountered the poor service delivery, understaffed and underfunded public schools, and unacceptably high crime rates they thought they had left behind. A resident of Yonkers, New York, the suburb immediately north of New York City, lamented that he and other residents "paid Scarsdale taxes and receiv[ed] ghetto services." Although African Americans escaped the inner cities in increasing numbers, they found that the promise of suburbia often went unfulfilled.[16]

## RISING ENVIRONMENTAL CONSCIOUSNESS

By the 1960s, white as well as black Americans were becoming aware of the imposing list of problems attributable to the rapid pace of post–World War II suburbanization. Suburban sprawl in the United States consumed an amount of land approximately the size of Rhode Island each year. The widespread adoption of mass production techniques accelerated home building, a wildly popular development at a time of inner-city decline and rising demand for suitable lodging but at considerable cost to the environment. In their relentless search for living space, builders indiscriminately fashioned housing developments in floodplains, wetlands, and agricultural land. Bulldozers and other heavy moving equipment flattened hills, filled riverbeds and creeks, wrenched vegetation from the sod, and otherwise cleared the land to make way for ranch houses and apartment complexes. The negative environmental consequences of such rapaciousness included soil erosion, flooding, and the reduction or elimination of endangered species. To save on construction costs, builders skimped on insulation that would have provided protection against extreme temperatures with resultant increases in the consumption of energy. Far removed from the sewer systems operated by existing municipalities, suburban tracts relied on septic tanks for the removal of household waste from the populous subdivisions. Leaky septic tanks and poorly designed suburban sewage systems polluted lakes and streams, contaminated groundwater, and generated outbreaks of disease. At a time when policymakers paid scant attention to the loss of arable farmland in the rush to expand metropolitan America, the environmental impact of suburbanization likewise seemed less important than adding to the housing stock and bolstering the construction industry.

Although much of the initial resistance to metropolitan sprawl emanated from aesthetic concerns with tract housing and a social critique of the bland sameness of suburban life, concerns about the environmental consequences of unbridled growth surfaced in the late 1950s and early 1960s as well. Throughout the country, grassroots campaigns developed to halt "the rape of the land." Activists challenged the right of builders and property owners to reconfigure the landscape without restriction, forging ties between the conservationists fighting against the despoliation of the American wilderness and suburban residents opposing environmental destruction on the borders between urban and rural landscapes. Many states approved regulations limiting where subdivisions could be built, and county and municipal governments passed ordinances that followed suit. Cities, counties, and intergovernmental authorities adopted policies to curtail the use of septic tanks and to establish more stringent construction standards. In a series of court cases, local governments won the power to regulate the development of suburban land by private developers. The growing environmentalism in suburban America constituted what the historian Adam Rome has called a "quiet revolution," yet a greater awareness of the costs of sprawl failed to interrupt the march of tract houses across the landscape surrounding metropolitan America. Even while environmentalists confronted the challenges of orderly and responsible growth on the metropolitan fringe, millions of Americans still preferred suburbanization to urban living.[17]

## METROPOLITANISM

The realization that suburbs as well as core cities confronted problems dealing with housing, race, environmentalism, and other matters led many business executives, urban planners, and policymakers to embrace the concept of metropolitanism during the 1960s. They came to believe that, rather than maintaining a strict demarcation between urban and suburban units of government, government officials in the central city and surrounding municipalities could best address problems in their communities through cooperation with others—even through varying degrees of governmental mergers. Arguing for the essential unity of city and suburb and contending that only artificial political boundaries precluded the kind of joint cooperative effort needed to solve problems that resisted piecemeal solutions, they called for an end to political fragmentation. Overlapping jurisdictions, duplication of effort, and questionable authority involving cities, suburbs, counties, school districts, public authorities, sanitary districts, forest and park preserves, and a host of other regulatory agencies, they believed, left any attempt at effective metropolitan governance in a shambles. Consolidation of governments, reasoned reformers, could only improve a harrowing situation.

In 1957, Florida pioneered in the formulation of a two-tiered government as Miami and Dade County began sharing responsibilities in an innovative manner. The area's governments remained separate, but Miami supervised public education, while Dade County assumed responsibility for providing water, regulating traffic, and delivering other public services. In 1962, Tennessee went even further with Nashville and Davidson County merging all functions of municipal government, and in 1967, Jacksonville, Florida, consolidated with surrounding Duval County. In 1967, Minnesota created the Twin Cities Metropolitan Council in the Minneapolis–St. Paul metropolitan region, integrating the work of 300 separate local and regional governments. Two years later, the Indiana legislature extended the jurisdiction of Indianapolis over much of Marion County in an arrangement called Unigov. Despite promising results in these instances, few other successful examples of metropolitan cooperation followed. Suburban residents frequently balked at assuming responsibility for dealing with urban problems—after all, many of these residents had recently fled inner cities precisely to avoid such obligations—and suburban and county governments cherished their political independence. Finding the proper balance between centralization and decentralization proved to be extremely difficult.

The problems associated with political fragmentation could be seen clearly in the St. Louis region, where, as in so many other urban areas, metropolitanism

failed to gain traction. The city and St. Louis County explored the possibility of consolidation under one government as early as 1926 and considered
a slightly different arrangement four years later that would have left some
authority in the hands of existing municipalities, but county voters rejected
both proposals. The wholesale population loss and rapid spread of blight in
St. Louis after World War II resurrected talk of metropolitan government
for the central city and the ninety-seven other communities in the county.
A referendum proposing the creation of the Greater St. Louis City-County
District, which would preserve existing municipalities but assume responsibility for transportation, sewerage, police, civil defense, and metropolitan
planning, failed in 1959 by a three-to-one margin in the county. In the early
1960s, reformers posited the merger of city and county into a single unit of
government, the Municipal County of St. Louis, divided into twenty-two boroughs; a mayor and legislative council would exercise power in representing
the interests of the boroughs. In a November 1962 statewide election to create
the Municipal County of St. Louis by amending the Missouri constitution,
the borough plan failed by a three-to-one margin; county voters opposed
the plan four to one. In both the 1959 and the 1962 elections, opponents of
city–county consolidation had successfully argued for home rule, small-scale
government, and decentralization in opposition to centralization, and no additional proposals for metropolitanism surfaced thereafter. "Despite mounting criticisms of fragmentation and a gradual increase in county authority,"
noted the historian Jon C. Teaford, "the suburban faith remained strong."[18]

## NEW TOWNS

The repeated failure to merge suburbs and cities in some form of consolidated
government led many reformers to forsake exiting metropolitan regions and
seek to create altogether new communities as the best solution for the future.
The new towns idea originated at the end of the nineteenth century with the
writings of Ebenezer Howard, a London court stenographer who became interested in urban reform and planning. In *Tomorrow: A Peaceful Path to Real Reform*, which was published in 1898 and reissued four years later as *Garden Cities
of Tomorrow*, Howard considered how best to improve the quality of life in
industrial societies and proposed the creation of new communities, surrounded
permanently by greenbelts, whose carefully planned residential, industrial, and
commercial sectors would guarantee the best of both urban and rural living.

During the Great Depression, the New Deal built a handful of greenbelt towns outside large metropolitan areas, but the limited experiment attracted little support in Congress or with the American public. Following the garden cities model, Great Britain and several Scandinavian countries designed and built new towns after World War II as an antidote to urban congestion. Looking at the European examples, American planners and architects hoped to terminate sprawl and create new towns that avoided the mistakes plaguing existing cities and suburbs. In contrast to the haphazard urban development of the past, in which planning had played a minimal role and municipal governments had paid virtually no attention to the impact of growth on the environment, each new town would be part of a comprehensive regional plan encompassing housing, transportation, public utilities, and leisure for residents from varied social and economic strata. Neither bedroom communities nor satellite cities entirely dependent on core cities, the new towns would enjoy solid economic foundations based on the existence of industrial and commercial as well as residential zones. Conveniently located near established metropolitan regions, the new towns would nonetheless function independently. In keeping with American traditions of rugged individualism and free market entrepreneurialism, private enterprise would take the lead in creation of the new towns.

In 1961, Robert E. Simon bought eleven square miles of land west of Washington, D.C., and the following year completed the plan for the nation's first post–World War II new town, Reston, Virginia. Designed to accommodate a population of 75,000 inhabitants, Reston opened three years later with residential neighborhoods of single-family homes and apartments along with distinct industrial and retail areas. (Refusing to be an absentee owner, Simon moved into Reston as well.) Consisting of seven villages connected by walking paths, the new town discouraged automobile use. Convinced of the importance of aesthetics, Simon insisted on the construction of distinctive homes and buildings as well as a pleasing landscape architecture that accentuated the natural topography. He also mandated that low-income families and racial minorities be included in the population mix. Reston attracted considerable attention for its striking architecture and its admirable devotion to social ideals but, unfortunately, also for its persistent financial problems. The Gulf Oil Corporation, the new town's principal creditor, ousted Simon in 1967 and succeeded in attracting more residents and increasing profit—but at the expense of the community's original ethos.

The developer of Columbia, Maryland, a new town built between Balti-more and Washington, D.C., espoused a similar vision. Shopping mall mag-nate James Rouse acquired 14,000 acres of land in rural Howard County by 1963 and proudly announced his intention of building a planned community that would both make a profit and sustain a wholesome living environment on a human scale. Columbia consisted of nine villages, each with schools and businesses in the center, arrayed around an urban downtown with separate areas for industry and recreation. In addition, the community set aside fully one-third of its acreage for open land. The community's projected 100,000 in-habitants would enjoy the vibrancy and amenities of metropolitan residence as well as the intimacy of small-town life. As with Simon in Reston, Rouse af-firmed that the new town would welcome home owners of all races and varied socioeconomic statuses—that Columbia "would have housing for everybody from the company president to the janitor." The first residents arrived in 1967, and, blessed with reliable funding from the Connecticut General Life Insurance Company, the Teachers Insurance and Annuity Association, and the Chase Manhattan Bank, the new town grew steadily through the 1970s. Neither the village centers nor the urban downtown ever developed into the lively communal centers envisioned by Rouse, and social integration lagged behind expectations, but reformers still proudly pointed to Columbia as proof that careful planning and sound management could create viable alter-natives to America's ailing metropolitan areas.[19]

Less idealistic in the articulation of altruistic goals, the new town of Irvine, California, sought to employ sound planning principles in the pursuit of profit. When Los Angeles's outermost suburbs crept closer to the 120,000-acre Irvine Ranch in Orange County, the Irvine Company opted to create a large planned community rather than divide the massive parcel of land into a number of smaller developments. As in Reston and Columbia, the new town would consist of a series of interconnected villages with attractive architec-ture and landscaping, bountiful recreation facilities, retail, and industry. The opening of a new branch of the University of California in the community un-derscored the importance of education. With no stated intention of providing low-income housing, Irvine developed as an upscale residential enclave that stood apart from the unplanned sprawl of southern California.

The enviable growth enjoyed by Reston, Columbia, and Irvine notwith-standing, the staggering cost of purchasing large tracts of land and creating entire infrastructures for wholly new communities and the attendant need to attract the necessary capital discouraged chary investors and planners. By the mid-1960s, developers called for assistance from the federal government in the form of tax breaks, low-interest loans, and other incentives as the only means to ensure the building of new towns. After several halting attempts at passing the necessary legislation, the Johnson administration succeeded in including a new towns provision in the Housing and Urban Development Act of 1968. Under Title IV of the law, the federal government could provide up to $250 million worth of "cash flow debentures," long-term loans with the repayment schedules for principal and interest tied to the income reported annually by the new towns. State and local agencies could also receive supplemental grants for up to 80 percent of the cost of providing facilities (streets, sewerage, water, parks, and the like) for the fledgling communities. Although the stimulus for new town development provided by Title IV far outdistanced earlier government packages for builders, reformers argued that the funds allocated would be insufficient to spark large-scale construction when the completion of Columbia, Maryland, alone cost an estimated $50 million. Expansion of the program, warned the critics, would require enhanced financial support from President Johnson's successor and subsequent administrations.

The new towns attracted considerable interest, at least in part because of the desperate search for an antidote to the urban crisis. Even as metropolitan regions continued to advance farther and farther into the surrounding countryside, policymakers and elected officials seemed incapable of devising reliable solutions to the problems confounding municipal governments. America remained an incredibly prosperous nation, yet curiously the quality of life in the cities lagged far behind expectations. The growing disparity in wealth, income, and power evident in the cities raised questions about society's ability to balance opportunity with equity. The list of intractable problems confronting the nation's metropolises—including racial antipathy, unsafe streets, unclean air, inadequate housing, underperforming schools, and a flawed governmental structure that undermined political leadership—portended ill for the future of urban America. In *The Unheavenly City*, a widely read and controversial book about the urban crisis published in 1968, Harvard University political scientist Edward C. Banfield offered a pessimistic assessment that predicted additional abandonment of the urban core, the relentless spread of blight throughout central cities and inner suburbs, and the continued flight of industry and commerce to the metropolitan rim. He concluded, "It is impossible to avoid the conclusion that the serious problems of the cities will continue to exist in something like their present form for another twenty years at least." Although a host of scholars disputed the particulars of Banfield's gloomy analysis, many agreed that a decade of liberal reform had left America no closer to solving the problems of the cities.[20]

# 5

# The American City in the Age of Limits: 1968–1990

American cities in the late 1960s and early 1970s experienced the death throes of a dying urban industrialism and the birth pangs of postindustrialism. Here and there, evidence appeared, especially in large cities such as New York and Chicago, that a new age of global cities had dawned. By 1990, the lineaments of this new global, postindustrial city had fully emerged. In many cases, the postindustrial city, with its glitzy office towers, corporate plazas, festival marketplaces, and scrubbed, rejuvenated, gentrified, and historically preserved neighborhoods, epitomized this revitalized urban world. Moreover, just beyond the boundaries of this new metropolis, where modern radial highways met multilane beltways such as Baltimore's I-695, Boston's I-495, and Washington's I-495, sprang up a new phenomenon, the so-called edge city, surrounded by an intermix of old garden apartment complexes, "New Urbanism" townhouses, and megamansion subdivisions.

However, whether glitzy edge cities—Washington, D.C.'s, Tyson's Corners or Philadelphia's King of Prussia, to name a few—or a rejuvenated Boston with its sparkling Faneuil Hall Marketplace or Baltimore with its dazzling Inner Harbor, behind that glitter in 1990 sat the horrors of inner-city life, a dystopia of crumbling housing, high unemployment, and soaring crime rates. Just blocks away from the modern postindustrial city, a corporate command center flaunting towering business headquarters, medical centers, research universities, and lavish downtown malls, drug wars raged, peeling lead paint claimed children's lives, and vandals plundered the sordid shells of abandoned houses.

Still, those depleted neighborhoods of the inner cities notwithstanding, in the minds of most Americans, cities in 1990 again seemed ascendant, a consummation hard to imagine twenty-two years earlier in 1968, the year when news of the Tet Offensive in Vietnam overshadowed the war on poverty, when besieged by protests President Lyndon B. Johnson declined to run for a second term in office, when Martin Luther King Jr.'s assassination triggered fiery riots in city after city, and when Richard M. Nixon's victory over Hubert H. Humphrey seemingly doomed even the fleeting hope for the future of Model Cities.

Richard Nixon's 1968 victory boded ill for a government-led rescue of besieged urban America. Indeed, Nixon promised to lead a retreat from the urban activism of the 1960s, from John F. Kennedy's New Frontier and Lyndon B. Johnson's Great Society with its war on (urban) poverty and the promise of Model Cities. The Community Action Program, the Job Corps, and the host of storefront advocacy agencies had in Nixon's eyes pampered the poor and exacerbated—not ameliorated—the urban condition. The flames from burning buildings that lit the night sky in Washington, D.C., following the death of Martin Luther King Jr. in 1968 consumed not only whole neighborhoods of the capital but also the faith that federal action could rebuild and revitalize the trembling carcass of the industrial city. Between 1968 and 1980, despite some urban initiatives during the Jimmy Carter presidency (1977–1981), Nixon's proclaimed policy of urban "benign neglect" generally prevailed.

## ACCELERATED DEINDUSTRALIZATION

During the late 1960s and 1970s, with few exceptions—the Sun Belt cities of Atlanta, Phoenix, Dallas, Denver, and Seattle, for example—American cities, especially the old northeastern industrial cities, those urban areas identified with the Rust Belt, slid inexorably into what might be called an urban abyss. Deindustrialization, a process already detectable in the 1950s and 1960s, accelerated in the late 1970s and reached cataclysmic proportions in the 1980s. Between 1977 and 1982, Chicago, Philadelphia, Detroit, Cleveland, St. Louis, and Buffalo each lost over 20 percent of their manufacturing jobs, while industrial employment in New York, Baltimore, and Minneapolis dropped over 10 percent. New York City lost over 20,000 manufacturing jobs in 1985 alone and 15,000 more in 1986. Between 1970 and 1985, 40,000 industrial jobs disappeared in Baltimore, a drop of 45 percent. Manufacturing employment in Cleveland fell 59 percent between 1947 and 1982. Meanwhile, the number of service-sector jobs rose; however, most of those service-sector jobs were found in the low-paying personal support services. This job hemorrhaging affected smaller cities as well as large. From 1974 to 1985, Indianapolis lost some 24,000 manufacturing jobs, most in durable goods. Between 1950 and 1980, plant closings and runaway industry in Louisville, Kentucky, plunged manufacturing in that city downward 40 percent.

## WHITE FLIGHT AND FISCAL CRISIS

White urbanites had been leaving cities since the 1920s, but the trend intensified in the 1970s. In the wake of the 1960s riots, cities such as Philadelphia experienced in the 1970s a massive white exodus from once heavily industrialized neighborhoods. By 1980, North Philadelphia had lost an average of nearly 40 percent of its 1960 population. Overall, Philadelphia's population declined from 2.1 million to 1.7 million (1960–1980), a loss that continued into the 1990s. Likewise, in Rust Belt Cleveland, plagued by plant closings in the 1970s, the population decreased 24 percent, a loss of over 177,000 people.

With white flight, urban population loss, and increased African American immigration, cities, especially those in the Rust Belt, grew blacker. In 1940, blacks made up 13 percent of Indianapolis's population; by 1970, that proportion had risen to 22 percent—actually 30 percent in the "Old City." Cities also grew more segregated and poorer, a phenomenon that sociologists Douglas S. Massey and Nancy A. Denton termed "hypersegregation."[1] In the 1970s, people of color continued to migrate to large cities despite the shrinking job base and limited housing options. In Chicago's Bronzeville neighborhood on the city's South Side, overcrowding had prompted the city's housing authority to erect two gigantic, all-black-occupied housing projects: Stateway Gardens and the Robert Taylor Homes. Deindustrialization and "incredible depopulation" (down 66 percent, 1950–1990) left an increasingly black neighborhood devoid of any means to support grocery stores, banks, restaurants, gas stations, medical clinics, churches, or any other basic human institution. Chicago banks had redlined Bronzeville, flagging the area as one to be denied either mortgages or home improvement loans. This only accelerated the problem of housing abandonment.

In the 1970s and 1980s, deindustrialization, population loss, neighborhood disinvestment, and hypersegregation all continued to erode further the viability of the historic downtown, what architect-planner Victor Gruen had called the "heart of the city." Despite the appearance of festival marketplaces in the 1970s, downtown retail continued to decline, and the growth and popularity of suburban malls remained strong. Between 1977 and 1982, retail employment fell in nine out of the twelve large central cities that he studied, including Chicago, Detroit, Baltimore, St. Louis, Buffalo, New York, Philadelphia, and Boston. It fell by over 20 percent in the first five cities mentioned. Setting aside Baltimore's booming James Rouse–developed festival market, Harbor Place, retail jobs in Baltimore plunged 29 percent between 1977 and 1982. Despite the opening of Detroit's massive Renaissance Center, retail employment in the industrially troubled Motor City dropped 27 percent, while retail sales there plunged almost 43 percent.[2]

The ultimate demise of the historic downtown department store explains much of this economic loss. Urban beltways and freeways linking city and suburb and huge modernist parking garages had failed to resuscitate downtown shopping. Suburbanites found it easier to drive to the satellite branch of department stores such as Philadelphia's John Wanamaker's or Chicago's Marshall Field. Tragically, these once palatial, architecturally distinguished edifices often made adaptive reuse difficult. Baltimore's flagship department store, Hochschild Kohn, closed its doors in 1977, the same year as Philadelphia's Lit Brothers and Detroit's Crowley's. Minneapolis's Powers Dry Goods closed in 1985, Cincinnati's Elder-Beerman and L. S. Ayers disappeared in the 1980s, as did Detroit's 91-year-old V. L. Hudson's. In 1986, the *Philadelphia Inquirer* described the city's once fashionable downtown as "a department store graveyard . . . a burial ground for retailers."[3] Retail shopping no longer involved a trip downtown on a train, bus, or subway line; it now required a car and a parking spot.

Deindustrialization, population loss, low wages in the emerging service economy, and a growing and hypersegregated African American community not only weakened downtown retail but eviscerated the urban tax base as well. Between 1970 and 1975, assessed valuations in Cleveland dropped $36 million from a 1959 high. They were down over $440 million in Chicago. Beginning in the 1960s, Rust Belt cities became increasingly dependent on state and federal aid for survival. Indeed, by 1970, New York, Baltimore, and Buffalo derived over half their general revenues from intergovernmental sources.

Despite intergovernmental infusions, shrinking tax bases and pressure from teachers, sanitation workers, and other organized public employees who used unionization to gain higher wages and better employee benefits inevitably led cities to the fiscal precipice and the specter of insolvency. Rising oil prices in the mid-1970s dealt cities yet another blow as elevated fuel costs increased inflation, fed unemployment, and stalled economic growth.

Thus, by the mid-1970s, American cities, especially those historic industrial cities of the old Northeast and Midwest, faced severe economic crisis. Some dared describe these places as moribund. Not only did many cities gaze into the abyss of bankruptcy, but in New York City's Bronx, North and West Philadelphia, Baltimore, Detroit, Cleveland, and Providence, Rhode Island, whole blocks of housing in the former thriving, working-class neighborhoods sat abandoned, their flooring, plumbing, wiring, and other salable materials plundered. Every Halloween in Detroit, vandals torched dozens of these derelict buildings, and understaffed fire departments often let the blazes alone. In unscathed but no less unkempt tenements occupied by jobless families or families struggling to survive on the growing rash of low-paid service jobs, death or learning disabilities awaited infants and small children ingesting flaking lead paint chips from the undermaintained units. All contributed to the aura of despair haunting inner-city neighborhoods by the 1970s.

## CHANGING FEDERAL URBAN POLICY

As the urban crisis intensified in the 1970s, Washington steadily retreated from its urban engagement rooted in the 1930s and capped by Lyndon Johnson's war on poverty in the 1960s. Advised by Daniel Patrick Moynihan, his counselor on urban affairs, Nixon was too politically cautious (despite his policy of "benign neglect") to preside over the dismantling of the federal support system. He did, however, scale down the Model Cities program and declare a moratorium on public housing construction. Nixon's Council for Urban Affairs emphasized better coordination of federal programs, the creation of intergovernmental cooperation with emphasis on local decision making, the improvement of service delivery, the decentralization of government responsibility, and the encouragement of voluntary organizations to deal with urban concerns.[4] Opposed to a top-down, federally controlled urban policy, Nixon, who owed his election to suburban—not urban—voters, saw cities as enemy territory where white ethnics and people of color clung to their old political loyalties. He sought to win them over by giving cities greater autonomy and flexibility over federal urban spending.

Nixon's New Federalism took definitive form in his 1974 Housing and Community Development Act, which made the Community Development Block Grant (CDBG) the chief instrument for urban revenue sharing. The CDBG consolidated all the existing urban community development programs, including urban renewal, Model Cities, water and sewer grants, rehabilitation loans, and Urban Beautification and Historic Preservation grants, into a single flexible "block grant" program. CDBG became the primary program for aiding cities with populations over 500,000 and urban counties with populations exceeding 200,000. The act also replaced conventional public housing and such federally subsidized housing programs as Section 23 and Section 221(d)3 with Section 8, a voucher program that shifted the responsibility for low-income housing supply entirely to the private sector. Under Section 8, local housing authorities distributed certificates or vouchers to qualified low-income families to obtain lodging in approved new or rehabilitated "affordable" units. Accordingly, tenants paid one-third of their income to these private-sector landlords, and the local housing authority compensated the owner for the difference between what the tenant paid in rent and the fair market value of the housing. Opting for vouchers as the principal means of dispensing housing aid to low-income families, the federal government ceased the construction of high-rise public housing projects.

## THE PARTIAL REVIVAL OF MASS TRANSIT

The rising disillusionment with urban renewal also extended to neighborhood-destroying federal highway building. Beginning in the mid-1960s and continuing in the 1970s, in a series of "highway/freeway revolts," citizens' organizations in New York, Philadelphia, San Francisco, and elsewhere rebelled against giant interstate highway projects that threatened to obliterate well-established old neighborhoods. Chicago's Dan Ryan Expressway precipitated "Negro Removal" when it ripped through the South Side of Chicago, and Interstate 95 dislocated Miami's African American Overton community. The freeway revolts of the late 1960s and 1970s built support for the federal Urban Mass Transit Assistance Act of 1970 and the Federal Aid Highway Act of 1973, bills that balanced highway building with mass transit funding. Buffalo's Niagara Frontier Transportation Authority in 1971 built a 12.5-mile rapid transit line to link downtown Buffalo with the Buffalo State University campus in suburban

Amherst. Greater Boston's Metropolitan Boston Transit Authority used almost $609 million in federal dollars to modernize Boston's mass transit, and in 1972 Chicago announced a $283 million mass transit modernization plan. With 80 percent funding from Washington, Philadelphia financed a downtown commuter rail tunnel creating a high-speed line linking West and East Philadelphia and providing a mass transit connection to the city's airport.

Public transit improvements remained secondary or supplementary to the construction and upkeep of the interstate highway system, however. Lawmakers and policymakers in Washington continued to earmark the lion's share of federal transportation dollars for expressway construction and maintenance. The Highway Trust Fund, created by the 1956 legislation that authorized the interstate highway system, remained a wellspring of funds reserved for expressways and closed to mass transit. Although public transportation served a vital function in many of the nation's largest cities, most Americans continued to navigate the daily commute to and from work in their automobiles.

## JIMMY CARTER VISITS THE BRONX

President Jimmy Carter took office in 1977 amidst profound pessimism about the future of American cities. The United States in the 1960s had boasted world economic supremacy; it then controlled the lion's share of world economic output (35 percent). By 1980, however, that share had been reduced to a mere 22 percent. Moreover, "stagflation" (rising inflation matched by increasing unemployment) badgered the nation. America's leaders would at one time have turned to the federal government for solutions, but public confidence was shaken in the wake of the Vietnam war and the Watergate scandal. A centrist, Carter had campaigned for the presidency in 1976 promising to balance the federal budget. With the political support of urban American and its African American voters, he insisted that Washington must help rebuild the nation's socially and physically blighted cities.

For his Department of Housing and Urban Development (HUD) secretary, Carter chose a black lawyer, Patricia Roberts Harris, who pledged to make the housing agency the servant of the urban poor rather than urban developers. Harris viewed with alarm disintegrating urban neighborhoods and sought to use HUD as a means of empowering communities to help bring about their revitalization. Carter's Urban and Regional Policy Group endorsed public–private partnerships and sought to use block grants, tax credits, and other incentives to help community development corporations invest in affordable housing ventures and to lure businesses and young professionals ("yuppies") back into city neighborhoods. To underscore the administration's sense of urgency at rebuilding cities, in October 1977 Carter traveled to New York City's Bronx neighborhood. Standing amidst the rubble of Charlotte Street in the fire-scorched South Bronx—an area that had been spotlighted in the movie *Fort Apache the Bronx* and in Tom Wolfe's novel *Bonfire of the Vanities*—he promised his administration's support in revitalizing America's inner cities.

In 1978, already politically besieged, Carter announced his pièce de résistance urban program, the Urban Development Action Grant (UDAG), a highly flexible urban assistance package that allowed cities to use federal grants and tax incentives as they wished to increase private investment in the city, including for new office towers, hotels, and shopping centers. Such projects were typically announced with promises of job growth but they seldom included funds to repair the aging infrastructure and improve ailing neighborhoods.

## SIGNS OF LIFE AMIDST THE RUINS

Carter's 1977 visit to the Bronx marked the nadir of the urban postindustrial plunge in fortunes. Although traumatizing for many—those workers in declining industries, unskilled and low-wage workers in general, and racially segregated minorities—the processes of deindustrialization and globalization (the creating of a competitive global marketplace for labor and services) aggressively, even ruthlessly, transformed cities in the 1970s. By 1980, old cities such as Pittsburgh, Boston, New York, Chicago, Milwaukee, and Indianapolis pieced together new economies built around research universities, health care, finance, insurance, real estate, business marketing, and corporate management. Many of the corporations that experienced growth during this time were directly or indirectly dependent on federal defense and other technology-related expenditures. They employed the "creative class": young, often unmarried or childless persons, single or couples, including gays and lesbians, drawn by the cultural opportunities that cities offered (theaters, art galleries, good music and other night-life entertainment, and exotic food) and by the many other allures of urban culture and urban life.[5] Meanwhile, south of the Mason–Dixon Line and in western cities such as Tucson, Phoenix, Los Angeles, Portland, and Seattle, federal military and aerospace spending made these urban places magnets for older Americans and job seekers from south of the border or the deindustrializing urban North.

Many manufacturing jobs drifted southward to the Sun Belt, but increasingly in the 1970s and 1980s, manufacturing jobs also moved offshore to low-wage developing countries. This decentralization created the need for transnational firms to locate in strategic places to finance, coordinate, and manage global operations. Thus, in the 1970s and 1980s, certain postindustrial cities remade themselves into global command-and-control centers, adept at information processing and in providing services to a workforce engaged in coordinating international business and far-flung markets. Such global control centers spawned dual economies—one consisting of high-wage managers, another of low-wage service workers. Pittsburgh, for example, once the home of the fictive Joe Magarac, the muscular immigrant steelworker who measured the consistency of ladled steel by tasting it, now became home to Carnegie-Mellon-produced robots, University of Pittsburgh heart transplant surgeons, and a host of advanced technology researchers, information processors, and other denizens of the information age. In the shadows of modern Pittsburgh, in the hollows that once sheltered the city's coal- and steel-producing economy, sat such grim urban places as Braddock, Duquesne, and Connellsville—the residuum of postindustrialism.

As cities economically adjusted to the decline of manufacturing and the decentralization of commerce, both capital and population shifted back into the city. In some instances, old abandoned neighborhoods with late eighteenth- and nineteenth-century Victorian housing stock suddenly excited real estate interest and investment. This evidence of life amidst the ruins of the old industrial economy became one sign that a creative class had rebuffed suburbia and rooted itself in the modern city, helping engender the first clear traces of urban revival as early as the 1970s.

This urban transformation of the 1970–1980 era commenced during a period of fiscal tribulation, one that called for effective political leadership. Washington's retreat from urban funding, the shredded tax base, and the imminence of bankruptcy forced city administrators to be creative. "Miracle mayors," such as Boston's Kevin White and Raymond Flynn, Pittsburgh's Richard Caligiuri, Cleveland's George Voinovich, New York's Edward Koch, and Baltimore's William Donald Schaeffer, utilized different strategies to cope with the crisis. Faced with declining federal aid as well as reduced state and local tax revenues, in the early 1970s mayors like Pittsburgh's Peter Flaherty and Boston's Kevin White, among others, slashed city payrolls. Flaherty cut Pittsburgh's payroll from 7,000 to 5,400 employees. Buffalo Mayor Stanley Makowski cut out 800 jobs, while White reduced Boston's payroll by 500.

For New York City and many other big cities, short-term borrowing became the most convincing way to confront the yawning budget deficit. New York's outstanding short-term debt had reached $3,416 million in 1974 before the city finally faced fiscal collapse in 1975. Only an eleventh-hour bailout engineered by the federal and state governments allowed the nation's largest city to avoid declaring bankruptcy. Philadelphia, Detroit, and Cincinnati stared over the same precipice in the mid-1970s, and Cleveland went into default in 1978. The crises in cities like Baltimore and Philadelphia, combined with the growing political strength of African Americans, produced black mayors such as Wilson Goode and Kurt Schmoke, well-educated men with reputations for administrative efficiency and budgetary skills. Yet by the late 1970s, the fiscal crisis all but vanished in most localities. Almost all these cities boasted new football stadiums, glitzy office towers, festival marketplaces, and examples of revitalized neighborhoods.

Some of the signs of urban resurgence at the end of the 1970s sprang from Carter's new "flexible" UDAG grants. Some derived from innovative tax increment financing (TIF), whereby mayors and state and city development agencies courted investment by insurance companies, pension funds, and other big investors with generous tax packages. And, finally, much came from the combination of the new young, research-oriented, global-coordinating workforce, the new urban gentry's interest in urban living and in revitalizing old neighborhoods, and interest perhaps sparked by the nation's 1976 Bicentennial celebration and by new federal tax incentives for historic preservation.

In any case, evidence of urban revitalization and of a new postindustrial city emerged across urban America, especially in the revitalization of the downtown retail sector, where over 100 downtown shopping centers opened in the late 1970s and early 1980s, including Crown Center in Kansas City, Omni Center in Atlanta, Renaissance Center in Detroit, Broadway Plaza in Los Angeles, the Galleria in Louisville, Kentucky, Gallery II in Philadelphia, and Copley Plaza in Boston. These developments marked the beginning of a rising hopefulness that central cities could be revived and attract new support for the gentrification of inner-city neighborhoods. Certainly, developer James Rouse, the moving force behind the festival marketplace movement, believed in the potential of a new postindustrial city and in the power of nostalgia to attract suburbanites and other shoppers back into the city. Indeed, many of these so-called festival marketplaces, such as Pittsburgh's Station Square, New York's South Street Seaport, Boston's Faneuil Hall, and San Francisco's Ghirardelli Square, were history and nostalgia oriented. Other nostalgic urban market ventures, such as 1890s-chic Underground Atlanta, Seattle's Pike Place, and Denver's Old West–themed Larimer Square, yielded uneven results.

The mixed record of the festival marketplaces left Rouse undaunted. He forged ahead with Faneuil Hall in 1976 and Baltimore's highly successful Harbor Place (in the city's inner harbor) in 1977. By the 1980s, propelled now by the Historic Preservation Act (1976) tax credits, Pittsburgh's Station Square, New York's South Street Seaport, and Portland, Maine's Old Port had all materialized. According to one historian, "historic preservation had become the hottest fad and the single most influential Main Street investment approach of the late twentieth century."[6]

Inner-city malls and nostalgia-themed marketplaces shared the new postindustrial urban stage with the new emblem of the global economy—towering glass, office skyscrapers, such as Minoru Yamasaki's 110-story World Trade Center in New York City; the Phillip Johnson–designed, forty-story glass, neo-Gothic PPG (Pittsburgh Plate Glass) Place in Pittsburgh; the Liberty Center in Philadelphia; the mammoth Renaissance Center in Detroit; Citicorp Plaza in Los Angeles; the 103-story Sears Tower in Chicago; and the Crocker Bank Center in San Francisco. Indeed, between 1970 and 1990, San Francisco underwent what could be called "Manhattanization" whereby thirty-one office towers arose in the downtown, including the forty-eight-story Trans America pyramid, the forty-eight-story California Center, the forty-story Chevron Tower, and the thirty-nine-story Citicorp Building. All these private office tower projects benefited from urban renewal action, TIF, or some other aid to private development. So did the new baseball and football stadiums and convention centers that appeared in cities such as Baltimore, Pittsburgh, Cleveland, and Detroit.

## WINNERS AND LOSERS: THE SUN BELT

The proliferation of skyscrapers, stadiums, and festival marketplaces offered a skewed view of urban growth during the 1970s and 1980s. Overall, between

1980 and 1986, eleven of the sixteen largest metropolitan areas in America's Rust Belt lost central-city population. Only New York, Chicago, Boston, Columbus (Ohio), and Indianapolis experienced growth. Both Cleveland and Pittsburgh lost population. Despite its huge Renaissance Center, Detroit, an exceptional victim of deindustrialization, endured not only population decline but also continued high joblessness, rising crime, and severe housing deterioration.

During the 1970s and 1980s, the greatest urban population increases occurred in the South and the West, a region now proclaimed to be the Sun Belt. This area, which had benefited most from World War II federal spending for defense, gained disproportionately from sustained military expenditures during the Cold War and from the emerging global marketplace. Rust Belt cities oriented toward manufacturing suffered in the 1970s and 1980s because of competition from abroad and were wrenchingly forced, often unsuccessfully, to restructure economically. Sun Belt cities such as Seattle, Houston, Phoenix, San Francisco, Los Angeles, Atlanta, Denver, and Miami built on a solid base of federal military and aerospace spending and on high-tech research centers such as Stanford University and California Tech, spawning America's computer hardware and software revolution. These cities also profited from their reputations as ideal retirement and tourist destinations.

Newer Sun Belt cities, unhampered by the rigidities of traditional northern suburban opposition to annexation, grew physically as their populations increased. Atlanta added eighty-two square miles to its size, and San Antonio, Texas, added 254 square miles of land in 1974. Unlike the more physically and politically constrained Rust Belt places like Philadelphia, Baltimore, and Boston, cities such as Los Angeles, Dallas, Houston, Denver, and Atlanta had room to embrace the growing aerospace, computer, and other twenty-first-century high-tech industries and benefit economically from their presence. For example, situated strategically on the Pacific Rim, Los Angeles in the 1970s and 1980s dominated in terms of federally funded research and development—as did San Francisco, an advantage that gave birth to the Silicon Valley and in the 1990s attracted such star-studded high-tech firms as Google.

Yet even as increasing numbers of people fled the declining Rust Belt cities and headed for southern and western climes, unchecked growth brought a series of problems to communities in the Sun Belt. Unequipped to handle rapid population increase, cities from Miami to San Diego suffered from housing shortages and inadequate infrastructure. Low taxes curtailed service delivery. Entirely dependent on automobiles, Sun Belt cities hurriedly erected multilane expressways and then suffered the crippling traffic jams and rising levels of pollution that new arrivals thought they had left behind in the Rust Belt. Crime rates rose dramatically as well, and soon southern cities such as Atlanta and Houston surpassed Chicago and New York City in the national homicide rankings. Transplants to Sun Belt cities were often frustrated with job market conditions in right-to-work states where workers often found only part-time employment at wages kept low by the absence of strong trade unions. The more salubrious climate aside, residents of Sun Belt cities soon found that they confronted many of the same challenges that plagued communities in other parts of the country.

## RONALD REAGAN AND THE RISE OF THE POSTINDUSTRIAL CITY

Republican candidate Ronald Reagan's victory over the beleaguered Jimmy Carter in November 1980 represented a victory for suburbia and for political conservatism. Reagan viewed his election as a mandate to retreat further from New Deal– and Great Society–oriented urban policy, a retreat that had continued under Carter's one-term presidency. As governor of California, Reagan had embraced and had been embraced by the state's upwardly mobile, consumption-driven suburbanites who abhorred taxes and railed against wasteful government spending and "welfare-cheating" black and Hispanic minorities. The former actor and General Electric spokesman, Reagan stood for old-fashioned limited government and greater individual freedom. Born in a small town (Dixon, Illinois) and educated at little Eureka College, Reagan showed not the slightest solicitude for cities and their problems.

Reagan ushered in a new era of robust laissez-faire conservatism that espoused unfettered entrepreneurialism. Once harnessed tightly to federal resources and centralized urban policymaking, cities during the Reagan years had to abandon any expectation of federal aid or top-down economic planning in favor of a broad concept of public–private partnership. The transcendent federal–urban linkage forged by the old pro-growth coalitions disappeared in favor of a new engagement with state and private corporations, universities, hospitals, and a widened nonprofit sector. To facilitate this privatization of urban revitalization, cities created development committees or corporations armed with a host of tax incentives and other emoluments to make cities as hospitable as possible to the new modern industrial parks, research campuses, hospital centers, stadiums, cultural centers, hotels, upscale condominiums, and other fashionable urban residential communities.

Cities formed development plans but were forced to put their expectations on hold as federal bureaucrats instructed municipal officials to make do with less. Economic recession—not boom times—followed in the wake of Reagan's inauguration. By 1982, unemployment had soared nationally to 10.7 percent, the highest since the Great Depression. For old industrial cities such as Pittsburgh, Philadelphia, and Milwaukee, the recession eradicated the last vestiges of the old manufacturing economy. In Milwaukee, which had managed to retain much of its old industrial base, the 1981–1982 recession proved devastating. Manufacturing in the old brewery capital plummeted over 22 percent. Not surprisingly, the recession hit blue-collar workers hardest. Joblessness among factory workers nationally reached 15.9 percent; among blacks, it crested at 20.2 percent. By December 1982, 12 million Americans searched for work, and homelessness in cities reached crisis proportions. Some 2.5 million homeless Americans slept in public shelters, in automobiles, in bus stations, and beneath bridges. In the City of Brotherly Love, the homeless made their beds on the steel grates lining Philadelphia's long Broad Street artery, grates that vented the warm air rising from the city's subway tunnel.

The recession accomplished one of Reagan's goals, however, curbing the runaway inflation that had tormented the Carter presidency. Joblessness and homelessness notwithstanding, Reagan cut federal spending in an effort to restore self-reliance to the inner cities, where he believed government programs such as Aid to Families with Dependent Children (AFDC), the Women's, Infants and Children (WIC) feeding program, and other federal aid had undermined urban morale and oppressed rather than helped the city poor. Reaganism shredded the proverbial "safety net." The administration ruthlessly attacked the already beleaguered public housing program, cutting $10 billion from Carter's proposed 1982 budget for low-income public housing. The Reagan administration slashed approvals for new and rehabilitated Section 8 rental housing by 45,000 units and, for families already living in public housing, raised rents from 25 percent to 30 percent of income. Reagan then sliced $17 billion in housing funds from the 1983 budget, declaring that the federal government would no longer finance either the construction of or the major rehabilitation of subsidized housing for the poor. He set a goal of eliminating 300,000 units of public housing by 1985. As for HUD's aid to cities, Reagan salvaged only the Community Development Block Grants for urban sewers and parks. Conspicuously, he left Carter's UDAG program for assisting urban shopping center, hotels, and other private commercial property untouched.

Reagan even targeted the suburban-oriented Federal Housing Administration (FHA), but it survived administrative scrutiny by aggressively curtailing vital urban programs. The administration sharply cut all direct aid to cities not only for housing but also for general revenue sharing for urban mass transit, public service jobs, job training, compensatory education, social service block grants, local public works, and economic development. In 1980, UDAG and other revenue-sharing grants covered 18 percent of urban budgets; by 1990, that percentage had dropped to 6.4 percent.

Reagan took his sharpest aim at federal welfare funding, which struck especially hard at struggling inner-city residents. His first budget reduced both the number of families able to participate in federal social programs and the amount of benefits. These cuts included food stamps, Medicaid, fuel aid, WIC, unemployment compensation, student loans, legal aid, and AFDC. In 1982 alone, food stamps were cut 11 percent, child nutrition 28 percent, AFDC 13 percent, and student financial aid 25 percent. Of the $11 billion cut from federal entitlement programs in 1982, over 60 percent came from programs for the urban poor. Although he failed to reach all his goals, Reagan sought to gut the panoply of Great Society social programs—Job Corps, Head Start, WIC, and legal aid, most notably—and replace them with "Workfare," which purportedly would restore dignity and ambition to the poor. His policies carried out in the shadow of deindustrialization, however, only aggravated urban poverty, highlighting, as sociologist William Julius Wilson argued, the plight of the "truly disadvantaged." It was during the 1980s that the plague of crack cocaine and the attendant violent crime wreaked havoc on inner cities. At the same time, an AIDS epidemic also struck inner cities, along with the skyrocketing incidence of homelessness. Thus, during the Reagan recession of 1981–1982, cities such as New York, Philadelphia, Baltimore, and Los Angeles suffered as the social service net collapsed and deepening poverty, crime, and social deterioration gripped inner-city neighborhoods.

Meanwhile, the new urban downtown with its nostalgic festival marketplaces and gentry-friendly, quaint neighborhoods sprang to life spurred by the marriage of tax incentive–armed private development corporations and private and institutional investors eager to capitalize on the debut of the new, sanitized corporate-dominated city. Reagan's tax policies greatly abetted this advent. His 1981 tax cuts—part and parcel of his supply-side economics agenda—reduced taxes (mainly for the wealthy) by 25 percent over three years. The law accelerated all kinds of investment by giving generous tax breaks to the oil industry; to savings and loan associations; to recipients of unearned income on stocks, bonds, and real estate; to married couples with two incomes; and, finally, to people with inherited wealth or wealth from gifts. Predictably, the 1981 Reagan tax cuts prejudiced the poor, the 31.9 million taxpayers with annual incomes in 1981 under $15,000, whose tax burden dipped only 8.5 percent while the 12.6 million taxpayers with annual incomes over $50,000 enjoyed a 35 percent bounty. The National Association for the Advancement of Colored People and other spokespersons for the poor blasted the cut as "welfare for the rich" but to no avail. Reaganomics officially launched the dual urban economy (a well-to-do urban information technology, management, finance, and professional sector juxtaposed with a low-paid urban service sector) whose basic form appeared by 1990.

### THE POSTINDUSTRIAL CITY

Unleashed by unrestrained privatism, by Reagan tax cut policy, and by federal, state, and local tax incentives as well as by generous federal UDAG grants that spurred expansive commercial development, the 1980s postindustrial city (forgetting the still-festering slums) bore little resemblance to its industrial predecessor. Surviving old school buildings, breweries, and cotton and candy factories had been transformed into offices and glitzy condominiums. Unlike the old urban-industrial economy, which clustered gritty mills and working-class populations in neighborhoods scattered throughout the streetcar-accessible periphery of the downtown, the new information-processing, finance, research, health care, and other service delivery jobs concentrated in glassy downtown offices. In this new global economy, corporations eyeing wider markets increased their white-collar workforces and set up regional headquarters and branch offices in big cities near financial advisers, lawyers, and public relations consultants. To meet the growing demand of corporate offices and other consumers for their services, the downtown firms performing these legal, financial, marketing, and other specialized tasks expanded and in turn further grew the service economy. For example, white-collar jobs in manufacturing firms, which had been about 20 percent of total urban employment after World War II, jumped to almost 40 percent in the 1980s.

The transformation from industrialism to postindustrialism revealed itself most dramatically in the changed use of urban space, a change clearly visible in the city skyline. In the early 1980s, office booms remade the cityscapes of cities big and small. Between 1980 and 1984, 4,325 new office towers rose in the downtowns of America's thirty largest urban areas, adding 550 million square feet of office floor space. New York City had once dominated as America's premier office center, supplying 29 percent of the nation's urban office space. By the mid-1980s, however, New York's share had dwindled to 17 percent, as Chicago, Washington, D.C., Houston, Dallas, San Francisco, Los Angeles, Boston, Denver, Philadelphia, and Pittsburgh all vied for a larger share of global business enterprise.

The cases of Philadelphia, Pittsburgh, and Cleveland further illuminate this 1980s urban transformation. During the Reagan decade, Philadelphia absorbed new office space at the rate of 1.4 million square feet per year. Philadelphia's Democratic mayors William Green (1980–1984) and Wilson Goode (1984–1992) welcomed the opportunity to use public–private partnerships to energize and reshape the downtown as an engine for postindustrial urban growth. Their vision embraced not only the conversion of the city's Delaware River waterfront into Penn's Landing, a verdant riverside promenade with floating restaurants, but also the downtown as an extravaganza of malls, Galleria I and II, a refashioned Independence Mall, and a host of new office towers. With a billion dollars in investment, the project was to generate 80,000 new jobs for the city. To the glee of the Philadelphia Industrial Development Corporation, the Greater Philadelphia Movement, and Greater Philadelphia Partnership, both American and foreign investors poured money into the city's downtown development.

Likewise, Reaganomics impelled the transformation of Pittsburgh from steel and glass industrialism into a modern, diversified service center, a metamorphosis orchestrated in the 1980s by "Miracle Mayor" Richard Caligiuri as Renaissance II. In addition to a cluster of new downtown office towers, Renaissance II shaped an architecturally rich area of the Golden Triangle into a cultural district and helped make the old, once-industrialized Monongahela, Allegheny, and Ohio riverfronts into a veritable playground for cyclists, joggers, lovers, and sports fans. Where blast furnaces had earlier spewed fire and smoke, a successful collaboration between Carnegie-Mellon University and the University of Pittsburgh spawned the Ben Franklin Technology Center, an incubator for high-technology innovation. In 1987, the University of Pittsburgh's Oakland hospital complex acquired a host of other city medical facilities to become the nationally known University of Pittsburgh Medical Center. By 1991, health care ventures in Pittsburgh employed 11 percent of postindustrial Pittsburgh's workforce.[7]

Cleveland, another Rust Belt city, also radically transformed itself in the 1980s. Energized like Philadelphia and Pittsburgh by private investment and by Reagan's cornucopia of UDAG grants, Cleveland converted its once-industrialized river and lakefront into marketplaces and playgrounds, including professional sports stadiums and the Rock and Roll Hall of Fame. Like Pittsburgh, Cleveland built a new employment base around universities (Case Western Reserve University and Cleveland State University) and medicine (the Cleveland Clinic).

## NEIGHBORHOOD REVITALIZATION IN THE REAGAN ERA

High-tech workers, information technology specialists, marketing gurus, and medical researchers and physicians—a lively, frequently international mix of often youthful (but some retirees), often unmarried people—flocked to these new cities seeking the arts, entertainment, and urban community. Here was the recipe for residential revitalization. These new urbanites made up a mix of middle- and upper-income families (urban gentry) that saw promise in the old nineteenth-century Victorian neighborhoods spared by the bulldozers of the 1950s and 1960s. In New York, Chicago, Philadelphia, Boston, San Francisco, Seattle, and elsewhere, historic preservation became a powerful force for revitalizing old neighborhoods like Philadelphia's Fairmount section, Pittsburgh's South Side, and Cincinnati's "Over the Rhine."

Historic preservation tax incentives, beginning with the 1976 Tax Reform Act, facilitated the process. The 1976 act catalyzed the process first by denying a tax deduction for demolishing historic buildings while simultaneously awarding accelerated depreciation for investors willing to "substantially rehabilitate" historic buildings. Two years later, in the Rehabilitation Investment Tax Credit Act, Congress went even further by giving a 10 percent tax credit for rehabilitating old buildings. But it was Reagan's 1981 Economic Recovery

Tax Act (ERTA) that made preservation big business. ERTA increased the Rehabilitation Investment Tax Credit to 25 percent for buildings certified historic (i.e., declared eligible for listing on the National Register of Historic Places) and allowed a 20 percent tax credit for buildings over forty years old or a 15 percent tax credit for those over thirty years old. Between 1982 and 1986, the 1981 law generated over $9.5 billion in urban investment in 13,000 historic buildings.

In 1986, Reagan again used tax legislation to boost and to preserve the nation's housing supply. Housing scholar Kent Colton called Reagan's 1986 Low-Income Housing Tax Credit, aimed at increasing the supply of "affordable" multifamily housing, "the clearest redirection of public housing policy toward preservation and private investment."[8] The act provided investors who provided equity for the building of or rehabilitation of affordable housing a ten-year federal income tax credit. In the twenty-first century, it remained the primary source of affordable housing.

Some downtown neighborhoods revived because of the efforts of gay and lesbian residents who frequently sought the freedom offered by life in cosmopolitan big cities. As families and upwardly mobile ethnic groups vacated homes in older sections of central cities, gays and lesbians acquired the aged housing, usually at very affordable prices, refurbished the dwellings, and often divided them into smaller living units. Neighborhoods such as Greenwich Village in New York City and North Beach in San Francisco became famous as cultural and artistic centers, not just as districts inhabited especially by gays and lesbians—a development repeated, though usually on a smaller scale, in other cities throughout the country.

## REBUILDING URBAN NEIGHBORHOODS: CDCS TO THE RESCUE

Reagan's individualistic New Federalism aimed to combat the recession that had buffeted his early administration and the nation. While downtown oriented, the tax incentive strategy embraced and revitalized urban neighborhoods. The New Federalism emphasized diminished federal intervention and glorified localism and public–private partnerships. Accordingly, the community development corporation (CDC) rose to prominence in the 1980s.

CDCs actually originated in the 1960s as part of the Community Action Program created under President Lyndon B. Johnson's 1964 Office of Economic Opportunity. CDCs were incorporated as a community empowerment tool into the 1966 Model Cities program, which sought to build more socially and economically viable inner-city neighborhoods. Mayors such as New York's Edward Koch and Baltimore's William Donald Schaeffer had pushed for neighborhood revitalization and made community action agencies, including CDCs, central to their efforts. During the hard times of the early 1970s, many community action agencies waned in influence, and some failed. Under Jimmy Carter and his HUD secretary, Patricia Roberts Harris, neighborhood renewal again took center stage, and community action agencies—including CDCs—assumed leadership roles. Harris wanted spruced-up, attractive inner-city neighborhoods to function as anchors to promote stability and to sustain growth. Harris fought FHA- and bank-induced disinvestment in poor black neighborhoods, an effort that culminated in the passage of the 1977 Community Reinvestment Act outlawing redlining and forcing banks to invest in the urban areas where they did business.

Tax incentives and other public and private support for CDCs launched a "block-by-block" rebuilding of neighborhoods in many American cities, including New York, Chicago, and Boston.[9] Social investment in nonprofit community development organizations as a tactic to rebuild ravaged inner-city neighborhoods had begun in earnest as early as 1968 with capital input into New York's Bedford-Stuyvesant Restoration Corporation, a prototypical CDC. In 1979, the Ford Foundation created the Local Initiatives Support Corporation (LISC), and a year later James Rouse of Harbor Place fame established the Enterprise Foundation for Neighborhood Development that generously funded 130 CDCs in sixty cities. By 1984, the Ford Foundation's LISC had backed 272 CDCs in ninety-three communities. By 1986, the LISC "colossus" had raised over $460 million from over 700 private corporations and foundations, assisted 777 CDCs, and leveraged $1.6 billion in additional funding. Collectively, the effort produced 28,000 new housing units and 6.4 million square feet of commercial space in once barely habitable inner cities.[10]

Following Jimmy Carter's 1977 visit to New York's South Bronx, nonprofit CDCs had demonstrated that with organized philanthropy and federal tax stimulus, such neighborhoods could be recovered. In the case of the South Bronx, the process began with a tough, politically savvy Catholic priest, Father Vincente Gigante, who made his South East Bronx Community Organization Development Corporation an agency for neighborhood rehabilitation and for converting into good housing hundreds of once rat-infested, boarded-up old apartment complexes. In 1982, another CDC with a somewhat sinister name, the Mid-Bronx Desperados, led by Genevieve Brooks and with LISC aid, federal and New York State subsidies, and the help of Boston and New Haven renewal guru Edward Logue, transformed Charlotte Street—the very place in the East Bronx where Carter had made his 1977 appearance—into Charlotte Gardens, a popular housing complex of picket-fence-surrounded prefabricated ranch-type homes, mimicking the suburbs.

Symbolically, Charlotte Gardens marked a turning point for the South Bronx and for the transformative power of CDCs backed by the Neighborhood Reinvestment Act, by Rouse's Enterprise Foundation, and by the LISC. In 1981, New York Mayor Edward Koch announced a ten-year plan to restore to livability New York City's enormous stock of abandoned apartment buildings. This so-called Vacant Building Program placed Father Gigante's and Genevieve Brooks's nonprofit CDCs on the front lines of neighborhood rebuilding. Another part of New York's assault against urban despair included the New York City Housing Partnership and the East Brooklyn Churches CDC. East Brooklyn Churches teamed with other community organizations to set up a $12 million revolving fund to construct low- to moderate-income row housing. This device, the so-called Nehemiah Program, had by 1984 developed the "Village of East Brooklyn," 2,400 two-story, single-family row homes. The project provided the model and set the stage for the federal 1987 Nehemiah Housing Opportunity Grants under the Housing and Community Development Act of 1987, which provided grants to nonprofit organizations to help moderate- and low-income families become home owners.

In the 1980s, outside New York City, CDCs became a key part of the inner-city revitalization effort in Boston, Pittsburgh, Chicago, San Francisco, Cleveland, and other big cities. For example, in 1979, Cleveland State University opened a Center for Neighborhood Development, and soon afterward the city utilized CDBG monies to underwrite the work of nonprofit CDCs, which by 1986 had emerged as the major representative of neighborhood involvement in the city's redevelopment process. Cleveland Mayor George Voinovich backed the city's neighborhood-based development effort, and in 1987, Cleveland Tomorrow (the city's corporation coalition for development), the LISC, and the Enterprise Foundation supervised a network of six Cleveland CDCs in undertaking a citywide, low- to moderate-income housing construction and rehabilitation effort. Nevertheless, several urban scholars called

Cleveland's CDCs mere "junior partners" in Cleveland Tomorrow's grander plans, which emphasized large-scale downtown development. Despite the hyperbole, these scholars noted, the CDC's housing enterprises involved little more than renovating about twenty-five homes per year.[11]

## THE POSTINDUSTRIAL CITY: THOSE LEFT BEHIND

By 1990, CDBGs and UDAG funds, tax incentives, and CDCs had transformed a number of once-shabby city main streets, nearly gutted downtowns, and once-burned-out, crime-infested, and rubble-strewn neighborhoods such as the South Bronx. In their place emerged glass-towered postindustrial Houstons, Atlantas, Philadelphias, and San Franciscos. Outdoor cafés adorned Carson Street on Pittsburgh's once-gritty, steel mill–enshrouded South Side; all bespoke the power of unleashed privatism, public–private partnerships, and philanthropy (once buttressed by federal tax policy) to remake the old, disfigured city into a new, gleaming, culturally lively, and economically transformed place. But the new gleaming facades notwithstanding, cities nurtured a dark side during the 1970s and 1980s. Beneath the glitter of a Harbor Place and the impeccably and historically preserved gentrified facade of Baltimore's Otterbein neighborhood sat poverty-ravaged black neighborhoods, steeped in drugs, crime, and failing social services and burdened by dysfunctional law enforcement and educational systems. Philadelphia, Los Angeles, Miami, East St. Louis, Providence, Rhode Island, and Camden, New Jersey, to mention just a few declining cities, harbored the same examples of deepening urban poverty, drugs, and despair. Sociologist William Julius Wilson thoroughly chronicled the tales of urban tragedy in his powerful 1987 book *The Truly Disadvantaged*. In the backwaters of the postindustrial urban economy, he recounted, dwelled those left behind, the low-paid service workers, the residue of deindustrialization, and people teetering on the edges of the global economy.[12]

The experience of Philadelphia Mayor Wilson Goode, the city's first African American chief executive, exquisitely illustrated the paradox of the Dual City. Goode became mayor in 1983 at the moment that the Reagan tax cuts, historic preservation incentives, and city industrial development corporations were remaking Philadelphia into a Paris on the Delaware. But Philadelphia's young information age, marketing, management, and technologically astute workforce, many of whom now enjoyed the urban culture of gentrified neighborhoods like Queens Village and the Fairmount section, resided in an increasingly poor black, Hispanic, and Asian American city with failing schools, underfunded services, and aging infrastructure. In 1980, blacks made up 75 percent of the North and West Philadelphia areas where over 20 percent of the population lived in poverty. An urban entrepreneur, Democrat Goode shared the vision of a sparkling postindustrial Philadelphia and pushed for the development of the One Liberty Place office tower, a modern city convention center, an enlarged airport, and the transformation of the old Lit Brothers Department store into the prize-winning, historically preserved Mellon Bank Center.

Goode's political fortunes foundered not on glitzy Market Street but in the declining black neighborhoods of West Philadelphia among the "truly disad-vantaged." MOVE, a militant black "back-to-nature" organization, had moved into a row house on Osage Avenue. Neighbors protested MOVE's unkempt living conditions, an armed confrontation with police resulted, and the be-sieged MOVE members (along with their families) barricaded themselves in their Osage Avenue fortress. To dislodge them, Goode fatefully approved an ill-advised "tactical" bombing of the house, resulting in an inferno that killed the MOVE members and their families and immolated every last home on the block. While Goode actually won a second term, the incident severely marred his reputation and tarnished Philadelphia's shimmering image as a city on the rise.

In Philadelphia, Cleveland, New York, and elsewhere in 1990s urban America, the emergence of the global, postindustrial city had not only failed to assuage poverty but actually exacerbated it. As Wilson observed, the 1980s trade imbalances had diminished the nation's support for less educated work-ers because production and routine clerical tasks were more easily transferred abroad. The lowering of unionization rates accompanying the demise of American manufacturing led to a reduction in wage and nonwage compensa-tion for the less skilled. Globalization in the 1980s heightened the importance and the demand for a more highly educated workforce; at the same time, new technologies, especially robotics and computerization, rendered many older jobs obsolete. Both forces prejudiced the low skilled in terms of both wages and job opportunity. In cities such as Baltimore and Philadelphia, this trend had a vicious impact especially on large, low-skilled African American popu-lations already found anchoring the tail end of the employment line. These were cities where the manufacturing base had been eroding since the early 1950s. Here, as in other cities during the 1980s, the proportion of nonpoor families and prime-age working adults decreased, and, unlike the 1950s and 1960s, joblessness became more and more strongly associated with poverty.

Within inner cities, lower incomes, high unemployment, poor schools, and property disinvestment contributed to massive housing abandonment and the loss of the last vestiges of community life. The growing disparity between the opportunity structure of the new information age and the despairing world of the inner city appeared on the graffiti-scarred walls of public buildings and on the side of urban bus and subway cars. It was also reflected in 1980 school dropout statistics. New York posted a school dropout rate of 50 percent, Chicago 45 percent, and Boston 40 percent. Poorly maintained public housing hulks in Philadelphia, St. Louis, Chicago, Boston, and Baltimore loomed as ugly, angry reminders that although the federal government under Reagan had abandoned conventional public housing and even retrenched support for Section 8 vouchers, in the 1980s these vestiges of the Great Depression and the age of urban renewal still housed a significant population of the city's low-income residents, white as well as black.

The inner-city economy that survived in the 1980s involved drugs, especially the highly addictive crack cocaine form, a narcotic not only available but also relatively cheap. The flourishing urban drug culture that infiltrated North Philadelphia, Chicago's Robert Taylor Homes, and New York's Bedford-Stuyvesant neighborhood engendered an epidemic of violent crime as well as AIDS. Statistics for 1984 showed 80 homicides per 1,000 among black males ages fifteen to nineteen; that number jumped to 180 per 1,000 in 1997. Drugs, crime, violence, the preponderance of female-headed households, and the absence of working males as models for inner-city youth all contributed to social isolation and the disintegration of social organization. Thus, while Washington and "miracle mayors" remained wedded to a faith in public–private partnerships and the power of CDCs and tax incentives and while glass towers mushroomed in downtowns and a new urban gentry revitalized historic neighborhoods, large swaths of the urban landscape sat untouched, unloved, and still seething during the 1980s; it was the landscape of the underground economy.

There remained yet another and final dark side to the postindustrial city that revealed itself by 1990. Space in the old industrial city had been largely public. Picketers for union recognition in the nineteenth century and most of the twentieth took their case to city sidewalks, city parks, and city streets. Civil rights protesters did the same thing. Much of the new urban space produced in the postindustrial city belonged to corporate owners of gallerias, festival markets, and giant corporate plazas, such as Citicorp Plaza in San Francisco, however. These showy places frequently offered a recycled version of history or reflected a strong desire for escapism in safe and secure surroundings, but they also raised serious questions about the privatization of urban public space and about the freedom of or limits to political discourse in the new global city. For example, did a union have the right to distribute flyers in an urban mall? A 1992 U.S. Supreme Court case ruled that that right did not exist.

Cities changed significantly between 1968 and 1990. Deindustrialization and globalization had been under way in 1968, but in that fateful year, few economists predicted that twenty-two years later, manufacturing would have essentially vanished and that education, research, the information and health sciences, finance, marketing, and corporate management would become the basis for urban economies. Government-orchestrated urban renewal in 1960 had begun the process of demolishing the old stone and brick industrial urban infrastructure of mills, warehouses, railroad sheds, stables, and coal yards. During the 1970s and 1980s, under Presidents Nixon, Ford, Carter, and Reagan, the federal government essentially stepped aside. Now private developers, lavishly praised by messiah mayors as partners in city rebuilding, encouraged by loosened zoning codes and permitting procedures, and generously aided by federal block and urban development action grants, as well as by the Reagan cornucopia of tax incentives, assumed more of the leadership for city rebuilding. Privatism produced glass towers, downtown malls, festival markets, art galleries, and the sports arenas that characterized the global, postindustrial city.

The creative economy incubated in corporate and university-housed research centers attracted a young, venturesome population back into the city, a population eager to consume urban culture and to live in recycled lofts in historic urban neighborhoods. Other neighborhoods like South Chicago and the Bronx, tucked close to the reviving downtown and blessed with politically astute community leadership, seized the opportunity to use CDC and Ford Foundation monies to undertake neighborhood revival. But, as this chapter has also explained, by 1990 the verdict on the success of neighborhood revitalization had been left undelivered. Poverty, abandoned houses, homelessness, drugs, crime, and poor urban education ravaged many inner cities in 1990, grist for future television dramas about the paradox of modern urban life.

# 6

# The City and the Image Made Real? The 1990s and 2000s

During the 1990s and 2000s, American cities were presented as gateways to economic and social mobility on the one hand and sinks of economic dependency and vice on the other. Public perceptions of American cities were drawn largely from television and movies until the mid-1990s when the growing popularity and sophistication of computer games and the availability of Internet connections meant that the city's image would now increasingly be shaped by other forms of electronic media. Millions of people began blogging on the virtues and frustrations of their favorite city. Others posted pictures of their favorite urban places and spaces on Flickr and social media sites. From the day it was dedicated, one of the most popular places in the United States for urban photography was Anish Kapoor's 110-ton *Cloud Gate* sculpture in Chicago's Millennium Park. Every day of the year, people come to photograph themselves or their friends as reflected in the sculpture and transmit the images all over the globe. They are a part of the continuous process of urban image making.

One event during this time period—the September 11, 2001, attack resulting in the destruction of New York City's World Trade Center; extensive damage to the U.S. Pentagon building in Washington, D.C.; and the downing of United Airlines flight 93 in Pennsylvania—surpassed anything that had ever taken place in the United States since the news came from Dallas in 1963 that President John F. Kennedy had been assassinated. Americans were unified in their fear and grief for the over 3,000 victims and their families. Economic, political, social, and cultural recovery from the events of 9/11/2001 took place at different rates in different parts of the country. The process of national healing was aided in some unusual ways. Joseph Temeczko, a Polish immigrant and self-employed handyman who passed away one month after the attack, donated $1.4 million in his will to the City of New York in honor of the victims. For some people, such as those who lost family, friends, and liveli-hoods as a result of the events of that day, the healing is an unfinished process.

The 1990s and 2000s further solidified three earlier trends. First, the line blurred between the city and the suburbs. It became more and more difficult to determine where the city began and ended. Did the city begin and end at its legal borders, or were the shopping malls and plazas, car dealerships, and apartment complexes located along "hamburger row" now a part of the city? Second, suburban growth during this period also made it harder to know how to measure the economic health and social vitality of cities. When examining joblessness in Washington, D.C., for example, should the District of Colum-bia be considered separately from northern Virginia communities such as Alexandria, Maryland's Rockville, and other places in the larger metropolitan area that experienced dramatic growth during the 1990s? Third, the period made more evident the concentration of poverty and the economic and so-cial problems associated with it in certain cities or particular neighborhoods. Detroit, which had experienced major race riots in both the 1940s and the 1960s, became the embodiment of urban poverty. News outlets publicized the persistence of unemployment, homelessness, substance abuse, and vio-lence that plagued the cities. Few of these reports pointed out that just miles away from some of Detroit's most troubled neighborhoods were suburbs such as Grosse Point, where affluent residents pursued a lifestyle that made it appear as through Detroit and Flint were in another country. In Pittsburgh, where the University of Pittsburgh Medical Center replaced U.S. Steel and other manufacturers as the city's leading employer, organ transplants and other cutting-edge medical procedures were performed just a short distance from the Hill District, a section of the city with long-entrenched problems associated with poverty. It was just as novelist John Dos Passos had written in the 1920s—there were two nations within the United States, and the border between them was social class and color. In American cities during the 1990s and 2000s, poverty and affluence existed side by side, and the middle ground seemed to be rapidly disappearing. Worse yet, neither the Democrats nor the Republicans were committed to developing and implementing a plan to reverse the situation. Both parties were unwilling to use their political capital to pass the legislation needed to launch a program similar to President Johnson's urban-oriented Great Society initiative.

## THE LOS ANGELES RIOT AND THE LIMITS OF THE POLITICAL RESPONSES TO URBAN DECLINE

From 1986 to 1994, one of the most popular shows on television was *L.A. Law*. Created by Steven Bochco and Terry Louise Fisher, it depicted the lives of the attorneys whose pursuit of money, power, and sex often complicates their efforts to represent their high-profile clients and cases. The image of Los Angeles as a city of easy money, fast cars, and shapely men and women stood in marked contrast to the city as it was known by millions of residents. Beneath the glitzy image was the reality of a deeply divided populace whose lives were heavily circumscribed by class, color, religion, gender, and national origin. The jobs in aircraft manufacturing, petroleum, chemicals, and shipbuilding that had brought thousands of migrants to the city during World War II disappeared from the 1950s through the 1980s. During his years as governor of California, beginning in 1967, former movie actor Ronald Reagan did little to slow down or halt the deindustrialization of the state's largest city. Pretending that Los Angeles—and the Golden State in general—was not heavily dependent on defense contractors and other military expenditures, the solution that he and his conservative political allies championed was to trim the size of government.

By the early 1990s, for the overwhelming number of Angelinos, especially those who lived in Central and East Los Angeles, everyday life bore little if any resemblance to the television depiction. The level of social and economic inequality that existed in the city was dramatically exposed in 1991–1992. On March 3, 1991, the California Highway Patrol apprehended Rodney King, an African American motorist who led them on a brief, high-speed chase through Los Angeles. When King resisted arrest, law enforcement officers shot him with a Taser gun, beat him with batons, and kicked him. A bystander captured the incident on video and released it to the news media.

A hospital report showed that King received more than ten skull fractures, a broken ankle, and permanent brain damage. Four police officers were charged with use of excessive force. Three of them were acquitted of all charges on April 29, 1992, and the fourth was to receive a retrial in federal court. Several hours after the verdict was announced, rioting began. Three days later, fifty-two were dead, and property damage totaled in excess of a billion dollars. Entire blocks of Los Angeles were burned to rubble.

Most media commentators saw the riots as a direct response to the trial verdict, but a government commission later found deep historical roots to the unrest among people of color in Los Angeles. An investigative report echoed the findings of the 1968 Kerner Commission Report. It identified "poverty, segregation, lack of educational and employment opportunities, widespread perceptions of police abuse, and unequal consumer services as the principal grievances which led to the civil disturbances of the 1960's. Little has changed in 1992 Los Angeles."[1]

Angered by the persistence of class and racial inequality within the American judicial system, in November 1992 voters in Los Angeles and large cities across the nation went to the polls to put an end to the twelve-year Republican lock on the White House. William Jefferson Clinton won thirty-one states and 357 electoral votes, while President George H. W. Bush captured only eighteen states and 168 electoral votes. Ross Perot, a billionaire defense contractor originally from Texarkana, Texas, likely helped Clinton by securing 19 percent of the popular vote.

Many urbanites hoped that after twelve years of Republican inaction and indifference, the cities would finally get the attention they needed and deserved. Now, at long last, the problems associated with deindustrialization—an eroding tax base and diminished federal support—would be addressed. It soon became evident, however, that the nation's metropolitan areas lacked the political clout they had once enjoyed. Even though the residents of many cities were still Democrats, outside the city limits were millions of suburbanites who lacked the party loyalty of their parents or grandparents.

The incoming Clinton administration not only had to address the deep-rooted economic and social problems in cities but also had to respond to evidence of a growing threat from terrorist organizations operating within and outside of the United States. On February 26, 1993, a bomb exploded in the parking garage underneath the World Trade Center in Manhattan, killing six and injuring more than 1,000. Shortly after the explosion, bomb threats forced the temporary evacuation of the Empire State Building and Newark

International Airport. The arrest of several suspects reported to be allied with radical Islamic groups followed. In June 1993, the FBI and New York City police worked together to halt a plot to bomb simultaneously the UN headquarters, the New York police headquarters, the Holland Tunnel, and the Lincoln Tunnel. Security measures were stepped up across the country.

As the United States became more aware of the threat of international terrorist plots at home, the number of mass shootings, many involving children or youth, appeared to be on the rise. A *Time*/CNN poll taken in 1993 indicated that 61 percent of all Americans thought that violent crime had increased in their communities within the past five years. An analysis of crime statistics showed that violent crime was actually going down in the largest, most densely populated cities and increasing in smaller ones with populations of less than 1 million persons.[2] In the aftermath of the April 20, 1999, mass shooting at Columbine High School in Littleton, Colorado, many city schools found it necessary to screen students for guns and other weapons. There was more national soul-searching about guns, youth, and violence, but in the final analysis, the Columbine shootings failed to launch a national gun control campaign.

On April 19, 1995, when a bomb blast ripped a huge hole in the Alfred P. Murrah Federal Building in Oklahoma City, many people initially believed that international terrorists were responsible. Americans were shocked to discover that the bombing was a case of domestic terrorism perpetrated by two disgruntled former members of the U.S. armed forces. After forty-three days of combing through the wreckage, authorities recovered 168 bodies. The victims included children from the day care center housed within the building and employees of numerous federal agencies.

Apprehension over terrorism and gun violence at home contributed to the tensions between police and urban dwellers long after the Rodney King case. People of color and immigrants alleged that law enforcement unfairly targeted them on the basis of racial, religious, and ethnic profiling. In 2000, angry protests and demonstrations were directed at the New York Police Department after the acquittal of police officers involved in the shooting death of Amadou Diallo, an unarmed African immigrant who was shot forty-one times by police officers in 1999. The case inspired rock-and-roll artist Bruce Springsteen to write a song about the incident. Symbolically, a step forward was taken in race relations in Columbia, South Carolina, in May 2000 when

Governor Jim Hodges signed legislation intended to end the dispute over the flying of a Confederate flag over the state capitol building. For many, however, this and other, similar incidents further underscored the division of not only cities but also the entire nation into two camps of haves and have-nots with people of color overwhelmingly concentrated in the latter.

The September 11, 2001, attack on New York and Washington, D.C., had a profound influence on national politics. Eager to identify those forces responsible, President George W. Bush convinced Congress that Iraq had aided the militants. Lacking a clear objective, the war in Iraq and military incursions into Afghanistan to seek and destroy terrorist bases and camps proved unpopular at home. Throughout the rest of his presidency, Bush sought ways to globalize the War on Terror.

## CHANGES IN URBAN POLITICS

The 1990s and 2000s raised questions regarding the influence of cities on national politics. Would city governments respond to the needs of immigrants and rural migrants the same way they had in the past? Would cities continue to serve as a jumping-off point to the larger state or national political areas for mayors and city council members from new American immigrant groups from Asia, Africa, the Middle East, and Central and South America as they had for the earlier generation of minority mayors, such as Chicago's Harold Washington Jr.? Would twenty-first-century U.S. cities be able to sustain old political dynasties or start new ones? Would they ever recapture the central role in American politics they once held?

A number of mayors gained national renown because of their efforts to guide cities through extremely difficult times. New York City Mayor Rudolph Giuliani won praise for lowering crime rates, for improving the delivery of basic services, and especially for his bold leadership in the wake of the World Trade Center attack. In 2000, seeking to parlay his fame into national office, he unsuccessfully sought the U.S. Senate seat that First Lady and later U.S. Secretary of State Hillary Rodham Clinton eventually secured. Two former National Basketball Association players, Dave Bing and Kevin Johnson, became the mayors of Detroit and Sacramento, respectively, in order to save the slumping cities from further economic decline. By 2002, New York had a new mayor, Michael Bloomberg, who gained political prominence, in part, by trying to make the world's largest city more environmentally friendly. His

2008, PlaNYC program included goals to cut greenhouse gas emissions by 30 percent by 2030, add bike lanes, convert taxis to hybrids, and impose a fee for automobile use in Manhattan. Bloomberg, a former Wall Street investor, also expressed a determination to improve city schools and reduce crime.

The nation's oldest urban political dynasty ended when Richard M. Daley, who followed in his father's footsteps as Chicago's mayor in 1989, announced in 2010 that he would not seek reelection in 2011. Daley governed autocratically and achieved only modest success in dealing with grave issues related to public education, low-cost housing, and crime but earned high marks for continuing the architectural reconstruction of downtown, instituting a number of "green" reforms, and easing the city's transition from an industrial to a service-based economy. In November 2010, Rahm Emanuel, President Barack Obama's chief of staff, announced that he would be resigning his White House post to run for the Chicago mayoralty. Emanuel was forced by his political opponents to spend precious time and money in late 2010 successfully proving his city residency but handily won election the following spring.

The 1990s and 2000s saw changes in voting patterns among urban dwellers. Election returns showed that the old pre–World War II pattern of most immigrants and migrants voting for Democratic Party candidates was altered. Cuban Americans who had fled the island after Fidel Castro's assumption of power in 1960 overwhelmingly voted Republican, for example, and became a powerful political force in southern Florida. Many of those newly arrived from India, the People's Republic of China, the Middle East, and eastern Europe were unlike earlier generations of European immigrants who were uneducated, unskilled, and often forced to take refuge in homogeneous neighborhoods close to downtown. By contrast, many new immigrants were white-collar workers with education or job experience in engineering, medicine, or computer science. They took up residence in the suburbs or moved to the urban fringe within a short time after their arrival. Gravitating toward the Republican Party, their political loyalties were at least in part explained by patterns of employment in "dot-com" firms and other businesses dependent on defense and other federal contracts. Many white-collar immigrant voters supported President George W. Bush's bid for reelection in 2004 over the Democratic challenger, U.S. Senator John Kerry of Massachusetts. The march of protest against the Iraq War that took place in New York outside the Republican Party Convention in August 2004 had little influence on Bush administration policy. Coral Cables, Florida; St. Louis, Missouri; and Tempe, Arizona, hosted presidential campaign debates, but none of these cities inspired the candidates to deviate from their scripted responses. Bush won a narrow victory thanks in large measure to rural and small-town voters.

In 2008, the Democratic Party's nomination of a Chicago resident, U.S. Senator Barack Obama, as its 2008 presidential nominee energized the urban electorate. Obama's nomination sparked increased political participation among people of color and youths. Rural inhabitants, especially white males, favored the Republican Party ticket consisting of Arizona Senator John McCain and Alaska Governor Sarah Palin. Voters who helped elect Obama to office might have optimistically hoped that having a person of color in the White House would bring about noticeable change, but they discovered that regardless of the goals or intentions of the president and the Democratic Party, without grassroots political organization and broad participation, employment, affordable housing, and quality education and training would remain beyond their grasp. During the congressional elections of 2010, this same group of voters gravitated toward the loosely organized "Tea Party" movement calling for less government and tax cuts. The Democrats lost control of the U.S. House of Representatives in the 2010 elections but retained a majority in the Senate. The Democrats lost President Obama's Senate seat as a result of racial backlash against what critics call "Obamaland," the places in white and black metropolitan Chicago where the president and his backers resided.

In 2009–2010, President Obama gave his support for aid packages that bailed out struggling banks and automobile manufacturers. General Motors and Chrysler Corporation accepted federal aid, while the Ford Motor Company, in better financial shape than its competitors, declined the offer. Although the American automobile industry had experienced a few profitable years, such as 1993, throughout the 1990s and 2000s, Japanese and other imported automobiles outsold automobiles produced domestically. When gas prices rose sharply in 2008, the market for domestically produced minivans, trucks, and sport-utility vehicles, the mainstays of the American market, declined sharply and recovered slowly. The 2010 automobile bailout somewhat helped the economically ravaged city of Detroit and dozens of other distressed cities in the upper Midwest where automobile and truck parts and accessories are made and distributed. By late 2010, General Motors emerged from bankruptcy and saw sales of its products increase in China and other developing nations. Meanwhile, in Detroit, Flint, and other cities where the auto giant had once employed thousands of unionized workers, the economic future continued to look bleak.

The changing patterns of immigration seen in American cities during the 1990s and 2000s contributed to shifts in the influence of religion on the political behavior of city residents. Before World War II, immigrants often contributed to the growth of political and economic power for Roman Catholic and Jewish institution. The immigrants who arrived in the 1990s and 2000s attended existing places of worship or built new Islamic mosques or Hindu and Buddhist temples in order to practice their faith. Some religious groups literally occupied the buildings that were formerly Christian churches. For many, the loss of Catholic power and prestige was best symbolized by the level of public outrage expressed when the Roman Catholic Archdiocese of Boston was forced to acknowledge that Church officials had covered up for priests who had sexually molested parish youth. These crimes, heavily publicized in 2001 and afterward, led to lawsuits that ultimately bankrupted the Archdiocese of Boston. Other cities were involved in what would soon become an international scandal.

## THE URBAN ECONOMY: CITY IS US

In the weeks and months that followed September 11, 2001, there was an outpouring of support and admiration for New York City from across the globe. At home from coast to coast, love for the city of New York (not Washington, D.C.) was expressed in songs, T-shirts, bumper stickers, and banners. The physical and psychological damage inflicted on the nation's capital city and its inhabitants was recognized, but for most Americans, "9/11" would forever be the day New York City was attacked. They viewed the film footage of the collapse of the towers knowing that it was not an image from a computer game or special effects from Hollywood but a scene of death, suffering, bravery, and kindness.

The nature of the September 2001 attack on New York City forced Americans to face the reality that the United States was an urban nation. Over a decade earlier, the 1990 census revealed that for the first time, a majority (50.2 percent) of Americans lived in cities of 1 million or more. This trend was expected to grow as cities in Florida, Texas, Arizona, and California experienced record growth. One out of every four Americans claimed Hispanic, Asian, African, or American Indian roots, up from one out of five just ten years earlier.

In 1992, when Arkansas Governor Bill Clinton defeated incumbent President George H. W. Bush, he promised to build political support for programs to improve the quality of urban life. Although the health insurance plan that he and First Lady Hillary Rodham Clinton advocated failed to secure sufficient congressional backing, it helped paved the way for the passage of President Obama's 2009 health care bill. The first Democrat to be president since Jimmy Carter and the Reagan Revolution of 1980 did not try to woo city voters who had abandoned the Democratic Party back into the fold. Neither Clinton nor his Republican successor, former Texas Governor George W. Bush, offered Utica, New York, Port Arthur, Texas, Richmond, California, and the hundreds of other cities like them help to retain the manufacturing that still existed and solve the environmental, economic, and social problems left behind by the departure of jobs in manufacturing and the decentralization of residential and commercial development. Regardless of how important a city was nationally or to the larger regional economy, each community had to develop and implement its own strategy for coping with the problems, such as blight and abandonment, that spanned city, suburb, and countryside. Identifying himself as a New Democrat and forsaking the urban liberalism of Lyndon Johnson's Great Society, Clinton echoed earlier Republican presidents in propounding a New Federalism that called for public–private partnerships, decreases in federal aid to cities, and an end to public housing construction.

One of the federal programs enjoying bipartisan support during this time period that had a marked influence on U.S. cities was Hope VI. Under this Department of Housing and Urban Development program, local housing and redevelopment authorities were granted federal funds to tear down or refurbish the low-income, federally subsidized public housing developments and turn them into mixed-income housing. The Boston Housing Authority, for example, used Hope VI funds to transform a public housing development built on the site of a former city dump on Columbia Point into a mixed-income development. With close proximity to the University of Massachusetts at Boston campus, the John F. Kennedy Presidential Library, and the Massachusetts State Archives, property values have increased despite the site's troubled environmental past. The Hope VI program offered limited aid to cities because it provided no funds or incentives to help them offset the overall loss of affordable housing units. Neither the Clinton nor the Bush years saw the emergence of a plan for urban and suburban job creation, housing, transportation, infrastructure improvements, or telecommunications.

During the 1990s, city leaders sought economic stability and growth in several ways, continuing in their efforts to court private and public funds for residential and commercial real estate development. Hotels, condominiums, hospitals, airport terminals, retail stores, concert halls, museums, and sports venues were built in both central business districts and prosperous suburbs. Although the construction boom created jobs—the rate of unemployment hit a thirty-year low of 3.9 percent in May 2000—unemployment remained a problem in long-troubled cities such as Camden, Detroit, and Oakland and certain sections of more prosperous cities such as Chicago and Los Angeles.

During the early 1990s, hopes were high for the growth of a new high-tech "e-economy." Business analysts were optimistic that the growth of telecommunications, health care, financial services, and other service-sector industries would fill the economic void created by the decline of union jobs in mass production industries such as steel and automobiles. As entry-level openings in industry all but disappeared, city dwellers whose education, skills, and work habits were incompatible with those demanded of employees in the growing economic sectors faced greater and greater difficulty making ends meet. How would their declining economic fortunes affect the cities where they resided?

By 1990, the cities of the upper Midwest—Detroit, Flint, South Bend, Duluth, and others—had already suffered the effects of decades of corporate and public policy that shifted the fabrication of heavy metals and the production of automobiles, machines, tools, apparel, and consumer products abroad. In December 1991, General Motors, with 1990 revenues at nearly $127 billion, announced plans to close twenty-five plants in North America and reduce its workforce by 19 percent. In October 1992, Sears and IBM announced major restructuring plans in order to cut costs. As the year drew to a close, unemployment stood at 7.6 percent. Some financial analysts expressed concern about the level of indebtedness among both consumers and banks, many of whom made financial decisions and commitments under the assumption that the jump in real estate values seen in many U.S. cities in the 1990s would continue. In certain metropolitan areas where the real estate market was hot, such as Miami and Las Vegas, real estate sales agents and mortgage lenders were busy until roughly 2000, when signs of a cooling market began to emerge.

The nation's largest cities—New York, Los Angeles, and Chicago—continued to be known as places for making and selling products and services, and
at the same time they sought to develop themselves as venues for entertainment, accessing transportation, and obtaining specialized services, such as
higher education and health care ("eds and meds"). During the mid-2000s,
the limits of pursuing economic growth or stability through the promotion
of real estate development and service sectors began to be evident. Dwindling
amounts of federal and state aid and voter hostility toward taxes made it difficult for mayors, city councils, school boards, and citizen groups to respond to
rising rates of unemployment, home mortgage foreclosure, troubled schools,
and aging roads, bridges, tunnels, parks, and water and sewage systems. The
September 2002 arrest of five men of Yemeni origin outside Buffalo, New
York, in a suspected terrorist plot raised concerns that cities suffering under
the crushing social and economic weight of deindustrialization might become
bases for terrorist or violently militant organizations.

Buffalo and nearby Lackawanna were examples of cities that by 2010 had
been written off by political and corporate leaders as unredeemable. They
were not unlike certain sections of other, more affluent cities where the poor
were increasingly concentrated. A 2011 press report revealed how while the
rate of poverty in the overall city declined by 2 percent between 2005 and
2009, in the section of the city known as Lower Northeast, which included
neighborhoods such as Tacony, the rate of poverty had increased by an astonishing 110 percent. The area had experienced an influx of poor Latinos
and African Americans and the departure of more affluent black and white
households. The percentage of residents on fixed incomes increased, and the
rate of unemployment (5.6 percent in 1999) reached 12.8 percent. Joblessness was particularly high among young adults who lacked education and
technical skills, and even those who had jobs received fewer hours of work or
found their benefits cut. Houses once owned by police officers, firefighters,
and workers in local manufacturing plants were now occupied by renters in
greater need of welfare and other social services.[3]

During the 1990s, public sector employment—so important to the
economic and social advancement of city residents, particularly recent immigrants and people of color—became less and less secure. Unlike large corporate employers, public sector employers could not relocate, were required
to employ more minorities, and were less resistant to unionization. Real

estate foreclosure, declining real estate values, and diminishing tax revenues combined with reductions in state and federal municipal aid, prompting many city departments and agencies to reduce staff and privatize or eliminate services. Layoffs in schools and public safety departments garnered the most public attention.

On April 14, 2,000 investors lost an estimated $2 billion when the Dow Jones Index fell 617.78 points in a single day. Protesters disrupted the meeting of the International Monetary Fund and the World Bank in Washington, D.C., with calls for global economic justice. Those who predicted that the downturn would be short in duration were forced to reassess their views in 2001 after the September 11 attack on New York and Washington, D.C. In the years that followed, economic conditions steadily worsened. Real estate and stock prices fell, and unemployment rates rose. In July 2004, when Kenneth Lay, the former chairman of Houston's failed energy giant, Enron, pleaded not guilty to eleven felony charges related to the financial collapse of the firm, an angry American public found it difficult to withhold judgment until the legal proceedings were over. Average wage earners saw their retirement and investment funds disappear in a sea of stock market losses, bond defaults, and bank closures. Leading investment firms lost billions of dollars; the once prominent Lehman Brothers investment firm went broke. In 2008, the country plunged deeply into economic recession, and economic woes in cities worsened. Some cities, most notably Detroit, teetered on the brink of bankruptcy. Fort Lauderdale, Houston, Phoenix, Las Vegas, and other Sun Belt cities were soon experiencing rates of mortgage foreclosure more typically associated with Detroit, Cleveland, and Youngstown, Ohio. So many people had fled the city and abandoned their homes and businesses that each of these cities discussed condemning the remaining private property, relocating residents and businesses, shutting off utilities, and closing some roads to traffic.

The efforts undertaken by cities to rejuvenate themselves economically were undermined or frustrated by the state of their public schools. The quality of U.S. schools and student performance rates had fallen behind those of less affluent nations. During the George W. Bush administration, much of the blame for failing city schools was placed on teachers and the unions that represented them. School administrators were also charged with not doing enough to make city schools places that prepared children for college or the workforce. Performance standards were created under the No Child Left

Behind Act, which mandated that failing schools lose federal aid if they did not improve their scores on standardized tests. City school boards were required to dismiss administrators and teachers who were unable to meet these standards. The program generated much publicity but revealed that there was no quick fix for deeply troubled city schools. The link between student performance, school budgets, parental involvement, and the rates of poverty and unemployment was identified as a factor that needed to be addressed in September 2010 when billionaire Mark Zuckerberg, the founder and chief executive officer of Facebook, donated $100 million to help Newark, New Jersey, improve its public schools.

## TRAVEL AND LEISURE AS URBAN ECONOMIC ENGINE

In June 1997, President Bill Clinton declared at the annual meeting of the U.S. Conference of Mayors that "our cities are back. We've got the biggest economic resurgence in cities since World War II; the unemployment rate down by a third in our 50 largest cities; more downtowns coming back to life with sports and tourism and local business booming."[4] The mayors of the nation's largest cities got the assurance they sought that the entertainment and tourism model for urban growth that many were pursuing was working. Business and leisure travel boomed during the mid-1990s. New York, Boston, San Francisco, Washington, D.C., Las Vegas, Chicago, and Los Angeles were among the cities most popular with travelers. Orlando's emergence as one of the largest cities in Florida was indicative of the ability of Disney World, Universal Studios, and other area attractions to contribute to urban growth—and urban problems such as traffic.

Leisure travel suffered in the months following the September 11, 2001, attack on the United States, especially in New York and Washington, D.C. Even after the shock began to wear off and the economy began to rebound, attendance at many cultural events, museums, and historic sites was lower than in the mid-1990s, when leisure travel was growing rapidly. A 2010 study showed that foreign travel to the United States continued to decline. In the months following the terrorist attack, the traveling public gradually became accustomed to long security lines at airports and security screening at certain events and cultural sites such as the Liberty Bell, exhibited to the public in Philadelphia by the U.S. Park Service. The need to improve security at the Statue of Liberty kept this important landmark closed until August 2004.

Issues of how privacy, free speech, and religious freedom have been affected by the increase in national security measures were addressed at the National Constitution Center, which opened in Philadelphia near Independence Hall in 2005. The museum that will be a part of the newly redeveloped World Trade Center site includes wreckage saved from one of the collapsed towers. Plans for the redevelopment of the site sparked international debate in 2010 when plans for the construction of an Islamic cultural center near the site of the former World Trade Center were announced.

Presented as a means of raising revenue, public tolerance for the legalization of certain forms of gaming grew during the 1990s, and its impact on the urban landscape was marked. Developers razed the famed Las Vegas casinos of the 1950s and 1960s, such as the Sands and the Aladdin, and replaced them with larger and gaudier hotels and casinos. Some contained "family" entertainments and attractions found at theme parks. In 1993, when the MGM Grand Hotel and Casino opened with over 5,000 rooms and per room development costs averaging $50,000, it was the largest in the world.

Atlantic City, New Jersey, the gaming capital of the East, also saw the construction or refurbishment of its casinos, but this infusion of investment did not reverse the city's overall economic and social decline. The city's economy, which revolved around one industry, suffered in part as a result of the expansion of Native American gaming. Atlantic City had more competition after Mississippi, Indiana, Pennsylvania, and other states legalized certain forms of gaming. In 2006, the city's troubles worsened when the Miss America Pageant moved to Las Vegas. Atlantic City officials soon discovered that their rival was not recession proof; by 2010, Las Vegas had a 15 percent unemployment rate.

During the 1990s, cities relied increasingly on revenue from leisure and shopping. Out-of-town visitors to Chicago might spend the morning at the city-owned Shedd Aquarium, the afternoon visiting a commercial entertainment venue such as Navy Pier or the American Girl Café and Theater or shopping on North Michigan Avenue, and the evening dining near historic Water Tower Place before retiring to a nearby room in a luxury downtown hotel. The family that drove into Baltimore from the suburbs in its Honda Odyssey to visit the National Aquarium in the Inner Harbor area or attend an Orioles game at the Camden Yards Stadium likely also shopped, dined, and photographed or commented on the experience using a "smart" telephone before they departed from the city that evening.

Chicago's Miracle Mile along Michigan Avenue and Boston's Prudential Center are examples of two upscale retail districts that thrived in the 1990s and 2000s because they successfully fused together elements of the suburban shopping mall and the old-fashioned downtown shopping experience. Located in the Back Bay section of the city, the latter included a full-sized chain grocery store with competitive prices, a rarity in most cities despite the economic incentives offered to help keep underserved city neighborhoods from becoming nutritional wastelands. Austin, Texas, with its affluent and educated population base, was typical of the type of city that saw the expansion of Whole Foods and other establishments serving specialty or niche consumers from suburban-like stores in small shopping plazas offering limited parking.

As downtown shopping disappeared, consumers learned to seek out smaller, more specialized retail and dining districts located along transportation routes or in new or revitalized waterfront, industrial, or warehouse sites. One of the more extreme cases of an attempted urban makeover was found in the small city of Homestead, Pennsylvania, located on the once heavily industrialized Monongahela River. The site of one of the most famous strikes in American history was cleared of the shuttered U.S. Steel plant and in its place, a retail and entertainment complex named The Waterfront in Homestead was erected. Only the plant's huge chimneys now remain, a reminder of the area's historic roots in the bygone industrial age.

During the 1990s, many cities erected new or refurbished old downtown convention centers. Some cities built convention centers to take advantage of waterfront sites or their proximity to other major attractions, such as sports arenas. Philadelphia's Convention Center has benefited from close proximity to the Reading Railroad Terminal, a bustling urban market offering locals and convention visitors alike a chance to purchase poultry from an Amish farmer, order a cheesesteak sandwich, or buy a used book.

Some urban districts became dining and shopping destinations for people who lived outside the neighborhood or even the city. The Italian section of Boston known as the North End, New York's Little Italy, and San Francisco's North Beach became popular as entertainment areas, altering their traditional residential base. During the 1990s, coffee shops, both independent stores and chain outlets such as Starbucks, joined corner bars and taverns as neighborhood meeting places. The appeal of the coffee shops, which typically offered free wireless Internet connections and a smoke-free atmosphere, cut across class, ethnic, and generational lines. By the mid-2000s, free wireless Internet access was offered in some museums, parks, libraries, transportation terminals, and even whole neighborhoods as a way to help build community by strengthening virtual ones.

Contributing to the allure of urban entertainment was the construction of new or the refurbishment of existing museums, concert halls, and other entertainment venues. In Omaha, Nebraska, for example, the 1992 completion of the Lied Jungle under the Henry Doorly Zoo's eight-story-high glass dome covering one and a half acres set new standards in zoos. During that same year, New York City refurbished Bryant Park and reestablished its aesthetic link to the New York Public Library. In December 2001, the Philadelphia Orchestra played for the first time in its new home, the Kimmel Center for the Performing Arts. Symbolic of the growing affluence of southeastern cities was the construction of new art museum buildings in Savannah, Georgia, and Wilmington, North Carolina. Major additions took place at the Nelson-Atkins Museum of Art in Kansas City, the Detroit Institute of Arts, and the Boston Museum of Fine Arts. During a 2002–2004 renovation project directed by architect Yoshio Taniguchi, a portion of the Museum of Modern Art's collection was temporarily relocated to a former Swingline Stapler factory housing in Long Island City in the borough of Queens. In 2008 and 2010, the Los Angeles County Museum of Art added two new buildings to its twenty-acre museum campus. Star architect Renzo Piano designed the Broad Contemporary Art Museum (2008) and the Resnick Pavilion (2010).

The expansion of popular entertainment venues during the 1990s and 2000s included the dramatic increase of new stadiums and sports arenas. The owners of professional sports franchises worked to convince city leaders that their teams were an important part of keeping the city—especially its downtown—economically vital. Prior to basketball star Michael Jordan's January 1999 retirement, millions of people around the world knew of Chicago because it was the city where he played for the Bulls. Convinced of the economic advantages that professional sports organizations provided, city and state officials rarely refused the demands of team owners, including when they threatened to move their organizations if taxpayers did not partially or completely finance the construction of new stadiums or arenas. City officials, developers, and team owners often defended their support for the use of public funds for stadiums and arenas by arguing that professional sports franchises created jobs, spurred economic development, and promoted a sense of urban identity. Between 1990 and 2008, owners opened nineteen new Major League Baseball stadiums, seventeen new National Football League stadiums, and twenty new National Basketball Association arenas in U.S. cities. Construction costs were often subsidized with public funds even in economically struggling cities.[5] A new appreciation for the need to preserve an old ballpark—Fenway Park—arose in 2004 when the Boston Red Sox swept the St. Louis Cardinals in four games to win the World Series for the first time since 1918. Time will tell whether this aging baseball landmark and Chicago's Wrigley Field will survive pressures for expansion or relocation to bring in more revenue.

Perhaps the most influential sports-related building project of the period opened in 1992. Orioles Park at Camden Yards in Baltimore was copied by other ball teams seeking to increase their popularity by bringing back neighborhood ballparks—stadiums designed to take advantage of public transit and fit snugly into the existing city neighborhood. When ground was broken for a new Detroit Tigers' stadium in 1997, team owner Mike Illitch stated that he wanted fans to feel that it was "their ballpark." With roughly 40 percent of the project costs coming from public sources, Detroit city planners hoped that the new stadium, named Comerica Park when dedicated in April 2000, would foster commercial and residential redevelopment in the surrounding neighborhood and "blend into the street life."[6] Meanwhile, the old Tiger Stadium was razed in 2008–2009 after an effort to redevelop the stadium—or at least the infield portion of it—for condominiums, offices, and stores fizzled for a lack of funding.

The selection of Atlanta as the site of the 1996 Summer Olympics made clear the relationship between this international sporting event and urban development and redevelopment. The oldest publicly funded housing development for low-income families in the nation, Techwood Homes, fell to the wrecking ball in order to protect real estate values in the newly redeveloped areas near the Coca-Cola corporate headquarters. Another indication of the economic allure that big sporting and entertainment events have on urban economies came in July 2000 when two members of the committee that persuaded the International Olympic Committee to select Salt Lake City as the site of the 2002 Winter Olympics were indicted by a federal grand jury on charges including conspiracy to commit bribery.

Cities worked in the 1990s and 2000s to attract new stadiums and sporting events mindful that they were only one part of the economic equation. City officials in Indianapolis, where hotels and restaurants depend heavily on the revenues earned in the weeks leading up to the annual Indy 500 race, concentrate on attracting conventions and promoting the growth of the downtown campus of Indiana University–Purdue University at Indianapolis, museums, and other attractions. Marathons, triathlons, walk-a-thons, and bicycle races in large and small cities brought together athletes, viewers, and sponsors to their host cities and generated revenue and publicity. On Patriot's Day (a holiday celebrated only in Massachusetts), when the nation's oldest road race, the Boston Marathon, takes place, a festive air prevails in the city, particularly in the neighborhoods along the course route that are heavily populated with college students.

During the 1990s and 2000s, the number and variety of hotels, restaurants, and other commercial establishments around airports, major highway interchanges, and rail and subway stations increased relative to downtown. Almost all the establishments serving travelers were part of large national or regional chains and have helped make the city more suburban in appearance. By the 1990s, large and well-established downtown hotels, such as Boston's Copley Plaza Hotel and Pittsburgh's William Penn Hotel, were no longer independent and had become part of nationally marketed chains.

The quality of urban life and food shopping has improved as a result of shifts in immigration patterns, the local foods movement, and the "greening" of cities. Frustrated in their attempts to find fruits, vegetables, and grains familiar to them, some immigrants from the Caribbean, South America, Africa, and Asia began turning private yards, parks, vacant lots, and brown field sites into gardens. Other city residents began or resumed gardening in order to gain access to more nutritious food, save money, combat urban blight, and build community. In Chicago and other cities, public housing residents planted gardens on vacant land owned by the local housing authority.

Aware of the difficulties in retaining grocery stores in impoverished areas, city planners encouraged the establishment or reestablishment of farmers' markets and urban markets. Some cities undertook efforts to publicize already established markets such as in Harrisburg, Pennsylvania, where workers, many of whom are employed by the Commonwealth of Pennsylvania, walk down Third Street every market day to a restored nineteenth-century building where they buy fresh and prepared foods from local vendors. Open early on Sunday, Dallas's produce and flower market attracts a diverse group of shoppers and visitors from the nearby convention center. Washington, D.C., acknowledged the importance of the city market in the South East district by restoring the building and reopening the market in 2007 after a fire. Each spring, lunch patrons wait in line to buy soft-shell crab sandwiches.

## URBAN ANCHORS: OLD AND NEW AND GREEN

By the 1990s, elected officials and urban policymakers no longer pinned their hopes for economic stability or growth on manufacturing; they looked to telecommunications, health care, higher education, tourism, and other potential employers. Seattle, Portland, and San Francisco boasted of their "green" or environmental consciousness and promoted themselves as great places in which to live and do business. The reality was, however, whether it was in Boston's Route 128 high-tech corridor or in northern California's Silicon Valley, the rise of the computer industry further accelerated the shift of investment toward the suburbs and away from downtown commercial districts. High-tech and defense contractors clustered in office parks and plazas during the early 1990s in so-called edge cities, such as Tyson's Corner, Virginia, outside of Washington, D.C., and Clayton, Missouri, outside of St. Louis; they were far less likely than financial services and insurance firms to be found in downtown Hartford or Houston. Owners of older office buildings in small cities often struggled to find the financial backing needed to make the updates necessary in order to be able to fulfill the computing and security demands of potential leaseholders. As the Internet's influence over business grew during the 1990s, numerous mergers between computer companies and telecommunications firms took place. Television networks and cable television providers were forced to reposition themselves to gain or retain a market share. For many cities, one of the most tangible signs or symbols of the revolution that had taken place in communications came with the demise of city newspapers. By the mid-2000s, many small-city newspapers had gone out of business, consolidated with others, or existed as shadows of their former selves.

During the 1990s and 2000s, the city landscape was dramatically altered by the growth of the medical, pharmaceutical, and health care industries; higher education; and airport and corrections-related construction. Hospitals, particularly university or research-based medical centers such as Houston's Baylor University Medical Center and Philadelphia's University of Pennsylvania Medical Center, were among the largest employers in their host cities. The Johns Hopkins University Medical Center in Baltimore became Maryland's largest employer by the end of the twentieth century. Certain hospitals and medical centers established dominance over whole sections of cities, prompting the organization of community and resident groups that owned or rented the housing and small businesses often leveled to make way for the expansion of hospitals, laboratories, office buildings, and parking garages. University medical centers and large research hospitals such as Harvard University, which by the late 2000s was spilling beyond the confines of Cambridge, have been forced to step up efforts to work in concert with neighborhood and community organizations to develop growth strategies and employment patterns that make them an asset to neighborhoods and cities. Duquesne University officials in Pittsburgh have tried to make the benefits of the growth of its School of Pharmacy available to impoverished local residents who live nearby by offering free or low-cost prescriptions beginning in 2010.

During the 1990s and 2000s, urban-based universities faced controversy regarding not only the growth of their medical and health care facilities but other expansion projects as well. When in the mid-2000s the University of Michigan decided that it wanted to increase the size of its football stadium, local residents organized to gain a few concessions. Overall, however, the university was able to increase the size of the "Big House" in 2010 pretty much as it wished. Some urban-based institutions of higher learning, such as the University of Massachusetts at Lowell, have maintained positive relations with city residents through a strategy that included the adaptive reuse of a former textile mill building into a dormitory and the conversion of a struggling downtown hotel into a dormitory and conference center.

During the 1990s, college and university presidents became more and more adept at showing city fathers just how much their institutions contributed to local economic and cultural life. In order to encourage incoming Western Michigan University students to shop and socialize in the central business district of Kalamazoo, a scavenger hunt was included as part of an orientation activity with prizes donated by downtown merchants. "Discover New York," a yearlong freshman program at St. John's University in Queens, was established by the university not only to help students learn about off campus educational opportunities but also to instill in them a civic consciousness and an enduring appreciation for New York City and urban life.

In 2010, while university campuses in Great Britain were awash with protests over government policies to make students pay a higher percentage of the overall cost of their education, campuses in U.S. cities were relatively free of protests over rising costs and cuts in federal and state aid. In the absence of a military draft and a high level of political engagement, campus police departments saw the greatest spike in student rowdiness when major sports championships were won or lost. Aware that many urban campuses suffer from higher rates of crime than surrounding neighborhoods, universities took measures to prevent sexual and other types of assault, stop vandalism and robbery, and prevent the theft of identity and intellectual property. In the wake of the mass shooting at Virginia Tech University in Blacksburg, Virginia, in April 16, 2008, some campuses developed or improved warning and signal systems. The student gunman had earlier warned of his plans and made a videotape explaining his motives. After shooting two students, he mailed the tape to NBC News in New York City and returned to campus, where he shot thirty others before killing himself. Students used cell phones and other electronic devices to alert each other. In 2010, the university was found to be remiss in its failure to alert students, faculty, and staff of the risk. In response to rising concern about campus crime, many schools began offering shuttle and escort services. The University of Nevada at Las Vegas instituted a nighttime campus shuttle service for the safety of students, faculty, and staff, for example, but by 2010, budget shortfalls had forced its elimination.

Cities sought to gain ground economically not only by boasting of the health care and higher education they offered but also by promoting themselves as transportation centers. The 1990s saw a marked increase in air travel improvements. Airport authorities in Pensacola, Florida, Minneapolis, Minnesota, and dozens of other cities built or expanded runways, terminal buildings, cargo facilities, and parking garages. Some city airports, such as Las Vegas's McCarran International Airport, grew so much during this period that they appeared to be under constant construction or reconstruction. In some instances, airport security demands following the 2001 terrorist attack became the driving force behind the work. Even before the successful emergency landing of a commercial passenger aircraft on New York's Hudson River on January 16, 2009, when the plane struck wildfowl and suffered engine failure, airports were working to reduce or minimize their environmental impact. New or varied flight patterns, the creation of wildlife refuges, systems of recapturing deicing fluid and other types of runoff, recycling programs, and the relocation of air cargo service to smaller regional or former military air bases have helped to make the nation's city airports slightly more ecofriendly. Traffic snarls around city airports, particularly in New York, Chicago, and Los Angeles, underscored the need for further improvements in public transportation between airports and key residential areas both within and outside the city. As a result, many metropolitan areas have extended public transit lines to airports to relieve traffic congestion on expressways.

Some cities began to examine their transportation and disaster planning in the wake of costly natural disasters. Many were shocked at the extent and cost of repairing the damage done by Hurricane Andrew, which devastated Homestead, Florida, and portions of coastal Louisiana in August 1992, and the human errors that contributed to the 2005 flooding that destroyed huge portions of New Orleans in the aftermath of Hurricane Katrina. Some cities have sought to foster economic growth by "going green" and embracing more environmentally sound development strategies, championing smart-growth initiatives that seek to contain urban sprawl, encouraging urban in-fill construction, and adaptively reusing historic structures. During the 1990s, the cities of northern California, Oregon, and Washington made the most headway in their attempts to keep downtowns from dying and undeveloped land on the outskirts of town from becoming paved over for another strip of automobile-oriented development.

Pocket parks, greenways, bicycle lanes and racks, pedestrian paths, and other outdoor recreational facilities and amenities increased in number all over the United States. Institutions of higher learning, museums, and corporations built "green" buildings designed to minimize the impact on the environment, reduce energy and water consumption, and capture rainwater or gray water. After fouling the water, soil, and air around its famous River Rouge Plant in Detroit for almost a century, the Ford Motor Company built a "green" roof for one of the largest buildings remaining in operation on the sprawling industrial site. The new roof is billed as an attraction, a part of the new visitor experience that has replaced the old plant tour with a simulation of the sights, sounds, and odors involved in auto and truck production.

The lack of metropolitan government or planning authority has hampered the ability of cities to work with the suburbs that surround them to keep growth contained and to preserve open space and agricultural land. One result of the unwillingness or inability of cities and suburbs to work together to stem sprawl is the destruction or loss of animal and plant habitats. News outlets note with amusement when whitetail deer, brown bears, moose, coyotes, and other wild animals are seen or killed in cities, but they seldom make the observation that these animals are evidence of failed policy regulating growth.

Architects, planners, and real estate developers who were proponents of the New Urbanism presented alternatives to energy-consuming suburban sprawl at several communities developed during the 1990s. Celebration, Florida, was designed and built beginning in 1994 by the Walt Disney Corporation to evoke, according to its promotional literature, the feel of a small village during the 1930s. Higher-density development, smaller lot sizes, the length of the setback from the road, and the use of front porches were among the architectural and planning features that promoters hoped would give rise to tight-knit communities where neighbors looked out for each other. When the city's first homicide arrest took place in 2010, critics remarked that they had known all along that it was not possible to plan crime out of existence.

## CONCLUSION

If you were to revisit the city where you were born—the very hospital where you were delivered—chances are that it would look different today than it did on the day of your birth. Perhaps the hospital has been enlarged, and there are medical professional buildings or a parking garage where houses used to stand. Can you imagine what the hospital and surrounding neighborhood will look like when your grandchildren are born? During the 1990s and 2000s, the process of rebuilding and redefining U.S. cities continued unabated. The more cities changed, the less they seemed to resemble the places your parents or grandparents knew, places where items were made and produced by wage earners who had, within a generation or two, migrated or immigrated to the city.

The challenges that face U.S. cities are daunting. The need for meaningful employment that offers a living wage and for improvements in medical care, transportation services, and housing, as well as the remediation of water, air, and soil pollution, are just a few. Some cities will soon be faced with the need to address rising tidal and water levels as a result of the increased water level in the oceans. Global climate change could ultimately mean the flooding of downtowns, airports, and interstate highways, forcing their relocation or abandonment. Not only do American cities drive the nation's economy and culture, but their impact is global as well. How will you help protect and enhance their future viability?

# Conclusion

The city that emerged in twenty-first-century America was bifurcated, a city of dark and despairing neighborhoods but also of shimmering glass towers, grassy, monument-studded parks, giant stadiums, and architecturally distinguished cultural centers. The authors are fully aware that this bifurcated image is hardly new. Charles Dickens, in *A Tale of Two Cities* and in many of his other books, such as *Oliver Twist* and *Our Mutual Friend*, portrayed London and Paris as places where opulence stood graphically juxtaposed against utter physical squalor and human degradation. Other writers, such as Tolstoy, Theodore Dreiser, and, more recently, Tom Wolfe in *Bonfire of the Vanities* and T. C. Boyle in *The Tortilla Curtain*, did the same thing.

But, as chapter 1 of this book has emphasized, unlike Dickens's, Tolstoy's, or Dreiser's city, the modern American metropolis unfolded in the full glare of media klieg lights. The key events—urban renewal, suburbanization, deindustrialization, racial rioting, municipal bankruptcy, and 9/11 terrorism, as well as the explosion of glitzy urban opulence, an opulence brilliantly illuminated by the collapse of Wall Street's titans in 2008—all took place while cameras (now mostly digital) clicked away.

Immediately after World War II, the media captured the stark images of a dark, unkempt city, its encrustation resulting from a decade and a half of Great Depression and wartime neglect. Film noir delivered those grainy images of the waning hours of an aging and popularly rejected industrial city through the shadowy, rain-swept scenes of Humphrey Bogart and Lauren Bacall in *The Big Sleep* or Marlon Brando in *On the Waterfront*. Other postwar films and television shows, such as *West Side Story*, *Guess Who's Coming to Dinner?*, and *All in the Family*, documented the racialization of the postwar city, as did television news footage of the school desegregation battles of the late 1950s and the "long hot summers" of the 1960s. Unfortunately, the cameras remained eerily absent when, in city after city, postwar urban redevelopment and renewal uprooted thousands of the black poor and rehoused them in such gigantic, sterile housing projects as Chicago's Robert Taylor Homes and St. Louis's Pruitt-Igoe, thus creating the "Second Ghetto."

Behind the images lay the facts of postwar urban change. Not only did World War II unleash a second great cityward migration of African Americans, but its legacy also included the GI Bill, an economic boom, the Cold War, and rising white middle-class expectations for mass consumption. America became a "consumer's republic." The newly entitled white middle class streamed from the city to suburbia, and the nation shifted from an industrial to a postindustrial urban economy. The old urban-centric "metropolitan tradition" of the late nineteenth and early twentieth centuries vanished, yielding instead the sprawling twenty-first-century megalopolis of suburbs, exurbs, edge cities, and decaying inner-city neighborhoods, eviscerated of their former opportunity-affording economic and institutional fabric.

Metropolitan regions—including suburbs as well as cities—changed dramatically under the influence of new immigration patterns that predominated by the last decades of the twentieth century. Although significant numbers of European immigrants still arrived in the United States, the enhanced flow of newcomers from Latin America and Asia transformed countless urban and suburban neighborhoods. Whereas immigrants had traditionally nestled at first into inner-city enclaves and established ethnic communities before venturing out to suburban residences—usually generations later—census data showed that the most recent arrivals more commonly moved directly to the suburbs. According to a 2008 Brookings Institution study, a majority of the foreign born lived in the suburbs of large metropolitan areas. The American Community Survey reported in 2010 that since 1990, more Hispanics than whites had moved to the suburbs. By the first decade of the twenty-first century, the influx of people from Asia, Africa, and the Middle East made suburban America more heterogeneous than ever before. Indeed, of the 13.3 million immigrants who moved to the suburbs between 2000 and 2010, approximately 2 million came from Asian nations. No longer refuges for the (mostly white) members of the middle class who were fleeing the problems of big-city life, suburbs had become ethnically and racially much more heterogeneous.

International migration patterns, the growth of global markets, and modern high technology operated to shape a new urban landscape, but, as this book has argued, so too did federal policy; housing and urban renewal programs, as well as extensive highway building, engendered more intensive patterns of racial segregation and accelerated the pace of deindustrialization. In the name of combating blight by excising slums, warehousing, alleys, coal yards, and the denigrated historic urban density of the past, postwar modernists, energized by eminent-domain powers and federal dollars, envisioned and then built the modern Corbusian city replete with glass office towers, high-rise apartments, and sprawling hospital and university complexes. Thanks to such key legislation as the Taft-Ellender-Wagner Housing Act of 1949 and the Interstate Highway Act of 1956, America's modern urban landscape, including Gateway Centers, Charles Centers, I-95 beltways, and Columbia Point housing projects, began to take center stage by the 1960s.

A host of critics, liberal and conservative—among them, Catherine Bauer Wurster, Jane Jacobs, Martin Anderson, and Herbert Gans—balked at what they saw as a hideous urban environment created recklessly by destroying a culturally rich, still socially and physically viable urban world. Not only had urban renewal demolished landmark buildings and uprooted healthy communities, but it had also failed to address the urban unrest that saw many cities in the 1960s literally aflame. Urban Rust Belt economies languished while, thanks to federal military spending and the preference of social security–armed senior citizens for balmy climates and beach-front living, Sun Belt cities flourished. Seattle, Los Angeles, San Diego, and Miami all experienced remarkable growth, even as their rapid population increase led to the social and environmental problems associated with the dense urban living common to older industrial cities in the Northeast and Midwest.

Policymakers in Washington, D.C., as this book has made clear, responded to the ongoing urban crisis. During the 1960s, the administrations of Presidents John F. Kennedy and Lyndon B. Johnson enacted a host of urban-oriented laws meant to improve life in economically depressed cities. These New Frontier and Great Society programs included the Office of Economic

Opportunity; the Job Corps; the Community Action Program; urban mass transit; the Housing Acts of 1961, 1965, and 1968; and Model Cities. A 1965 law created the modern Department of Housing and Urban Development (HUD). Sensitive to the critics of large-scale slum clearance and renewal, HUD shifted more and more federal dollars to private-sector strategies for urban rebuilding, especially housing for moderate-income families and for the elderly.

However, despite the great civil rights triumphs of the 1960s—voting rights, affirmative action, open housing, the use of court-ordered busing to achieve school desegregation, and key legal victories, such as *Gautreaux v. The Chicago Housing Authority*—urban housing patterns in the 1970s and 1980s grew more—not less—segregated. The image of American cities such as Philadelphia, Detroit, Newark, Baltimore, St. Louis, and Washington, D.C., as squalid receptacles for a black urban underclass and as lawless wastelands of drugs, violent crime, and welfare dependency only deepened in the public consciousness.

The Kerner Riot Commission Report (1968) confirmed the multiple failures of urban housing programs, schools, law enforcement, and the opportunity structure as well as the pernicious lingering effect of racism and hypersegregation. The Community Action Program, the Job Corps, and Model Cities aside, deindustrialization and discrimination inexorably left cities devoid of opportunity for racial minorities and rendered urban mayors—many of whom, such as Philadelphia's Wilson Goode, Gary's Richard Hatcher, and Cleveland's Carl Stokes, were black—helpless to counter the ravages. In the 1970s, many of the African Americans who did manage to get an education and succeed—and the numbers rose—joined their white counterparts and began their flight to suburbia. Some moved to the small number of New Towns built by private investors and the federal government, but suburbanization remained largely an unplanned movement. At the same time, the problems of the cities began to spill over into inner suburbs even as more affluent populations moved farther from urban cores to the metropolitan rim.

The paroxysms of urban decline crested in the late 1970s and early 1980s. By then, cities such as Baltimore had lost over 40 percent of their industrial jobs. Between 1960 and 1980, the population of once heavily industrialized North Philadelphia declined 40 percent. Housing abandonment increased, and homeless people, wrapped in dirt-soiled blankets and sleeping on city streets, often over the heating vents of big-city subways, became a familiar sight. In a highly publicized televised event in October 1977, President Jimmy Carter visited Charlotte Street in the notorious South Bronx. With the cameras rolling, Carter beheld rubble-strewn lots and blocks of abandoned, often burned-out and scavenged brick apartment houses, a scene of modern urban America that seemed to resemble firebombed Dresden, Germany, in 1945.

But forces operated in 1976 that turned much of—albeit hardly all of—urban American away from the abyss. In some cases, it was the "miracle mayors," such as Boston's Ray Flynn, Pittsburgh's Richard Caligiuri, Baltimore's William Schaeffer, and Cleveland's George Voinovich, who forged public–private partnerships with corporate leaders to revitalize languishing downtown economies. In the Bronx, Boston, Pittsburgh, Philadelphia, and elsewhere, community development corporations, aided by federal rehabilitation and below-market-interest loans, helped resurrect blocks of scabrous housing. Impelled by excitement over the nation's bicentennial and by tax incentive legislation making historic preservation a profitable tool for urban development, festival marketplaces and gentrified neighborhoods, such as Philadelphia's Society Hill and Boston's Faneuil Hall, made lofts, townhouses, and other forms of modern urban living a viable alternative for young professionals drawn to the urban universities, hospital complexes, high-tech businesses, and high-finance firms constituting the new "creative economy." Downtown malls, office plazas, new "retro" baseball stadiums, cultural districts with experimental theaters, and, as in Milwaukee, a magnificent, architecturally unique art museum also helped to revivify and buttress once sagging downtown commerce. Moreover, the new city airports with rapid-transit access to the central business district, the glitzy downtown hotels, the Michelin three- and four-star restaurants, and the local history museums all made urban tourism another very important dimension of the postindustrial urban economies.

But, paradoxically, this same bifurcated metropolis, the modern global city of glass towers, privately policed neighborhoods, sculpture gardens, and immaculately preserved historic neighborhoods, nurtured and still nurtures deep in its bowels grotesque, abject poverty. The modern American city of immense wealth houses a host of jobless, underemployed, and desperately poor families. These are families of the thousands of urban residents, men and women, incarcerated in rurally situated state and federal prisons, the families

of the nonunionized, low-wage black and Hispanic custodial, kitchen, clerical, and service staffs that constitute the functional workforce of the modern
global city. Bereft of the old-fashioned industrialism that for over a century
and a half made the American city a beacon of opportunity for millions of European immigrants and shorn of the middle-class tax base that once made city
schools engines of upward mobility and made city political organizations a
determining force in national politics and thus a partner with the federal government in city building, today's globalized, bifurcated city struggles against
a cancerous inequality and social fragmentation that undermines any claim it
might make to being a true community. The economic travail of the "Great
Recession" of 2008–2011 has only exacerbated that inequality. Without its
earlier grit—minus the factories, warehouses, trolley cars, and rail-switching
yards that characterized cityscapes in 1945—urban America in the twenty-
first century looks vastly different from its mid-twentieth-century ancestor.
However, one feature of the modern city remains unchanged from the past
and as deeply embedded in the twenty-first-century city and suburb as it was
in the twentieth: poverty. The question remains whether the metropolitan
America of today is any more prepared to confront poverty, inequality, and
social injustice than it was in the postwar, post–Great Depression city of 1945.

# Suggestions for Urban History Research, Writing, and Public History Projects

Your professor will likely assign—or has already assigned—a research project that will culminate in a traditional paper, website, virtual exhibit, or documentary. Regardless of whether your research will be directed to a scholarly or popular audience, the best way to get started is to identify a series of questions about cities in general or a particular city or group of cities to help frame your research.

1. *Urban Images*: How has the view of U.S. cities changed since the 1950s? Are they presented as desirable places to live and work? What factors shape the image of a particular city? How has gambling shaped perceptions of cities such as Las Vegas and Atlantic City? Is Dallas still associated with the assassination of President John F. Kennedy? How have Oakland, Newark, Detroit, and other cities been affected by the highly publicized race riots of the 1960s? What makes or breaks a city's image? How influential are computer games, movies, television, radio, novels, magazines, and newspapers in shaping the reputation of cities?

2. *Sectionalism and Regionalism*: How were cities influenced by sectionalism and regionalism in the decades after World War II? What did it mean to be a Sun Belt or Rust Belt City in the 1970s and 1980s? Are there differences between southern, western, midwestern, and eastern cities? Can today's cities be distinguished from their larger metropolitan areas?

3. *Geography and Environment*: How were cities affected by the larger ecosystem? Why did Americans allow air, water, and soil in their cities to become polluted? How and why did suburban sprawl change after World War II? What prompted cities to rediscover waterfronts, parks, and neighborhoods that had deteriorated? How will cities likely respond to global warming and rising oceanic water levels?

4. *Planning and Urban Growth*: Which cities grew and which declined during the postwar years? Why did most downtowns decline while the suburbs grew? Who lost and who gained from the shift in investment to the city outskirts? How did government influence patterns of urban growth? Who or what was previously located downtown and on the edge of town? What was the impact of urban renewal in the 1950s and 1960s? Do streets, parks, and plazas named in honor of minority members of the community serve as cultural unifiers or dividers?

5. *Population*: Who lives in cities, and how have urban demographics changed since the 1940s? What immigrant groups came to cities after World War II, and why? What type of aid or infrastructure existed to help them? How did immigrants and other newcomers to the city differ by social class, color, gender, nationality, religion, skill, education, and income? What type of household arrangements have they made for themselves?

6. *Residence*: What patterns of residence emerged in the decades following World War II? Why did most affluent Americans (regardless of color) move to the suburbs and leave the most impoverished people in the city? What influence did federal policies have on city neighborhoods? What types of dwellings were built after 1950? For whom were they built? Why were most new houses detached dwellings located in subdivisions without sidewalks and community centers? Where were apartment complexes, condominiums, manufactured housing developments, and retirement or extended care villages built and why?

7. *Occupation*: How did urban employment trends change over time? During the postwar years, who worked in the city, and who worked in the suburbs? At what levels were city workers compensated, and what education or skills were demanded of those who found work in cities? What kind of employment benefits did they enjoy, and what risks did they face? Has unemployment or underemployment been a persistent problem, or have these conditions varied over time? How will the growth of joblessness likely affect cities? Will commuting decline as telecommunications improve?

8. *Transportation*: How has the city been affected by the postwar rise of the automobile and the demise of mass transit? What was the impact of the improvement in municipal, county, and state roads and the construction of federally subsidized interstate highways? Did the city benefit from increased air travel or improvements in light rail, subways, and commuter rail systems in the postwar period? How will increased fuel prices and environmental concerns likely shape future transportation patterns?

9. *Politics*: How effectively have urban issues and interests been promoted by the states and the federal government? Have local, state, and federal elected and appointed officials done a good job of solving the environmental, economic, and social issues that diminish the quality of urban life? How involved are urban residents in politics, and do they see the electoral system as offering them a voice? Will the Internet and changes in information technology change urban politics and help make government more responsive to urban needs?

10. *Economy*: How did urban economies change in the decades after World War II? Why are some cities wealthy and others impoverished? Why is there such a disparity within cities—why such extremes of wealth and poverty? Why do cities that exist in such close proximity to each other, such as Philadelphia and Camden on the East Coast and Oakland and San Francisco on the West Coast, have such different economic profiles? How have our cities been affected by disinvestment in manufacturing and processing?

11. *Recreation and Leisure*: How have recreational and leisure trends altered since the 1940s? What accounts for the rise and fall in the popularity of home versus commercial recreation? How did class, color, gender, nationality, religion, income, and other factors affect recreation and leisure? What happened to public parks and recreational programs in the wake of the civil rights movement? How dominant were sports teams in shaping public images of cities? Will cities of the future be places of work, play, or both?

12. *Corporations*: How has the role of corporations in America's cities shifted during the postwar years? Is the fate of certain cities and corporations intertwined? How did the postwar years redefine notions of what cities owe corporations and what constitutes good corporate citizenship?

13. *Families and Households:* How have families and households changed in the postwar years? How has the very definition of a family evolved? What

factors led to the increasing concentration of the elderly in older city neighborhoods? Why do many of today's newest immigrants settle in the suburbs? Why have older ethnic neighborhoods become tourist attractions? How will shifts in household composition likely shape the demand for urban services?

14. *Commemoration:* Did cities commemorate World War II? How? How many cities commemorated the September 11, 2001, terrorist attack? What other individuals and events were commemorated from the 1940s through the 2000s? Who were the builders and sponsors of postwar commemorative markers and monuments? What motivated them? What patterns did they follow?

15. *Crime:* What has happened to urban crime since 1945? Is crime fundamentally an urban problem? What has happened to suburban crime rates in recent decades? How did perceptions of vice and crime respond to the Black Power Movement, protests against the war in Southeast Asia, and changing attitudes toward illegal drug use? How are perceptions of crime shaped by television, movies, and computer games?

16. *Technology:* How have cities been affected by postwar shifts in technology? What cities have grown as a result of the explosion in electronics technology from the transistor to the supercomputer? Will telecommunications ultimately contribute to greater urban decentralization? Will electronic technology contribute to greater economic and social inequity?

In order to answer these and other questions regarding late twentieth-century cities, it will be necessary for you to undertake a research effort that in all likelihood will be different from those you might have previously undertaken. Gathering research materials on postwar American cities will make you aware just how little postwar documentary and nondocumentary sources have yet found their way to archives, museums, and special collections libraries. Part of the problem is that many of these institutions lack the staff and funds needed to collect and process such material. A 1970s Model Cities project report may not be offered to a museum or a library, for example, because it might be perceived as too recent and not "historical" enough.

The volume of material pertaining to postwar cities in archives and libraries will likely continue to be affected by shifts in donations and giving to museums, libraries, and archives. E-Bay, television programs such as *Antiques*

*Road Show*, and Internet sites have convinced many people that they or a family member might realize financial gain by selling papers, letters, and printed material known as ephemera instead of donating it to a local, state, or regional historical society, museum, archive, or library.

Postwar urban history will likely require you to undertake fieldwork; you cannot sit at your computer or visit your university, college, or public library and assume that you have done a good job looking for material. You will have to visit the records available to the public at city, county, state, and federal office buildings, courthouses, and offices. Research on postwar urban history may also require you to conduct oral history interviews. Why not talk directly to the people who were involved in a 1960s urban renewal program, led or participated in a civil rights demonstration, or served on a human relations commission? Most colleges and universities have boards that review such research. Human subjects institutional review boards often provide information about professional practices and ethics regarding the collection of oral history testimony. You can learn more about oral history ethics and procedures through professional organizations such as the Oral History Association and the American Folklore Society. Fieldwork also involves responsibly walking, biking, or driving the city's streets and alleys. Researchers who tour city parks, cemeteries, factory sites, retail areas, wholesale districts, and neighborhoods are best suited to learn how to read or decode the urban landscape and seek vestiges and clues from the past.

The process of getting to know a city is an endless one that can take a lifetime. Just when you think you know what makes Topeka or Spokane tick, it is rebuilt or something happens that makes you think again. There is no single source for understanding the city; the sources of insight are numerous and range from documentary sources to nondocumentary sources, such as material culture, architecture, the landscape, art, music, and drama. Studying the city is a demanding and highly rewarding task that will help you contribute to a national goal of keeping U.S. cities livable, vibrant, and uplifting.

# Notes

**PREFACE**

1. "Detroit Census Figures Confirm a Grim Desertion Like No Other," *New York Times*, March 23, 2011, 1; "Many U.S. Blacks Moving to South, Reversing Trend," *New York Times*, March 25, 2011, 1.

**CHAPTER 1**

1. The arrangement could have been inspired by the Fort Pitt Tunnel, Pittsburgh's dramatic gateway. Fred Rogers retired in November 2000 and died in 2003, but the show is still on the air in reruns.

2. "Are You Lonesome Tonight?," in *Life Decades of the Twentieth Century* (New York: Life Books, n.d.), 110.

3. *This Fabulous Century, 1950 to 1960*, vol. 6 (New York: Time-Life Books, 1970), 250.

4. *This Fabulous Century*, 136.

5. "Larry King," in *Time Annual, 1992: The Year in Review* (New York: Time Books, 1993), 128.

## CHAPTER 2

1. See Robert Fishman, "The Metropolitan Tradition in American Planning," in *The American Planning Tradition: Culture and Policy,* ed. Robert Fishman (Washington, DC: Woodrow Wilson Center Press, 2000).

2. Kenneth Jackson uses the term "crabgrass frontier" in his seminal *Crabgrass Frontier: The Suburbanization of the United States* (New York: Oxford University Press, 1985); see also Herbert Gans, *The Levittowners: Ways of Life in a New Suburban Community* (New York: Columbia University Press, 1982), and Bennett Berger, *Working-Class Suburb: A Study of Auto Workers in Suburbia* (Berkeley: University of California Press, 1960).

3. On suburban malls, see Richard Longstreth, *The American Department Store Transformed, 1920–1960* (New Haven, CT: Yale University Press, 2010); on suburbia, see Scott L. Bottles, *Los Angles and the Automobile: The Making of the Modern City* (Berkeley: University of California Press, 1987).

4. Arnold R. Hirsch, *Making the Second Ghetto: Race and Housing in Chicago, 1940–1960* (Cambridge: Cambridge University Press, 1983), 27.

5. Robert M. Fogelson, *Downtown: Its Rise and Fall, 1880–1950* (New Haven, CT: Yale University Press, 2001), 381.

6. Jill Pearlman, *Inventing Modernism: Joseph Hudnut, Walter Gropius, and the Bauhaus Legacy at Harvard* (Charlottesville: University Press of Virginia, 2007).

7. Jon C. Teaford, *The Rough Road to Renaissance: Urban Revitalization in America, 1940–1985* (Baltimore: Johns Hopkins University Press, 1990), 54; Mark I. Gelfand, *A Nation of Cities: The Federal Government and Urban America, 1933–1965* (New York: Oxford University Press, 1975), 158–59.

8. Fogelson, *Downtown,* 375.

9. Fogelson, *Downtown,* 373.

10. Fogelson, *Downtown,* 376–77.

11. Fogelson, *Downtown,* 378.

12. Miles Lanier Colean, *Renewing Our Cities* (New York: Twentieth Century Fund, 1953).

13. Marc Fried, "Grieving for a Lost Home: Psychological Costs of Relocation," in *The Urban Condition,* ed. Leonard J. Duhl (New York: Basic Books, 1963), chap. 12.

14. David Freund, *Colored Property: State Policy and White Racial Politics in Suburban America* (Chicago: University of Chicago Press, 2007); Thomas Sugrue, *The Origins of the Urban Crisis: Race and Inequality in Postwar Detroit* (Princeton, NJ: Princeton University Press, 1996); Amy Hillier, "Searching for Red Lines: Spatial Analysis of Lending Patterns in Philadelphia, 1940–1960," *Pennsylvania History* 72 (Winter 2005): 25–47.

15. Colin Gordon, *Mapping Decline: St. Louis and the Fate of the American City* (Philadelphia: University of Pennsylvania Press, 2008), 100.

16. John F. Bauman, *Public Housing, Race and Renewal: Urban Planning in Philadelphia, 1920–1974* (Philadelphia: Temple University Press, 1987), 180.

17. Editors of Fortune, *The Exploding Metropolis: A Study of the Assault on Urbanism and How Our Cities Can Resist It* (New York: Doubleday, 1958).

18. Michael Harrington, *The Other America: Poverty in the United States* (New York: Scribners, 1997); Dwight McDonald, "Our Invisible Poor," *New Yorker*, January 19, 1963, 18–132.

## CHAPTER 3

1. Quoted in Mark I. Gelfand, *A Nation of Cities: The Federal Government and Urban America, 1933–1965* (New York: Oxford University Press, 1975), 306.

2. Quoted in Gelfand, *A Nation of Cities*, 318.

3. Quoted in Carl M. Brauer, *John F. Kennedy and the Second Reconstruction* (New York: Columbia University Press, 1977), 43.

4. Quotations from Wendell E. Pritchett, "Which Urban Crisis? Regionalism, Race, and Urban Policy, 1960–1974," unpublished paper in possession of Roger Biles.

5. Quoted in Oral History Interview with Robert C. Weaver, November 19, 1968, Lyndon B. Johnson Presidential Library, Austin, Texas, 21.

6. First quotation in "Debacle," *Newsweek* 59 (March 5, 1962), 24; second quotation in Gelfand, *A Nation of Cities*, 446 n. 77.

7. Quoted in Gelfand, *A Nation of Cities*, 347.

8. First quotation in Irving Bernstein, *Guns or Butter: The Presidency of Lyndon Johnson* (New York: Oxford University Press, 1996), 95; second quotation in James

T. Patterson, *Grand Expectations: The United States, 1945–1974* (New York: Oxford University Press, 1996), 535.

9. Quoted in *Public Papers of the Presidents of the United States: Lyndon B. Johnson, 1963–1964*, vol. 1 (Washington, DC: Government Printing Office, 1965), 114.

10. Quoted in Daniel Patrick Moynihan, *Maximum Feasible Misunderstanding: Community Action in the War on Poverty* (New York: Free Press, 1969), 170.

11. Quoted in Robert Dallek, *Flawed Giant: Lyndon Johnson and His Times, 1961–1973* (New York: Oxford University Press, 1998), 111.

12. Quoted in Eric F. Goldman, *The Tragedy of Lyndon Johnson* (New York: Alfred A. Knopf, 1969), 91.

13. Quoted in *Public Papers of the Presidents of the United States: Lyndon B. Johnson, 1963–1964*, vol. 1, 705.

14. Quoted in Randall B. Woods, *LBJ: Architect of American Ambition* (New York: Free Press, 2006), 665.

15. Quoted in Charles M. Haar, *Between the Idea and the Reality: A Study in the Origin, Fate, and Legacy of the Model Cities Program* (Boston: Little, Brown, 1975), 35–36.

16. Quoted in *Congressional Record*, 89th Cong., 2nd sess., October 13, 1966, vol. 112, Pt. 20: 26628.

17. Quoted in Joseph A. Califano Jr., *The Triumph and Tragedy of Lyndon Johnson: The White House Years* (New York: Simon and Schuster, 1991), 276.

18. Quoted in Lyndon Johnson to John McCormack, April 5, 1968, White House Central Files, Confidential File, Box 66, Folder LE/HU2, 4/1/68–8/31/68, Lyndon B. Johnson Presidential Library.

19. Moynihan, *Maximum Feasible Misunderstanding*; Humphrey quoted from a memorandum to Ken Gray, August 25, 1967, Hubert H. Humphrey Papers, Box 150.D.20.7(B), Folder General. Project Files. Model Cities, 1967, Minnesota Historical Society Library, St. Paul.

20. Quoted in Wendell E. Pritchett, *Robert Clifton Weaver and the American City: The Life and Times of an Urban Reformer* (Chicago: University of Chicago Press, 2008), 323.

## CHAPTER 4

1. Quoted in Jane Jacobs, *The Death and Life of Great American Cities* (New York: Vintage, 1961), 4.

2. Quoted in Mark I. Gelfand, *A Nation of Cities: The Federal Government and Urban America, 1933–1965* (New York: Oxford University Press, 1975), 222.

3. Quoted in Robert A. Caro, *The Power Broker: Robert Moses and the Fall of New York* (New York: Alfred A. Knopf, 1974), 849.

4. Raymond A. Mohl, "The U.S. Department of Transportation and the Freeway Revolt, 1966–1973," unpublished paper in the possession of Roger Biles.

5. Arnold R. Hirsch, *Making the Second Ghetto: Race and Housing in Chicago, 1940–1960* (Cambridge: Cambridge University Press, 1983).

6. Quoted in Allen J. Matusow, *The Unraveling of America: A History of Liberalism in the 1960s* (New York: Harper and Row, 1984), 360.

7. Quoted in Robert M. Fogelson, *Violence as Protest: A Study of Riots and Ghettos* (Garden City, NY: Anchor Books, 1971), 27.

8. Quoted in Harvard Sitkoff, *The Struggle for Black Equality, 1954–1980* (New York: Hill and Wang, 1981), 203.

9. Quoted in James B. Lane, "Black Political Power and Its Limits: Gary Mayor Richard G. Hatcher's Administration, 1968–87," in *African-American Mayors: Race, Politics, and the American City,* ed. David R. Colburn and Jeffrey S. Adler (Urbana: University of Illinois Press, 2001), 57–58.

10. Quoted in the National Advisory Commission on Civil Disorders, *Report of the National Commission on Civil Disorders* (New York: Bantam Books, 1968), 1.

11. Quoted in Roger Biles, *Richard J. Daley: Politics, Race, and the Governing of Chicago* (DeKalb: Northern Illinois University Press, 1995), 146.

12. Quoted in J. Harvie Wilkinson III, *From Brown to Bakke: The Supreme Court and School Integration, 1954–1978* (New York: Oxford University Press, 1979), 230.

13. Quoted in Maurice R. Berube and Marilyn Gittell, *Confrontation at Ocean Hill-Brownsville: The New York School Strikes of 1968* (New York: Praeger, 1969), 174.

14. Quoted in Andrew Wiese, *Places of Their Own: African American Suburbanization in the Twentieth Century* (Chicago: University of Chicago Press, 2004), 211.

15. Quoted in Wiese, *Places of Their Own*, 212.

16. Quoted in Wiese, *Places of Their Own*, 244.

17. Quoted in Adam Rome, *The Bulldozer in the Countryside: Suburban Sprawl and the Rise of American Environmentalism* (Cambridge: Cambridge University Press, 2001), 4.

18. Quoted in Jon C. Teaford, *Post-Suburbia: Government and Politics in the Edge Cities* (Baltimore: Johns Hopkins University Press, 1997), 116.

19. Quoted in Jon C. Teaford, *The Metropolitan Revolution: The Rise of Post-Urban America* (New York: Columbia University Press, 2006), 158.

20. Quoted in Edward C. Banfield, *The Unheavenly City: The Nature and the Future of Our Urban Crisis* (Boston: Little, Brown, 1968), 255.

## CHAPTER 5

1. Douglas S. Massey and Nancy A. Denton, *American Apartheid: Segregation and the Making of the Underclass* (Cambridge, MA: Harvard University Press, 1993), 74–78.

2. Jon C. Teaford, *The Rough Road to Renaissance: Urban Revitalization in America, 1940–1985* (Baltimore: Johns Hopkins University Press, 1990), 290.

3. Quoted in Teaford, *The Rough Road to Renaissance*, 294; see also Alison Isenberg, *Downtown America: A History of the Place and the People Who Made It* (Chicago: University of Chicago Press, 2004).

4. See Bernard J. Frieden and Marshall Kaplan, *The Politics of Neglect: Urban Aid from Model Cities to Revenue Sharing* (Cambridge, MA: MIT Press, 1975), 200.

5. Richard Florida, *The Rise of the Creative Class* (New York: Basic Books, 2002).

6. Isenberg, *Downtown America*, 272.

7. Roy Lubove, *Twentieth-Century Pittsburgh: The Post-Steel Era* (Pittsburgh: University of Pittsburgh Press, 1996).

8. Kent W. Colton, *Housing in the Twenty-First Century: Achieving Common Ground* (Cambridge, MA: Harvard University Press, 2003), 160.

9. Alexander Von Hoffman, *House by House, Block by Block: The Rebirth of America's Urban Neighborhoods* (New York: Oxford University Press, 2003).

10. For quotations, see Lubove, *Twentieth-Century Pittsburgh*, 100.

11. Dennis Keating, Norman Krumholz, and John Metzger, "Cleveland: Post-Populist Public-Private Partnerships," in *Unequal Partnerships: The Political Economy of Urban Redevelopment in Postwar America*, ed. Gregory D. Squires (New Brunswick, NJ: Rutgers University Press, 1989), 126–36.

12. William Julius Wilson, *The Truly Disadvantaged: The Inner City, The Underclass, and Public Policy* (Chicago: University of Chicago Press, 1987).

## CHAPTER 6

1. http://www-lib.use.edu/~anthonya/la/rebcauses.htm.

2. "America the Violent," *Time Annual 1993: The Year in Review* (New York: Time Books, 1994), 114.

3. Michael Matza and John Duchneskie, "Poverty Surges in Lower Northeast," *Philadelphia Inquirer*, January 3, 2011, A1, A9.

4. Clinton, quoted at http://frwebgate3.access.gpo.gov/cgi-bin/PDFgate.cgi?WAISdocID=IQQzbE/0/2/0&WAISaction=rerieve.

5. http://www.america.com/archive/2008/april-04-08/a-closer-look-at-stadium-subsidies.

6. http://mlb.mlb.com/det/ballpark/information/index.jsp?content=comericapark.

# Index

# About the Authors

John F. Bauman is visiting professor of community planning and development at the Muskie School of Public Service, University of Southern Maine, and professor emeritus of history at California University of Pennsylvania.

Roger Biles is professor of history at Illinois State University.

Kristin M. Szylvian is associate professor of history at St. John's University.

CPSIA information can be obtained at www.ICGtesting.com
Printed in the USA
BVOW042322131111

275918BV00004B/2/P